DIANA

The Killing of a Princess

Nicholas Davies

Pen Press Publishers Ltd

First published in Great Britain in 2006 by
Indepenpress (Pen Press Publishers Ltd)
39, Chesham Road
Brighton
BN2 1NB

ISBN 1-905621-48-5
978-1-905621-48-4

Printed and bound in the UK

A catalogue record of this book is available from
the British Library

Cover design by Jacqueline Abromeit

About the author

Nicholas Davies is many-times published and a New York Times best-selling author for his book *"Diana: A Princess and her Troubled Marriage"*.

Nicholas Davies has close contacts within the royal circles – he doesn't write to be sensationalist but he pulls no punches. All his previous royal books have proved to be both accurate and factual. His writing is always balanced and yet challenging, even to those who are avid readers of royal books.

Previous titles by Nicholas Davies

*

Dead Men Talking
Death Before Dishonour
Diana: Secrets and Lies
The Terminators
William: The Rebel Prince
Street Warriors
Deadly Affair
Not By Strength By Guile
William: King for the 21ˢᵗ Century
Ten Thirty Three: The inside story of Britain's secret
killing machine in NI
The Year Zero
Elizabeth: Behind Palace Doors
Diana: The People's Princess
William: The man who will be King
Queen Elizabeth II: A woman who is not amused
Fifty Dead Men Walking
Violent Delights: Love story of an SAS hero and a Provo IRA girl
Princess who changed the world
Roll The Dice: The Aristocrat Who staged a £2m sting
Diana: The Lonely Princess
The Nemesis File
A Deadly Kind of Love
Diana: A Princess and her troubled marriage
Death of a Tycoon: An insider's account of the rise and fall of
Robert Maxwell
**The Unknown Maxwell: His astonishing secret lives
revealed by his aide and close companion**
Rebel Royals

Contents

Foreword

William and Harry learned of their mother's death at some time after 8 am, just six hours after the hospital confirmed that Princess Diana had died. While on their way to breakfast a serious-faced Prince Charles called them into his suite of rooms in Balmoral Castle, saying he had something to tell them.

As gently as possible, Charles then broke the news of their mother's death, explaining how she had been killed in a car crash in Paris in the early hours of that morning. Charles later recalled his sons were stunned by the news, at first unable to say anything or comprehend that their mother was dead. The lads looked at each other, not knowing what to say as their minds took in the horror of what their father had just told them.

Briefly, Charles explained what he knew of the crash, telling them that Dodi and the driver had also been killed. Wills asked how the accident had happened. Charles replied that he didn't yet know all the exact details but as soon as he knew, he would tell them. He then told his sons that he would be flying to London within a couple of hours and then on to the hospital in Paris to see Diana and bring her body back to London for the funeral. He told the boys they would be staying at Balmoral with their grandparents and he would phone them.

It was at that moment that the awful reality of what Charles was telling them hit Harry and he burst into tears, his body shaking as he sobbed. Charles put his arms around

Harry and hugged him to his chest while his young son cried and cried. Somehow, William remained calm for a few moments, slowly shaking his head from side to side, looking down at the floor and repeating: 'I can't believe it, I can't believe it.' Harry's uncontrollable sobbing affected William and he too needed a handkerchief to wipe the tears that had begun to stream down his face.

Now, nine long years after her death, William and Harry and every other member of the Royal Family still do not know for certain how Diana died. They do not know precisely what happened to her; why the car crashed and how it came about that Diana died when she was sitting in the rear passenger seat of a Mercedes, a car renowned for its safety. To the two young princes, who have since grown to manhood, it is beyond belief why the official British investigation - an inquest into her death conducted under British law by the Royal Coroner - has never been held.

Meanwhile, the British police investigation into the circumstances surrounding Diana's death, given the title of 'Operation Paget', drags on relentlessly. Former Metropolitan Police Chief Lord Stevens, formerly Sir John Stevens, was put in command of 'Operation Paget' and a team of detectives assembled.

Earlier this year I was invited to Scotland Yard and asked to give evidence to the team and explain to them the reasons why I believed Princess Diana had been killed by British security forces. During an interview lasting several hours I explained how I had been told Diana's killing was planned and executed. I readily gave them the evidence I had collated in researching this book. The interview was taped.

According to the French police, the death of Diana,

her lover Dodi Fayed and their French chauffeur Henri Paul had been a simple, straightforward road accident which had occurred because the driver was drunk and had been driving too fast.

And now it seems there may never be an inquest into her death. No date has been fixed and yet no reason has been given by the Royal Coroner why an inquest has not been held.

There are many who believe an inquest would re-open the myriad of questions that still surround the car crash and Diana's death. And that is the last thing the Royal Family, the Establishment and those in command of our intelligence agencies would want exposed to the scrutiny of the press.

It seems the fact that Diana's two sons might want to know how and why their mother died in that crash are ignored, indeed, treated with disdain. It seems a decision has been taken that no inquest will ever take place. But who has taken that decision is unknown and will, more than likely, remain a secret.

The French investigation, conducted as is customary by a presiding magistrate, was thorough; within weeks the evidence surrounding the car crash was collected and collated by the French police. A little over two months later, the police submitted their report to the presiding magistrate. As is common practice in France, this report, along with all the available evidence gathered by the French police, was then sent to the Royal Coroner so that a full inquest into her death could be held in the UK and a verdict reached. At the British inquest, witnesses, experts and police officers would present their evidence and be cross-examined by lawyers representing the Royal Family as well as the Spencer family. At the end, the Coroner would sum up the evidence and announce his verdict. The matter would then be closed, for ever.

But not in the case of Diana's death.

There has been no inquest into her death. The fact that nine years have passed and no inquest held into a tragedy which rocked the British nation is, of course, a scandal. Making William and Harry wait for so many years to discover what really happened to the mother they adored is outrageous and extraordinarily unfair on the young princes.

In 2001, my contacts within the intelligence services, who had corroborated with me on other books, informed me that the death of Princess Diana was no accident. These contacts informed me that Diana's killing was organized and carried out by MI5 with the assistance of the French DST – La Direction de la Surveillance du Territoire, the French equivalent of MI5.

This book is the result of the investigations I have since carried out, both in France and the United Kingdom, in a bid to discover all the circumstances surrounding Princess Diana's death and to substantiate the reasons why it was considered necessary by those in charge of British security to order her killing.

Chapter One
Sacrificial Lamb

The innocent, virginal Diana Spencer had no idea that she had been offered to the late Queen Elizabeth, the Queen Mother, as the future bride of Prince Charles, the heir to the British throne. Diana was oblivious to the behind-the-scenes discussions that had been going on for a couple of years between the late Queen Mother and her own grandmother, Lady Fermoy.

The Queen Mother had always been close to Prince Charles, far closer indeed than his own mother, for, in fairness, the Queen was too busy to find the time to sort out a bride for her eldest son. So the Queen Mother made it her business.

Lady Fermoy was a close confidante and friend of the Queen Mother and had been so for most of her life. She worked at Clarence House under the quaint, ancient title of 'Extra Woman of the Bedchamber', and was only too keen to help the Queen Mother find Charles a suitable bride; she was keener still that one of her own granddaughters might fill that role, for it would achieve one of the Spencer family's most cherished ambitions – they would finally become an integral part of the ruling Royal House of Windsor.

It was Lady Fermoy's second attempt to provide a bride for Prince Charles, the first attempt having ended in disaster. Lady Fermoy had first offered Diana's elder sister,

Sarah, as a potential wife. Sarah dated Charles and shared his bed for some twelve months.

Charles had rather taken to Sarah, whom he found fun-loving, bright, good company and sexy. They not only had many laughs together, but Charles discovered that Sarah had ignited the rather dormant side of his sexuality. Young Sarah was the dominant partner in this romantic relationship, a role-reversal she enjoyed and Charles found exciting and fulfilling. He rather liked such treatment. But Sarah was a rather emotional and challenging character and the more time they spent together, the more Charles came to realize that she was very strong-willed with a mind of her own. Petty arguments, which Charles has always loathed, became more frequent and Charles decided to call an end to the affair. They parted on good terms.

Undaunted, Lady Fermoy tried again. She knew the Queen and Prince Philip were more keen than ever that Charles should find a bride, for as time rolled by they feared that their eldest son, then in his thirties, was too at ease with himself, too content to remain a bachelor, and not terribly interested in young women except as occasional dinner dates and bedmates. Indeed, Prince Philip had tried on a number of occasions to press and cajole Charles into finding a bride – for the sake of the House of Windsor. Philip had become somewhat exasperated that his eldest son never seemed that interested in young women and appeared oblivious to the fact that it was his duty to find a bride.

Following the disaster over Sarah, the Queen Mother had to plead with Charles to date Diana and he only agreed to do so to please the grandmother he had always adored.

The fact that Charles took up with Sarah's younger sister somewhat riled Sarah and she never completely forgave her little sister for 'stealing' her prince. That, of course, was an exaggeration but from time to time Sarah would tease Diana that she had 'stolen' her man.

It was the assassination of Earl Mountbatten in August 1979 that shook Charles out of his lethargy and dramatically changed his outlook on life. Mountbattten had been Prince Charles' mentor and father-figure, and his despicable murder by the IRA – when they detonated a bomb in his fishing smack in Ireland, killing Mountbatten and other members of his family – was a terrible and dramatic blow, not only to Charles but also the entire Royal Family. At a stroke, every member of the family came to realize that they had become prime targets of the ruthless, murderous IRA, who seemed prepared to kill anyone in their bid for a united Ireland.

Almost overnight, the thunderbolt of Mountbatten's death woke Charles from his lassitude towards marriage, for he suddenly realized it was urgent, perhaps even vital, for him to marry and produce heirs for the Royal House of Windsor in double-quick time. As Charles himself put it, 'One never knows whom the next bullet will hit.' For the first time in his life, he realized that he might well be the IRA's next target. Speed was now of the essence. To Charles, Diana's arrival on the scene looked as if the Gods, with perfect timing, had provided an immediate answer to his prayers.

It had been a year or so since Charles had last seen Diana, whom he remembered as 'the other Spencer girl', the young one he had met a few times in his life but had not taken much notice of because of their thirteen-year age gap. He had danced with her once at a Sandringham house party organised by the Queen in January 1979, but that dance had only taken place because Charles was

7

expected, out of politeness and tradition, to dance with every woman attending the party.

Within weeks of Mountbatten's murder, Diana was invited by the Queen, who had been tipped-the-wink by the Queen Mother to ask Diana to another party at Sandringham. This time she found Charles more charming, more attentive and more interested in her. Not only did they dance together on several occasions, but Charles chatted to her for much of the evening.

Diana was rather stunned by this attention, for on previous occasions when they had met at informal gatherings, she believed Charles had hardly noticed whether she was in the room or not. He had always been polite but had showed no interest whatsoever in her as a woman.

To his delight and surprise, Charles found the more mature Diana enchanting and, importantly, he sensed in that first serious encounter that she was more amenable and less argumentative than her sister Sarah. Almost overnight, and after conferring with his grandmother, Charles convinced himself that Diana would make a wonderful wife and mother for his children. He also knew that his decision to target Diana would have the full approval of his parents, who would probably sigh with relief that Charles was finally to take the plunge. In that moment, Charles determined that the relationship with Diana would work, and that they would marry as soon as practicable.

But he never told Diana this.

It was ironic that throughout her sister Sarah's affair with Charles, the inexperienced teenage Diana was openly jealous of the relationship. Indeed, since puberty, Diana had always had a crush on Charles and later she would confess that from an early age she had dreamed of marrying him – not because she wanted to be a member of the Royal family nor because she wanted to be Queen of England, but simply because she was so in love with the dashing, handsome man-of-action.

In retrospect, however, Diana's marriage was over before it began. The love she had felt for Charles during those wonderful months together before their glorious wedding was real enough. Diana had felt she was floating on air, the luckiest girl in the world. She saw Charles as her knight in shining armour: a highly intelligent, articulate public speaker whom everyone listened to and admired; a man of action, piloting his own aircraft and helicopters, playing high-goal polo, skiing *off piste* and, in his quieter moments, reading academic books, fly-fishing and listening to opera and classical music. In the late 1970s Charles was the acknowledged darling of the nation whom people in their hundreds turned out to catch a glimpse of. The nation admired him, for his image was not that of a stick-in-the-mud, old-fashioned royal but a daring and dynamic sportsman who happened to be a member of the Royal Family.

From Diana's viewpoint, Charles was not only a dynamic sportsman but, more importantly, the world's most eligible bachelor who had unbelievably plucked her, a skinny, shy, self-conscious teenager, to be his girlfriend. At that time Diana saw herself as someone with no ambition and no idea what she wanted to do in life, except that she wanted to live in London and was prepared to do the most menial tasks in order to earn enough money to feed and clothe herself. Unlike the fashion icon she would later become, in the late 1970s, she cared little or nothing for clothes and did not have much in the way of dress sense. She was just an innocent, naïve young country girl with no sophistication and no confidence, simply getting on with her dull, unadventurous life as an unknown nanny living a quiet, unobtrusive life. Indeed, the teenage Diana had few friends and, importantly, no boyfriends. To cap her lack of self-esteem, Diana hated her looks, especially her hair, and was embarrassed by what she perceived as her big nose.

And yet within a few months everyone who watched her world-wide televised wedding ceremony was impressed by the beauty and elegance of the young woman who, almost overnight, had become sophisticated, dazzling and a stylish role model for women everywhere. All wished the couple well and silently hoped that their marriage would be long, happy and fruitful. Champagne toasts to the royal couple were made not only in Buckingham Palace but in homes, pubs, bars and cafes nationwide and across the globe. Tears of emotion were shed that day by women everywhere for the innocent, natural, unaffected and lovable Diana, who in a matter of a few months had won them over with her shyness and apparent vulnerability. People everywhere felt they were not only a part of the couple's wedding day celebrations, but also somehow involved in the marriage itself as they heard and witnessed the prince and his bride declare their solemn vows.

But only a handful of people had any idea of what was really going on in Diana's heart and mind that day. Many viewers noticed that she looked nervous and uncertain, but most dismissed her troubled demeanor as natural, given the extraordinary circumstances that had catapulted this unknown and bashful young woman into the stark, glaring limelight of the world's most prestigious Royal Family, the House of Windsor.

The young Diana was indeed a worried and anxious woman that lovely summer's day in July 1981. Emotionally she was in turmoil. Her natural instincts were telling her that she should not go through with the wedding ceremony, while her head was telling her that she must. She believed she had no alternative. In those few days before the wedding, Diana found herself in an impossible situation. The world was ready and waiting to witness and enjoy the royal marriage – her marriage – and she felt that she could not let them down. As her wedding day dawned Diana, alone in her room in the palace, felt physically sick because she knew it was simply too late to pull out. There was no escape.

For weeks, such doubts had been gathering in her mind, and as the big day approached, the more nervous and unsure Diana became. She kept telling herself over and over that she was only suffering the normal pre-wedding nerves that many brides experience, but her nerves were in shreds because this was no ordinary wedding. In those weeks, major problems had surfaced that worried Diana greatly but she hadn't the nerve to pull out or run away. And she was too nervous to raise these doubts with her husband-to-be. She felt trapped, unable to escape the inevitable.

But it had not always been like that. At first, Diana had been thrilled, flattered and delighted that each and every night she was going to bed with her dream lover, Prince Charles, the young man she had thought about on and off for years but never for a moment believed would actually invite her on a date. After he had asked her to marry him she had loved their quiet, intimate dinners in his apartment at Buckingham Palace, where they would drink champagne before dinner and share jokes, Diana laughing at his wit, adoring his attention, overcome by the intimacy and his words of love. Diana was a young, inexperienced and naïve young woman, totally in love, and she reveled in her good fortune.

It was the first time she had been in love. Indeed, the innocent Diana had never before enjoyed a relationship with any man, for she had never had a steady boyfriend. She was 19 and still a virgin at a time when most of her girlfriends were dating, falling in love and enjoying love affairs. Diana's experience with men was so limited that even a passionate kiss from a man was rare and, understandably, she yearned to be like the other girls with whom she shared an apartment in London – dating, dining out and enjoying the companionship, love and passion of a man. Such intimacy had been a mere dream for Diana before, out of the blue, Charles invited her to accompany him to a Sunday polo match.

Later, Diana would confess that when Charles phoned to invite her to the palace, she dared to wonder whether there was a chance that he might actually fancy her. As she arrived for that first date, she suspected that Charles only wanted to chat to her about her elder sister Sarah, with whom he had been enjoying a year-long, on-off intimate relationship. Diana knew the couple were happy for most of the time, but she also knew that Sarah was an emotional and often challenging person who needed careful handling..

But those feelings of joy and elation that Diana had enjoyed when Charles asked her to marry him had turned to tears, nervousness and a sense of desperation by the morning of the wedding. In her heart Diana knew it wasn't simply pre-wedding nerves. The reasons for her apprehension were far more fundamental.

On her wedding day, she was awake at the crack of dawn after a sleepless night tossing and turning and she peeped through the curtains to see the crowds gathering in the Mall. It was at that moment the tears fell, she explained later. Diana knew they weren't tears of simple emotion or apprehension of what lay ahead that day. Her tears cascaded and her shoulders shook in the full knowledge that she could no longer escape her destiny. She sat on the edge of her bed, fearful of her future, and cried alone. The dreadful realization had arrived too late, and she knew the moment had passed when she could bring a halt to the proceedings that now horrified her. She had no option but to go ahead with the wedding and marry Prince Charles – a man she no longer loved.

Weeks before the wedding, Diana had come to the realization that she would never find true happiness with Charles. But Diana hoped it was all just nerves. Later, she would tell her close friends the reasons why the marriage had gone so wrong, but it was only with a few very close friends that she discussed the principal reasons why she knew *before* the wedding that she could never be truly happy.

There were, in fact, three main reasons. The first was the dreadful realization that she could never again enjoy any freedom, privacy or obscurity; the second that Prince Charles had so many duties and responsibilities that they had little or no quality time together; and the third, equally important, was sexual.

Over the previous decade Prince Charles had enjoyed the companionship of many young women, including a couple of friendly lunches with Camilla Parker Bowles, a relationship which over the years would develop into a lasting friendship, and later still to a measured, loving affair with both Charles and Camilla enjoying a deep commitment to each other. Charles had also enjoyed perhaps some 20 or more romantic affairs with young women, which he knew would lead nowhere. Many of those relationships Charles had managed to hide from the prying eyes of the press as well as the public. The press understood that he should be permitted to conduct his love life in private – he was simply enjoying the life of a bachelor sowing his wild oats – until he found the woman he wanted to marry. From the moment there was a real likelihood that Prince Charles was viewing Lady Diana Spencer as a potential wife, the press felt they had been let off the leash and from then on they were never to leave her alone. Not even in the moment of her death.

For her part, Diana was totally unprepared for the reality of becoming the world's number one target for the newspaper and magazine editors who quickly realized that here was a delightful, wholesome, good-looking, engaging yet shy young woman who sold their papers and magazines like no one before her. Many editors, and media accountants, could see from their sales charts that an issue with a cover picture of Diana sold far more copies than those without her. They demanded more and, as a result, a new industry took off as photographers discovered that pictures of Diana sold for high financial rewards.

None of the photographers, however, spared a thought for Diana, save as a prize milch-cow. Diana had lived in obscurity; a nonentity, who, to make ends meet in London, cleaned other people's homes and lavatories to earn a crust. All her short life, this country girl from an aristocratic background had been bashful and nervous meeting strangers, and would go to pieces when confronted by a camera. Diana's upbringing, quiet country-life and private boarding schools had simply not equipped her to cope with such extraordinary attention, catapulted overnight from peace and obscurity onto the front pages of the world's media. At first, the intensity of interest frightened her. She had never expected such attention and never wanted it.

Diana's life had been spent on the large private family estate of Althorp in Northampton, some 50 miles from London, with only two older sisters for company; and they mostly ignored her. The arrival of brother Charles, three years her junior, gave her life some form and she lavished her love and attention on him. But at the tender age of five ,Diana discovered to her horror that her mother was leaving the family home, their father and her four children to go away and live in London.

It is difficult to exaggerate the effect that single event had on Diana, deserted by the one person who had shown her love and affection and protected her from her two older, bossy sisters. For the remainder of her life, Diana could never forget and she never forgave her mother for deserting her in her hour of need. Later, Diana would confess, 'I never could forget that my mother had walked out on me. I don't think I ever got over it.' That horrendous shock was followed by life at boarding schools, where most of the time she lived a quiet, unadventurous life. She was poor at learning and not very sporty.

From the moment of the announcement of her official engagement in February 1981, there was no hiding place for Diana. From the minute she delightedly accepted his offer of marriage, Diana found herself physically confined to palaces and royal households, cut off from the outside world, unable to participate freely in her favourite pastime – shopping – and never permitted to walk or drive anywhere without an armed police bodyguard. She hated losing her freedom and hated being unable to hide, unrecognized, in a crowd, a shop, a street or a restaurant. Diana had always lived a very private life and she cherished her privacy, wearing ordinary, comfortable, unfashionable clothes so that she would never stand out or draw attention to herself. It was for that reason that Diana hated being tall and, at 5ft 10, she had always been one of the tallest girls in her school year.

It was unfortunate for Diana that her fame arrived in the early 1980s, a time of real and genuine concern that IRA terrorists were targeting the Royal Family. She understood that following Earl Mountbatten's murder there was real fear among those responsible for guarding the Royal Family that IRA killer squads might target another member of the family in a bid to obtain maximum worldwide publicity for their cause. Those senior MI5 officers responsible for royal security fully realized that if the IRA gunmen managed to kill the young Diana, her murder would be hailed as a magnificent success by the IRA leadership and might even bring closer the day of a united Ireland. Those responsible for Diana's safety knew the very real danger and, of course, they could take no chances with her safety. They escorted her everywhere and they were always armed. There was no escape, though Diana constantly begged to be allowed to go shopping on her own.

This realization that in agreeing to marry Charles she had totally sacrificed her own private life for ever and a day was disturbing enough for the young Diana, but there were other matters, equally important, that would have a profound effect on her personal life.

She had never fully realized just how many royal duties Charles was called upon to perform each and every week, sometimes from early morning to late at night, leaving him very little time to spend with her. His was no nine-to-five job. His day would usually start at 6 am because he would need to travel some distance to his first appointment. More often than not he was out most of the day, welcoming visiting dignitaries, chairing meetings, attending official lunches, opening factories, schools or hospitals, running the Prince's Trust, talking to those who ran his estates, farms and properties, writing official letters and reading the government papers that arrived throughout the day, every day. And once a week or so he would have to attend some official dinner or some other function. On those occasions he would be fortunate to be home by ten o'clock – a sixteen-hour day dictated by duty.

Charles' life was hectic. Sometimes, he might need to return to the Palace to change his clothes perhaps four times a day, dashing in, changing and then away again to the next call of duty. To Diana, the word 'duty' became abhorrent for she quickly came to understand that meant separation from the man she loved. Duty, the moral obligation that bound Charles to serve his country because he was the Queen's first son, drove a wedge between the couple and the innocent Diana simply could not cope with the loneliness.

Yet those few months of her engagement, when she all but lived with Charles in his apartment at Buckingham Palace, were happy despite the fact that she saw very little of the man she was about to marry because her own life was hectic. Diana rarely had a moment to herself, her day one long series of appointments, meetings, conferences and fittings. She got on famously with the helpful staff of Vogue magazine who happily accepted the challenge to change Diana from the innocent, country girl to one of the most sophisticated and beautiful women in the world.

Diana confessed later that the task of buying an extensive new wardrobe of clothes was more enjoyable than anything else. For the first time in her young life she could buy whatever clothes she wanted, not having to think for a moment of the money she was spending. She had no idea what anything cost because all bills simply went straight to the accountants taking care of the Prince of Wales' finances. She didn't even have to sign a card or see a bill.

However, it still took some weeks after her engagement for it to suddenly dawn on her that she could now have whatever clothes she wanted – for the rest of her life. And that realization changed Diana overnight from a girl who hardly spent a penny on her wardrobe to a fashion-conscious icon the world came to admire for her style, elegance and choice of outfits.

In those early months of 1981, from the moment Diana awoke until she happily climbed into bed beside Charles for some love, affection and sometimes sex, Diana hardly had a moment to herself. 'I hardly have time to grab a bite,' she would happily tell her roommates, 'life's absolutely wonderful.'

One of the principal reasons Diana so enjoyed her life during those months was the fact that she was never on her own. As a result of her secluded upbringing in the country and the desertion of her mother, Diana always feared being left to amuse herself, fend for herself, care for herself. Diana would explain that whenever she was left alone she felt she had been deserted, and found it hard to cope with that haunting feeling. It was one of the reasons she had been so shy about becoming involved with a young man, for fear that one day he might dump her. Diana knew that she couldn't face being deserted. Nothing terrified her more. She came to understand that she needed a man who would love and cherish her totally, a man capable of giving her the confidence and emotional support she sorely needed.

Immediately following the engagement, it was decided that in an effort to escape the media circus Diana would leave her London apartment and, until her wedding day, move to Clarence House in the Mall, the Queen Mother's London home, a hundred yards from the Palace. Unknown to the world, however, within days Diana had moved from Clarence House to an apartment next to Charles' rooms in Buckingham Palace and the two young lovers spent the next five months living together. Diana was blissfully happy, dining by candlelight most nights in private with Charles, falling in love and making love, and sleepily kissing him goodbye in the morning when he would set off on his royal duties. Later, Diana would rise and shower and ready herself for another hectic day preparing for the great event.

Those were possibly among the happiest times Diana ever enjoyed. She was unashamedly in love, adored Charles and believed he was the most wonderful man in the world. Whenever Charles was making a speech, Diana would look at him with adulation, admiring everything about him and brimming with love for the man she was to marry. She would tell her friends, 'I'm the luckiest girl in the world and Charles is just wonderful.' During these months Diana idolized Charles, unable to find fault with the man she was to marry.

Such adoration would not last, could not last, and did not last.

The more Diana saw of Charles, the more she realized that he was fallible after all. His halo began to slip and, within weeks of the wedding, Diana was faced with the stark reality.

It was some weeks after their wedding that Diana came to the realization that the problems with their sex life seemed insurmountable. She became agitated and nervous because she had no idea how to bring back their wonderful love-making of the earlier weeks and months before they were married. She hoped it was simply the fact that she had become pregnant within weeks of their wedding. But it was not to be.

Subsequently, Diana confessed to Howard, a City banker who for some months became her lover in the 1980s, that she and Charles had had problems with their sex life shortly before they married and these continued afterwards. Diana told him that at the beginning their love life had been wonderful because she was so in love with the man, but because she was a virgin and totally inexperienced, she knew nothing else. In time, however, she came to realize that the earth wasn't moving for her and had, in fact, never done so.

Diana read sex books and manuals in the hope that she could find the missing ingredient that would produce the orgasms and fulfillment that she realized were missing. But they didn't seem to help. Understandably, she also found it all but impossible to raise the subject with Charles, and later she confessed to Howard that she sometimes faked orgasms so that he believed she was in seventh heaven whenever they made love. But that proved to be a short-term solution and she found herself becoming more agitated, frustrated and nervous. Their lovemaking deteriorated and Diana found herself making excuses. Where once she had been willing to make love 'at the drop of a hat', she now found herself wanting to do anything to avoid sex. At the time, however, Diana didn't mention this problem to anyone but kept her secrets to herself. She was simply too embarrassed to broach the subject with anyone.

Later, Diana would also confess to Howard that Charles had showed her kindness and understanding and had tried everything to help her, but nothing worked. She convinced herself that she was at fault because she had no experience and felt guilty and worried. Diana told Howard that when Charles left in the mornings she would sometimes break down in tears, feeling so frustrated and angry with herself. As a result, a rift developed between them which Diana believed was one of the main causes for the marriage breakdown. She told him that their problem was no one's fault as such and they tried to sort it out but failed. 'It just wasn't right,' Diana told him.

Some years later, Diana would confess that she came to blame Charles for their sex problems simply because he was the man and she believed that he should have taken responsibility for ensuring that she was enjoying her sex life as much as he seemed to be. Within a matter of weeks the respect and adoration that Diana felt towards Charles had all but drained away and the two found themselves in a loveless marriage with little physical contact between them.

Her first pregnancy helped. Diana was thrilled at the thought of soon having a baby of her own to love and that expectation of motherhood gave her confidence a much-needed boost. As Diana focused on her pregnancy, the problems of their sex life faded. Charles continued with the daily round of never-ending royal duties and the couple began to drift apart.

Charles appeared the more capable of putting up with this unfortunate and deteriorating state of affairs. He had his full-time job, his duties to perform as heir to the throne as well as his extensive charity work, including, of course, the Prince's Trust. There was also another problem in that Charles had very limited experience of long love affairs and had never had to cope with a young woman suffering from such sexual anxieties. Once William was born, Diana told her friends and relations how much she revelled in nursing and caring for him. As the months went by, however, Diana began to feel agitated again, feeling cut off from her friends and desperate for more love and affection from Charles. And as the months rolled by she came to realize that Charles was simply not cut out to be a loving, caring husband. Diana needed a man who showed his love for her, cuddled her, kissed her with passion and made her feel loved and wanted.

At times, Diana believed she was going mad, for she had nowhere to turn and no one to turn to. She was now too embarrassed to discuss her problems with Charles because she didn't think he really understood. She felt she couldn't talk to her mother about the situation because she had never felt close to her, and she didn't want to talk to her sisters or her brother Charles. And because of her natural shyness Diana didn't want to confess her personal problems to former roommates and friends. She felt utterly alone.

In desperation, Diana made friends with the servants and the cooks in the same friendly way she had always done back home at Althorp. The staff were taken aback by her visits to the kitchens because they knew it was simply not appropriate for any member of the Royal Family to chat with maids and cooks as though they were her friends. To Diana's astonishment, they didn't want her there. After a dozen or more visits to the kitchens, senior staff objected to her frequent appearances and demanded an end to them. One day as she popped into the kitchens, the Yeoman approached, pointed to the door, and told her, 'Through there, Ma'am, is your side of the house; through here is our side of the house.'

A shocked, embarrassed Diana was unsure how to respond to this blunt piece of advice. The Yeoman stood his ground, in effect barring Diana from moving further into the kitchen. Diana looked around for a friendly face but there was none. She blushed madly, turned and fled through the door, never to return. It seemed the one set of people with whom she could enjoy a friendly chat had put an abrupt end to any chance of any friendliness. She felt even more isolated.

For Diana, weekday mornings became the bane of her life. She came to dread them. The problem was Edward Adeane, Charles' private secretary. A confirmed bachelor, a barrister and a highly efficient royal aide, Sir Edward Adeane would knock on the door of their private quarters to discuss official matters with Charles, check his diary arrangements, go over the plans, timetables and speeches for that day and evening, and discuss plans for the days and weeks ahead. Most mornings Sir Edward would need to spend at least 30 minutes to an hour with Charles on his own, with no distractions.

This had occurred every weekday since Charles began his royal duties after leaving the Royal Navy. It was of course necessary. But that made no difference to Diana.

She hated the daily ritual. She barely coped with the intrusion in the early months of their marriage, but after she became pregnant and, even more so after the birth of William in June 1982, she did her utmost to put an end to the early morning meetings.

Diana believed this was a defining moment in her marriage. She saw Edward Adeane as her rival, almost as the enemy whom she must defeat. And she determined to prove that she was the more important. Diana would plead with Charles to change the time of the morning meeting until later and stay with her for an hour. Her pleading became desperate and she would quite often scream and cry, sometimes physically restraining Charles, tugging at his clothes, begging him to stay with her and William.

In a raised voice, Diana could be heard saying, and sometimes screaming through her tears, 'I need you here; William needs you here. For God's sake, can't you tell him to go away and leave us alone? You're the bloody Prince of Wales, one of the most important people in the whole country and you can't do anything you want. They always tell you what to do and you go along with that. Can't you tell them to go away just for an hour or so?'

Charles would try to calm her, explain to her that his life was not his own; that he had duties to perform, royal obligations, which he could never defer – whatever domestic crisis might be afoot.. Time and again Charles would tell Diana, 'There is no alternative. There are no 'ifs' and 'buts' in my life. I have duties I must perform and which take precedence over everything.'

Later, during some ferocious spats, Diana would accuse Charles of not loving her or William, shouting through her tears, 'If you loved us you would stay here with us.

Even when I beg you to stay, you don't. What kind of man are you?'

Charles was in an impossible situation. For the majority of the time, he would try to calm the situation, constantly explaining that he had to adhere to a strict timetable and that he could never be seen to keep people waiting. He explained that he had to go; he had no choice in the matter; that was his job, his duty. When Diana realized that Charles was not going to alter his routine to please her, she turned on his senior advisers and particularly the man she saw as her implacable foe, Edward Adeane, whom she came to treat with venom, sarcasm and obvious loathing.

On occasions she would verbally attack Sir Edward, blaming him for ruining her marriage. It was therefore not surprising that the highly intelligent Sir Edward, an honourable man, eventually quit the job. He came to realize that he couldn't win in such a situation and, furthermore, he wondered whether staying around the couple might in fact be detrimental to their relationship.

As the world now knows, the effect of these traumas culminated in Diana becoming ill and refusing to eat properly, which led to her bulimia and anorexia. Diana became a classic case of *bulimia nervosa*, eating mountains of a single food at one time – for example, scoffing an entire 2lb carton of ice cream – and then making herself sick by putting her finger down her throat. She would later claim that making herself ill made her feel in control of her eating habits and, she claimed, relieve the inner tension she felt. At the height of her anorexia, which lasted on-and-off for some four years, Diana's weight plummeted from around 8 stone 9 lbs to under 7 stone 2lbs. At these times Diana would describe herself as 'a bag of bones'.

To make matters worse, some weeks after William was born, Diana suffered from post-natal depression. This psychological reaction to the birth triggered more black moods. Understandably, she found it impossible to cope with the depression and her bulimia. Her mood swings, which had started during the latter months of her pregnancy, returned with a vengeance and her personal staff never knew from hour to hour how they would find her. At times, of course, Diana was wonderfully happy, the life and soul of the party, joyful and smiling and great company, particularly when cuddling and playing with William. At other times, and for no apparent reason, her euphoric mood would change in an instant and the black cloud of depression, irritability and self-loathing would descend again, frequently accompanied by floods of tears. Charles became seriously worried and so did the Queen and Diana's close relatives.

It was time for action. Doctors, psychiatrists, counsellors and psychologists were called in to advise on Diana's emotional problems in a bid to help the princess rid herself of these inner conflicts, encourage her to eat normally, and somehow come to terms with her life as the wife of the Prince of Wales, the mother of the future king. But Diana didn't really want to know. Sometimes she would be happy to see these people for she rather enjoyed being the centre of attention, but on other occasions she hated the idea of feeling like a goldfish in a bowl with hordes of different people with different medical skills queuing up to gaze at her, examine and question her.

Whenever Diana felt like a goldfish, she simply refused to see them or talk to them. She would leave the room and go to her bedroom, refusing to come out while eminent doctors, physicians and psychiatrists would wait patiently in an adjoining room in the hope that the Princess of Wales might change her mind. But Diana hardly ever did change her mind on those occasions, and they would have no option but to leave without having seen or talked to her. From time to time, various different drugs were prescribed and proffered and, on occasion, Diana would take them. But then, for no particular reason, she would refuse to take any more drugs complaining they were either 'useless' or doing her more harm than good. Consequently, the doctors who prescribed them would tell her that if she wanted to get better she should heed their advice. Such advice, however, had no effect on the stubborn Diana. She simply did what she wanted when she wanted.

In the autumn of 1983, however, a year after the birth of William, Diana seemed to be making a recovery. Her moods became less black, her eating habits less bizarre, and she appeared happier and more content with herself. The change came about some months after she met a dashing young Guards officer by the name of James Hewitt.

Chapter Two
The Prisoner Rebels

The gilded cage never suited Diana's temperament or character. The girl who had once roamed in freedom around her father's country estate in Northampton found real problems coming to terms with having to reside in an open prison – despite the fact that her prison was a palace. Of course, Diana was permitted to move around the palace and the grounds but, because of the constant IRA threat, forbidden to leave the sanctuary of home.

On one famous occasion, shortly after moving to Kensington Palace, Diana decided to go for a walk, desperate to escape the confines of the palace and to breathe some fresh air. She would later tell what happened, explaining how she had simply walked out of the house and down the drive to where the police were on guard. Instead of stopping, she just kept on walking. Apparently, the officers looked at each other, unsure how to react, and Diana kept on walking towards Kensington High Street, one of her old shopping grounds. As she was wearing a coat and scarf, she hoped no one would recognize her. She managed to walk some 200 yards before the police officers gave chase. As they ran towards Diana, she quickened her pace, determined to try and lose herself in the crowded street. But just as she was about to dive into the first shop, the officers caught up with her. 'Excuse me

Ma'am,' said the first breathless officer, 'but I've been instructed to escort you back to the palace.'

Diana pleaded with them, saying she only wanted to look at some clothes before returning to the palace. The police officers, of course, were in an impossible situation. They had been ordered to apprehend Diana and escort her back to the palace. 'Ma'am,' said the other officer politely, 'we can't permit that. It would be worth more than our job to let you go shopping on your own and we can't accompany you dressed in uniform. We'll have to ask you to accompany us. I'm sorry.'

Diana later recalled that she had pleaded with the officers to let her go but they were adamant. For a moment she thought of making a dash for freedom but she looked at the concern on their faces and realized that would be unfair. Reluctantly, she returned, escorted by the two officers and seething with rage at such treatment.

Later Diana would laugh at the incident, 'I walked back towards the palace sandwiched between the two officers and I felt as though I was under arrest, being escorted back to prison.'

As Diana's pregnancy continued, she became more disillusioned with her life, seemingly cut off from her friends and only seeing her husband in the evening. Once again she felt lonely and unloved. Indeed, Diana would recall, that before William was born, she had reached the conclusion that Kensington Palace had become her prison and she wondered whether she would ever be able to escape.

In her growing despair, Diana tried to persuade her personal police bodyguard, senior courtiers, Sir Edward Adeane and Charles to order the police to permit her to go shopping on her own or, perhaps, with a girlfriend. Of course, Diana could go shopping whenever and wherever she wished but only if accompanied by armed police officers, usually dressed in civilian clothes. But she hated that idea; it made her feel awkward, embarrassed, as though she couldn't be trusted to shop alone.

It was an argument that never went away, causing a running sore between Charles and Diana. Understandably, Diana hated the idea of being confined to live under armed guard from which there was no escape. This led to frequent rows between the royal couple, some of which were heated and very vocal. What really riled Diana was the fact that Charles kept telling her he could not give her permission to go out alone because her safety was not his responsibility but the responsibility of the police officers whose duty it was to protect and guard her at all times.

'But you're the bloody Prince of Wales!' Diana would shout at him. 'They must obey you, they have to obey your f***ing orders!'

In his agonized, desperate manner, Charles would try to calm Diana, telling her that the police were not under his authority and that he could not tell them what to do and what not to do. He tried to make Diana understand that the officers had to obey the orders given to them by their senior officers, which he could not countermand. It was their job, their duty.

These non-stop arguments contributed to a rapid erosion of their relationship. From Diana's standpoint it simply showed that Charles had no real power or authority. She finally came to the conclusion that her husband was little more than a figurehead. As a result, she began to see Charles less as a leader of men, a man of authority, but rather a man with zero influence. And, of course, she quickly came to realize that situation could never, and would never, change.

For some years Diana was convinced that if Charles *really* wanted to be his own man, there was no way anyone could stop him. She knew that Charles could, if he wished, simply tell them to 'f*** off' and leave him alone – convinced the police and his staff would obey such an order because they were trained to obey orders. It took a number of years for Diana to fully understand that Charles, like her, was a prisoner of the system from which he too could never escape

She also came to understand that Charles would never order an adviser, a bodyguard, a police officer or any member of his staff to carry out an order he knew went against their duty, whereas Diana knew that if she had been in her husband's position she would have happily issued such orders to all and sundry.

Somewhat unfairly, Diana saw this as a lack of courage in Charles' character, rather than the fact that he was hidebound by his upbringing, his position and his respect for the system. The sad reality was that this particular argument, which never reached a conclusion, drove a wedge between the two of them, forcing them further and further apart. On occasions Diana's frustration would explode and she would plead with Charles to break the rules, demand his freedom and go shopping or take a walk with her on their own, with no bodyguards. And it would drive Diana into a fury because Charles refused to even contemplate such action, let alone agree to it.

As Charles told Diana a thousand times, he wouldn't do so because it would be 'grossly unfair' to those responsible for their safety, and he would never put them in that impossible position. Of course, Diana would disagree, sometimes shouting and pleading with him, but Charles would not be moved.

Sometimes Diana became so desperate to escape on her own that she would make a break for freedom, leaving the palace in disguise, pretending to be one of the office workers employed at Kensington Palace taking a lunch break. She would wear a long coat and a scarf over her head in an effort to hide her face. She would walk with her hands in her coat pockets, her head down, in the hope that she could escape the notice of the officers on duty as she slipped past the barrier. But every time, she failed. Diana became convinced that the police manning the barrier were tipped off by palace staff who had seen her walk out in her disguise. She discovered her theory was right and that really angered her. Diana hated the ignominy of being stopped and instructed to return to the house like some schoolgirl playing truant and she would return to the palace angry and depressed.

It is difficult to emphasize how important this issue of personal freedom was to Diana and how it affected her relationship with Charles. She felt she was living in a prison without bars. She would say to friends, to her family, 'There are armed guards who physically stop me from walking out of the place and they then insist on escorting me back again just like any prison officer would if a prisoner tried to escape from jail. There really is no difference, no difference at all.'

Diana believed her enforced confinement was responsible, in large measure, for causing her bulimia because there was nothing for her to do all day but sit around Kensington Palace, watch television, listen to music, phone friends, read magazines, gorge chocolates or, as many bored people do, eat any food to hand. And

Diana had never really enjoyed reading at any time in her life, probably because she had never been encouraged to do so during her formative years. As a youngster she had tended to watch television. So she became bored. Of course, once William was born, she had him to bathe, dress, play with or cuddle but there were always nannies and nursery maids scurrying around carrying out those duties for her.

As a result, Diana found herself constantly raiding the refrigerator, picking at things, having a snack or eating fruit or sweets in an effort to stave off the relentless boredom that ground her down. 'I'm bored, bored, bored to death!' she would yell at Charles. 'Don't you understand that? There's nothing for me to do, nothing except watch bloody TV and eat! Don't you understand that I want my freedom, I need my freedom, otherwise I'll go stark raving mad stuck here all day in this God-forsaken place!' Quite often, such outbursts would be punctuated by a number of her favourite swear words, the word 'fucking' being one of them.

So Diana would raid the pantry and munch away until the feeling of guilt struck her and she would throw away whatever food she was eating and make herself sick. For a while that would re-establish her equilibrium, her peace of mind, but the gorging quickly became a vicious circle. The downward spiral had begun but, at that time, Diana didn't recognize the symptoms.

She became convinced that if she had been allowed to go shopping on her own, to spend a couple of hours alone buying clothes, wandering around her favourite stores, having lunch alone with a friend, she would have been happy. She would tell friends that being given some time alone would have made her feel relaxed and contented because, if she was enjoying herself, there would have been no compulsion for her to stuff herself full of food she didn't want in a bid to bring some pleasure into her dull existence.

In fact, Diana was allowed to go out shopping or see a girl-friend for lunch in any London restaurant on the understanding that an armed police officer was in attendance at all times. But Diana wanted her freedom. The argument that IRA gunmen might try to kidnap or kill her cut no ice with her. She considered the idea so preposterous, she thought it was simply an excuse for insisting that she had to be accompanied by a man with a gun whenever she left the palace grounds.

Diana would argue that she could never relax when under the constant, watchful eye of an armed bodyguard. She didn't want some policeman going into shops with her when she was buying clothes or whatever. She didn't want him sitting at a nearby table whenever she lunched with a friend, watching everything she did, listening to her private conversations. As Diana put it to some of her girl-friends, 'Does a girl really want some policeman standing by watching her while she buys her bra and knickers?'

Her friends would laugh, but to Diana it was no joke. To most of her young friends, of course, Diana was the luckiest young woman in the entire world, the envy of everyone – married to the Prince of Wales, with servants, chauffeurs, cooks and maids, magnificent homes to live in, wardrobes full of designer clothes, never wanting for any material goods and all the money she could spend. But not to Diana.

The youthful, miserable Diana wasn't the only non-royal married to a member of 'The Firm', as the royals refer to their own close family unit. There were others who shared her anxieties, who yearned for freedom, found life unbearable within the tiresome confines of royal protocol. The present House of Windsor is littered with broken marriages and one of the primary reasons for those casualties is not the personal relationships themselves, but the never-ending life of duty, obedience, confinement and living their lives in a goldfish bowl with the world examining – and more often than not, criticising – their every movement, remark, every dress and outfit, every hairstyle or makeover.

From the day she became queen in February 1952, Elizabeth wanted her family to be the epitome of a loving, caring nuclear family, a beacon of moral example to the British people. Born in 1926, Elizabeth grew up convinced that divorce was an abomination, a sin in the eyes of the Christian church which had never been tolerated by the Royal Family. Royal courtiers also accepted that situation and they saw their duty as upholding the good name of the monarchy to ensure standards never slipped. Throughout Elizabeth's early life, divorcees had been treated like lepers, ostracized by the court, forbidden to ever meet a member of the Royal Family. Indeed, no divorced person was permitted to be in the presence of the monarch, in the same room or even in the same residence. Divorcees were never invited to attend the Queen's summer tea parties on the lawns of Buckingham Palace, even if they had attended earlier parties before being divorced.

When Elizabeth became monarch at the tender age of 26, she understood that two world wars had weakened the nation's moral fibre as well as a sense of duty and obligation. She determined to do all in her power to persuade the British people to return to the golden age when no divorces were even contemplated, let alone condoned by any section of society. Guided by her strong-willed Scottish mother, Elizabeth determined to uphold such principles.

In 1967, fifteen years after her coronation, Elizabeth's attitude to divorce was still unforgiving and, in a remarkable demonstration of her principles and belief in the old moral code, Elizabeth acted in a draconian fashion towards the divorce of her own cousin, George Lord Harewood, with whom she had been on close family terms. His wife, the beautiful and talented concert pianist Marion Stein, wanted to divorce Lord Harewood after he met a striking Australian model, Patricia Tuckwell, who, in 1965, bore him a son. Harewood went to see Elizabeth to seek permission for a divorce but she refused, calling in the Prime Minister Harold Wilson and the Archbishop of Canterbury in an effort to gain their support and to dissuade her cousin from such action. She was adamant that as a matter of principle, no close member of the Royal Family should be allowed to divorce. In the end, Elizabeth did agree to a divorce but only because the young woman had borne Harewood a child. However, the consequences were brutal for Harewood. They were intended to be so as a warning to all other members of the extended Royal Family.

Elizabeth ordered that Harewood be banished from court and her draconian action of total ostracism ended much of his public life. On her explicit instructions, Harewood was forced to resign his position as Chancellor of York University and also as artistic director of the famous Edinburgh Festival. And yet, in an ironic twist of fate, only two years later, Elizabeth had to sign into the law of the land her government's 1969 Divorce Reform Act, permitting easier and quicker divorce with no blame attached to either party. She had no choice, of course, for the unwritten British Constitution gives Parliament the right to pass laws as they see fit and the Sovereign must sign such Acts of Parliament into the law of the land. Under no circumstances is the British monarch permitted to refuse to bring any new Act of Parliament into law.

With that Act of Parliament, divorce rocketed in Britain over the next 20 years. And Elizabeth was soon to find herself in the most embarrassing situations. In 1978 Princess Margaret, Elizabeth's only sister, divorced Lord Snowdon. Worse was to follow. In 1980, Elizabeth was shocked to be confronted with a marital problem much closer to home and even more shameful. Her only daughter, Princess Anne, then sixth in line to the throne, was involved in a sexual relationship with her personal police bodyguard, Sergeant Peter Cross. Unnerved at the revelation, the Queen ordered a close watch be kept on the couple and she demanded weekly reports of the lovers' trysts. On hearing that the couple were having a full-blown affair, Elizabeth ordered the immediate removal of Peter Cross from royal protection duties.

The gutsy Anne was furious, turned on her rather meek husband, Captain Mark Phillips – whose nickname inside the Royal Family was 'Fog' – and accused him of telling tales behind her back. Eventually, Mark confessed that he had told the Queen's own personal bodyguard about Anne's adultery, which infuriated Anne further.

However, Mark Phillips had never really enjoyed his high-profile position that came with being married to the

Queen's only daughter. He had never felt comfortable being a member of the Royal Family, and had steadfastly refused to become involved in any royal matters at any time during their marriage. And so, to all intents and purposes, Mark Phillips kept in the background, out of sight and out of the royal limelight.

At that time, however, neither the Queen nor Mark Phillips knew Anne was pregnant and that the father of the unborn child was Peter Cross. After being withdrawn from royal duties, Cross resigned from the police protection squad and was then free to see Anne at any time. Anne's daughter, blue-eyed, blonde-haired, feisty Zara, was born in 1981. Only when the Queen finally learned that Peter Cross was Zara's father did she permit Anne and Mark to divorce. In those circumstances, of course, she had no real option but to grant the divorce, but she was mortified that her own daughter had let her down by committing adultery and having a baby out of wedlock.

However, the Queen was determined to show her daughter her displeasure, refusing to permit her to live openly with Peter Cross until some time had elapsed after the divorce – for the public had no idea that Zara was not Mark Philips' daughter. However, after Zara's birth, Anne and Cross continued to see each other and Anne would phone him at his office using the name Mrs Wallis. (It was Anne's mischievous idea to use the name of the most famous adulteress known to the House of Windsor, the American divorcee Wallis Simpson, who married King Edward VIII after he abdicated the throne in 1937). However, Cross did not want to spend the rest of his life as Anne's secret lover and became convinced the Queen would never permit her only daughter to marry a 'mere cop'. So he began looking for another woman and, eventually met and fell in love with a dental nurse. A distraught, tearful Anne had to accept that she had lost the man she loved and she was furious with her mother for taking such action, driving away the father of her beloved Zara.

The Queen found it difficult to accept that divorce had entered her own family. But as the world now knows, Anne's divorce was only the start of a catastrophic period for the Royal Family and a particularly difficult one for the Queen herself as the nation looked on gripped by the revelations of scandals, affairs, betrayals and the intimate details of royal shenanigans in the tabloid press. In the space of a few years, the marriages of two of her sons and her daughter fell apart amidst dreadful scandals and bitterness, which gripped the attention not only of the British nation but much of the western world.

The feisty, flame-haired Sarah Ferguson, daughter of the late Major Ronald Ferguson, who played polo with both the Duke of Edinburgh and later Prince Charles, had arrived on the royal scene with big smiles and great enthusiasm, but little decorum. Overnight, Fergie, as the world came to know her, caught the eye of Prince Andrew and within weeks the two were inseparable, apparently spending the majority of their time in bed together. Andrew was bowled over by the audacious, bubbly, boisterous Fergie, who enjoyed the reputation of being a very sexy lady.

A matter of months after their first date, in the summer of 1986, Andrew married Fergie; two years later Beatrice arrived, and in 1990 Eugenie. But royal life never suited the extrovert Fergie. She was too outgoing, too boisterous, too full of life, too headstrong; and there seemed no possibility that she would ever calm down and lead a quiet background existence, dutifully carrying out royal duties by Prince Andrew's side. Fergie also discovered that Andrew was not the man she had hoped would be able to quench her sexual appetite and she had begun to look around for other likely prospects. It didn't help their marriage, of course, that Andrew had spent most of their married life away at sea with the Royal Navy, providing Fergie with a free rein to indulge herself.

In November 1989, when three months pregnant with Eugenie, Fergie went on an official royal visit to Houston, Texas, to represent the Queen at the British Festival at the Houston Grand Opera. There she met Steve Wyatt, 35, a serious, athletic, handsome man with a mahogany suntan who did not smoke, drink or take any form of drugs. Fergie became smitten by his seductive talk of karma, astrology, divinity and other New Age subjects, interests which were dear to her own heart and a million miles from the conversation she usually had with Prince Andrew. She spent much of the evening dancing with Steve. It was a real-life fatal attraction.

Fergie invited Steve to London, escorted him on a personal tour of Buckingham Palace and arranged invitations for him to lunch at the palace and dinner at Windsor Castle. She even introduced her new 'friend' to Prince Andrew when he was home on leave and, apparently, they all got on famously – having supper and barbecues together. Months after meeting Wyatt, Fergie took Bea and Eugenie on holiday to Morocco and she brazenly invited Wyatt to join them. Unknown to Andrew, the couple were enjoying a passionate fling, which continued when they returned to London.

Eventually, Fergie's illicit sex exploits reached the ears

of senior courtiers at the palace, and by the autumn of 1990 the Queen was informed. Fergie was summoned by the Queen's Private Secretary, Sir Robert Fellows (Diana's brother-in-law), informed that the Queen knew of her affair with Wyatt and ordered to end the matter forthwith. Fergie took no notice, seemingly oblivious to the fact that this potential scandal could be ruinous to her reputation and her marriage as well as deeply embarrassing to the Queen.

The influential powers of Buckingham Palace, however, had more of an effect on Wyatt. He was discreetly taken to one side and advised to end his relationship with Fergie and leave Britain on the next plane. He took the advice and fled. Unhappy and upset that the 'love of her life' was deserting her for no apparent reason, Fergie was convinced that the Establishment had been surreptitiously at work in the background. She was furious that they had the audacity to interfere in her private life.

The departure of Wyatt brought Fergie to the edge of a nervous breakdown, for without Wyatt she felt vulnerable and defenceless. She believed her phones were being tapped, her mail checked, her meetings with everyone spied on. Even the ebullient, cheery Fergie couldn't take the pressure and towards the end of 1991 she began to fall apart.

In a remarkable interview for the society magazine *The Tatler*, Fergie confessed, 'I just have to get away from The System and people saying to me all the time 'no you can't, no you can't'. That's what The System is like. I can't stick to all these guidelines, to all the rules, because they're not real. It's not a real life living in a palace. And I feel so inhibited.

'I don't even feel happy at our home at Sunninghill. Some nights I ask every member of staff to leave so that we can be a family, on our own, like any normal family.'

The interview continued:

'I like to get away but I feel I can't. If I lived in Europe no one would be any the wiser – if, for example, I went to the mountains. I could go skiing for the weekend and no one would bat an eyelid. But here, everyone thinks skiing is an elitist sport. The mountains are my security. I love them. The mountains talk to me and they give me strength. But I'm not allowed to go because of being seen, because of what people might say or write, and all because I'm now owned by The System. Therefore I don't go and I feel trapped. And it is The System that is trapping me.'

Diana, who enjoyed an on-off-on friendship with Fergie, totally sympathized with the latter's frustration and her description of life inside The Firm, and phoned Fergie to congratulate her, telling her she wished she had the courage to write something similar. She congratulated Fergie for telling the world what life was really like inside the Royal Family, everyone thinking its members all enjoyed the most wonderful life, never realising that life - at least for some of them – was really 'bloody awful'.

Despite Elizabeth's obvious displeasure at the goings-on of the younger generation, it seems an extraordinary irony that for many years she stoically accepted Prince Philip's adultery with her own cousin, Princess Alexandra. It has, of course, been a hugely embarrassing part of Elizabeth's life, the affair lasting some twenty years from 1955 to the mid-1970s. The Queen had no option but to live with the painful knowledge of that deeply embarrassing and hurtful liaison. Though she had been told of the affair by her Private Secretary in the late 1950s,

Philip had simply refused to end the relationship, thus causing a severe rift in their marriage.

Philip was of course aware that Elizabeth, as Queen, could do nothing about it. Those close to the Queen, who knew the facts of Philip's relationship with Alexandra, were outraged that her husband, seemingly so dutiful, had continued the relationship despite appeals from his wife to end the affair because of the appalling embarrassment it would cause her and the entire Royal Family if it ever became public knowledge. Some who knew of the secret affair considered Philip had acted like a 'cad and a blackguard'.

Of course, Diana had come to learn of it and she knew the Queen had been placed in an impossible position, unable to do anything but appeal to the better natures of the two lovers. And yet they had continued their affair.

This knowledge revealed to Diana how far the Queen and her courtiers would go to protect the image of the monarchy. It gave her more confidence to continue her own affair, safe in the knowledge that the Queen would go to extraordinary lengths to keep such matters secret. And as Diana found herself becoming ever more popular with the British people, so she felt increasingly confident in continuing her love affair. The crowds, the cheering mums and their daughters, gave Diana the confidence and determination to cock a snook at the Royal Family and enjoy a life independent of them. As the mother to the heir to the throne, Diana knew she was in a powerful position and she began to enjoy her new-found confidence.

On occasions, Diana would say that she could almost feel the love and esteem in which the British public held her. She witnessed their feelings towards her every time she made public appearances. But that was no accident of fate. Diana had set out to woo them to her cause, to win their support, their friendship and their love, because she understood that women nearly always gave their support to a woman whose husband had cheated on her.

And they believed that Charles had cheated on Diana.

Diana knew the great majority of British women supported her and she knew that when the world heard Charles had walked away from their marriage into the arms of his old flame, they would support her as one of them. She would also show them that she had become a victim of the Royal Family, a 'non-person' who had to yield to the orders of the 'The Firm' and their courtiers, and be subjected to their demands as well their rigid rules of royal protocol.

It was shortly after Harry's birth that Diana first conceived her bold plan. She put it into operation almost immediately, testing the ground to see how popular she had become. She soon discovered that the British people had taken her to their collective bosom. To many women Diana had become 'that darling girl'. Although she was born an aristocrat, with family trees even more royal than the House of Windsor, the British people considered Diana one of them because she had worked as a char woman, a nanny and a kindergarten teacher and, importantly, they came to believe that, like tens of thousands of other British women, she had been betrayed by her husband. That meant Diana was one of them. In such a scenario Charles didn't stand a chance.

In the early years of her marriage Diana's shy smile and bashful appearance won the hearts of most people, but even Diana was astonished by the adoration the women of Britain showed towards her whenever she made public appearances. As a result, Diana came to enjoy the great majority of her royal visits and official engagements, even those she feared would be boring because those who turned out to see her, to wave their flags and cheer, were growing in numbers. And the courtiers knew full well that the crowds were increasing almost exclusively because of Diana's presence. When Charles undertook official engagements without her, the crowds diminished, sometimes as much as 80 per cent.

The television news showed crowds welcoming the royal couple but chanting in unison: 'Di-an-a, Di-an-a!' as the royal car drew up. Sometimes, that chant would continue unabated until after she had been driven away – sometimes some 30 minutes later. She took great comfort in that enthusiasm and support, and, importantly, it gave her courage. That was why, on many of those obligatory occasions that she had originally feared and hated so much, Diana was seen happy, smiling and genuinely enjoying herself.

In the early days of her marriage she had proved herself, making public appearances while pregnant with William, and portraying the image of a happy, smiling mum-to-be, even though she was suffering from terrible bouts of morning sickness. These public appearances won her praise and affection.

Before Diana, most royal women never appeared in public when pregnant, preferring to hide their bulging waistlines. But Diana was different, and British womanhood took her to its heart – she who, by chance, happened to have married a prince.

However, for some years the British public had little or no idea that trouble was brewing in the royal marriage. But they were soon to find out.

Chapter Three
Desperate for Love

In 1983, Prince Charles was told by his Private Secretary Sir Edward Adeane, that the Princess of Wales had become involved with a young Cavalry Officer. Adeane did not reveal the officer's name or rank, nor did Charles ask; but Adeane did tell Charles that he not only knew the Officer's name, but confirmed the man was still serving with the Life Guards in the Household Cavalry.

Charles was shocked and somewhat unnerved by the news. He knew that the faithful Sir Edward would not have given him such a delicate and shattering piece of information unless he was absolutely certain that Diana and the unnamed Cavalry Officer were romantically involved. Charles guessed that the information had probably been passed to Sir William by one or other of Diana's police bodyguards, as it was their duty to inform Sir Edward of what was going on.

As is the case with all royal bodyguards, Diana's bodyguard's sole duty was to protect the Princess of Wales. He would have been made well aware that it is never the duty of a police protection officer to judge anyone's morals. Diana's bodyguards had been drilled to understand that the private lives of the royals must remain private. If any of the royals they were protecting had affairs, committed adultery, took drugs or attended wild parties, it was none of their business. The royals had to be permitted to have private lives and feel assured that they could indulge themselves in whatever sexual pleasures or dalliances they wished, safe in the knowledge that such behaviour would remain secret. Police officers were under orders never to reveal such extra-marital matters to their superior officers unless there was an overriding reason for doing so.

Unfortunately for Diana, in the Britain of 1981 there was an overriding reason. The IRA had begun its bloody campaign of bombings and killings in a bid to make Northern Ireland ungovernable and drive the British out of the Province. Terror, bombings and shootings were their weapons and they used them ruthlessly with not a care for those they killed, maimed or wounded. The IRA had already successfully targeted and assassinated one senior member of the Royal Family, Earl Mountbatten, along with three other family members while they were on holiday in Ireland in August 1979. As a direct result of Mountbatten's murder, all police protection officers were ordered to take extra care when guarding their principals and to consider the possible consequences of any untoward behaviour for those they were protecting. As a result of all this, Diana's romantic relationship with a Cavalry Officer was judged a possible threat to her safety; and it was deemed that her secret meetings might expose her to danger. The Household Cavalry, as well as other British regiments, were constantly targeted by the Provisional IRA.

Due to his concern for Diana's safety, her police protection officer had decided that he had no option but to pass on his knowledge of her clandestine movements outside the palace gates to his superior officer. In turn, Sir Edward Adeane was informed.

Perhaps it was hearing this news that caused Charles

to accept the inevitable: that his marriage to Diana was over in all but name. They had been married barely two years and Charles had no idea what had gone wrong or who was to blame. He came to the conclusion that the marriage and their love life had begun to go downhill shortly after she had become pregnant with Prince William, just a few weeks after their wedding.

To give Charles some credit, he had tried everything to please his young bride, and he hoped and prayed that her pregnancy would not only rekindle her love for him, but that having a baby to care for would bring her happiness and contentment. Before their wedding, Diana had talked of the thrill of nurturing and loving a little child of her own for she had understood that she and Charles were expected to have a family. Diana had always loved babies. Hadn't she happily looked after her baby brother Charles when she was only five years of age? The reason she worked for so little money as a London kindergarten teacher was because it involved caring for very young children.

Diana had eagerly looked forward to the prospect of motherhood, and had told girl friends she hoped to have a large family. She understood that one of the reasons Charles needed to marry was so that he could, God willing, produce not only an heir for the House of Windsor but also a vibrant young family. They had talked about all these matters well before their engagement was announced.

After the bitter experience of his own childhood, Charles wanted his children to lead a happy, free life without the dreadful restrictions that had been imposed on him by his parents since the age of four. Diana, too, wanted her children to be part of a loving family, unlike her own lonely childhood after her mother fled the family home.

During former relationships with a number of young women, Charles discovered that because of his position as heir to the throne, some of those affairs ended in disaster. A number of the young women soon discovered that dating the Prince of Wales could be awkward and restrictive and not at all idyllic. Charles was a straightforward, regular, heterosexual man with what he gauged was a healthy sexual appetite – as probably a dozen or more women can testify.

And yet, despite his interest in the opposite sex, Charles himself openly recognized that he wasn't in any way a 'ladies' man'. He always felt somewhat awkward, even gauche, in the presence of a young woman, particularly one he found attractive and felt a strong sexual attraction towards.

One of his first girlfriends, Caroline Wisley, whom he dated in the 1970s, confessed: 'We had some fun together and he was wonderfully polite and well-mannered, but when it came to going to bed together he seemed unsure of himself, even embarrassed, and yet he had no reason to be. The other problem, which really seemed rather stupid, was that I had been advised that I should call him 'Sir' on all occasions. Every girl can imagine how off-putting it would be to have to call her lover 'Sir' throughout all the passion and love-making. It totally put me off.'

With some young women, however, he felt no embarrassment whatsoever, particularly with those women who enjoyed his jokes and who were interesting conversationalists with bright, sharp minds and a sense of humour. Indeed, Charles found he actually enjoyed such women far more than those he simply fancied physically, usually because he discovered that though he had found them sexually attractive, there had been no meeting of minds.

And now Charles wondered whether he had been foolish in rushing to marry Diana so soon after they began dating. He realised that when they became officially engaged they barely knew each other. But he also recognised that he had been under enormous pressure to wed a suitable young woman because of the real fear amongst the Royal Family and their advisers that the ruthless IRA might well target another member of the family at any time. 'Marry in haste, repent at leisure' was the phrase he couldn't get out of his head.

Before Diana moved in with Charles some months before the wedding, he had never actually lived with a woman. Indeed, he had hardly ever spent more than a long weekend with a young woman he found attractive at any time in his life. Charles had been a typical bachelor and thoroughly enjoyed being a single man. Indeed, if he had not been heir to the throne and subjected to constant badgering from his parents to marry and produce an heir, it is fair to say that Charles might well never have married at all.

Since leaving the Royal Navy at the age of twenty-eight, Charles had gathered a team of men around him to organize his life; to run his office, to organise his diary, to manage his hectic official duties, to manage the multi-million-pound Duchy of Cornwall with its large farms and its property empire in London; to run the Prince's Trust for less fortunate young people seeking a new life; and to take care of his homes. Each day, government papers were delivered to his home informing him, as heir to the throne, of exactly what the government was doing on a day-to-day basis. Like his mother, who also received these daily reports, he was diligent in reading them, though many of the papers were dull and mundane.

In his spare time, Charles relaxed by playing polo, shooting birds and game, fishing for trout in Scottish rivers and, of course, hunting foxes with various hunts throughout Britain. He also found time to attend the theatre in London and enjoyed opera and classical music. From time to time he threw informal parties, usually for his polo friends and others. He also found time to date occasionally but that never seemed to be a priority. He was declared the world's most eligible bachelor who could offer a young woman great wealth, a future kingdom and, one day, the probability of a crown along with the title 'Queen of England'.

But Charles was no ordinary man and could never be one. He had never really enjoyed a normal life. He had never enjoyed a mother-son relationship with the Queen because she was far too involved with her daunting job as monarch to spend much time with any of her children. The love and warmth that most children receive from their mothers was missing and though his nannies were kind, loving and gentle, Charles' only true family relationship was with his father, Philip, who, time has shown, proved a disaster in the role.

At the age of seven, Charles was sent to boarding school. When he turned thirteen, he moved on to the tough Scottish school of Gordonstoun, which was totally unsuitable for a boy of Charles' temperament and where he was never happy. That unfortunate experience was followed by three years at Cambridge University, studying anthropology and archaeology, where he worked hard to achieve a lower second class BA honours degree. But during his years at Cambridge he largely kept himself to himself, meeting a few girls but never becoming involved with any of them. He went on to the RAF flying school at Cranwell in 1971 and not only became a member of the select Ten Ton Club (piloting an aircraft at more than 1,000 mph) but he also learned to parachute. In September 1971 Charles moved on to the Royal Naval College at Dartmouth, joining as a lowly acting sub-lieutenant. Just twelve days before his 23rd birthday he joined his first ship, the guided-missile destroyer HMS *Norfolk.*

It was while serving on *Norfolk* that Charles was introduced to the seamy, raunchy side of life. One night when at anchor in Toulon, southern France, Charles joined a small group of petty officers and ratings for a night on the town. They took him drinking in low dives, touring the red-light district, chatting in his schoolboy French to the girls who were sitting half-naked in the brothel windows. He walked along the quay and saw the prostitutes in the cafes and in the streets plying their trade. Three prostitutes offered themselves to Charles and his group as they walked slowly along the quay but an embarrassed Charles blushed madly and waved them away. At one nightclub he sat at a table drinking a beer for 30 minutes while watching a couple of naked girls dancing immediately above him, gyrating their naked pelvises within a few inches of his face. Charles told the group of ratings that he was amazed at such goings-on, believing it was more like a film set than real life. But he did the decent thing, buying everyone in the party a few rounds of drink before heading back to the ship.

Charles was to spend five happy years at sea in the company of men and naval officers whom he respected.

(At that time, no women were permitted to serve on Royal Navy ships.) In today's world it seems extraordinary that Charles should have led such a life almost bereft of female company and with such little knowledge of the real world. As a baby and young boy, Charles spent very little time with his mother and was cared for by nannies. He only saw his sister Anne in the school holidays As a result, Charles had little or no understanding of women. He was twenty-eight years of age when he finally emerged into the real world where 50 per cent of the population was made up of the female sex.

With that start in life, it is not surprising that Charles never felt he ever understood women; never felt comfortable in their presence and was usually painfully shy when left to chat to an attractive young woman one to one. He only seemed to feel at ease with them on a cerebral level, and, on the few occasions he actually felt sexually attracted to someone, the introductions were usually carried out on his behalf by his closest adviser who would ask the young woman in question whether she would like to dine privately with the Prince in his rooms. On occasions, a lusty romp might follow an excellent dinner where the wine flowed. But more frequently than not, his nights of passion would end up being a one-night stand.

Throughout his life Charles has made some close, long-term friendships with women; usually women with whom he enjoyed a cerebral relationship; women he could trust, enjoy a laugh with or discuss all manner of subjects but who were sensible and down-to-earth types. He never liked frivolous or coquettish women. Indeed, Charles' initial interest in Camilla Parker Bowles was as someone with whom he could enjoy a laugh and a serious conversation, someone who was witty but not overawed chatting to the Prince of Wales. They became friends after Camilla's then boyfriend, Andrew Parker Bowles, who played polo with Charles, introduced them.

Another life-long friend has been the actress Susan George, who still takes tea with Charles perhaps three or four times a year. They are good friends and Charles treasures such open, confidential friendships, mainly because he has so few of them.

Unfortunately for Diana, Charles' character was not conducive to sitting on a sofa in front of a roaring log fire enjoying long cuddles and chats, happily engrossed with the young woman at his side; or spending hours over a romantic candlelit dinner with a lover; or lying in bed together making love for hours at a time. To her horror, Diana quickly discovered that such romantic ideas were never a part of Charles' thought processes. Diana soon came to believe that Charles had never learned how to woo or make love to a woman, never learned to make a girl feel relaxed, happy and secure in a loving relationship; never indulged in little intimacies or affectionate kisses. He didn't seem to understand that young women love to be romanced, seduced and made love to, not simply invited to take part, and, hopefully, enjoy the act of fornication. Diana soon discovered that Charles, though kind and considerate, was no passionate lover. And Diana, brought up in boarding schools, living a secluded, almost solitary existence in the countryside, had never had a boyfriend, and had no sexual experiences whatsoever save for the occasional fumbled kiss at a party.

During the months she lived with Charles before the wedding, however, Diana had discovered her true sexuality and she had become someone who yearned for a passionate relationship. The problem was that Charles was no Lothario!

After the marriage ended in tears, Diana told Sarah, who was married about the same time as Diana, but is now divorced, 'I found much more romance and affection in a magazine story than I ever found with Charles and that made me really sad. It was all such a terrible waste. Basically, Charles is a nice guy but he simply hasn't any idea, any idea at all how to treat a woman.'

Diana told a girl friend some five years after her marriage, 'I accept that it's not his fault; I accept that the whole Royal Family is lacking in affection, warmth and kindness. Poor Charles inherited the family traits and he has to live with that… The trouble was that I fell in love with the whole idea of marrying Prince Charles, perhaps because he was heir to the throne. I had always thought him the perfect man but I just didn't see the personal problems and all the royal baggage that came with him… Stupid, stupid me… I just went into it with my eyes shut, believing the fairy tale would come true… I really did think that the Prince had fallen in love with the girl he had been searching for all his life and that we would live happily ever after.'

This was at the heart of what *really* went wrong with the marriage. With her unfortunate upbringing, with no mother around to love and care for her, and a father who had the will but little or no idea of how to bring up three young daughters in a loving way, Diana was desperate for a close, loving relationship. Charles was the first man who had ever shown her any real commitment and she fell in love with him, hoping that he would give her the confidence she lacked and the love for which she yearned. It is difficult to exaggerate Diana's fundamental need for

55

a caring, loving relationship with someone following her loveless upbringing and what she always considered was her mother's desertion. Unfortunately for Diana, the dutiful, lukewarm and passionless Charles was simply not the man capable of fulfilling those needs. Seemingly, he had little or no idea how he should treat his wife. His own personality faults, perhaps as a result of his own loveless upbringing, prevented him from having a caring, exciting relationship with any woman – let alone an inexperienced, bashful, shy young woman like Diana

Charles was kind, considerate and loving towards Diana, but he simply had no idea of her needs. He never showed Diana the passion, the raw lust for which she yearned and so, unwittingly, he failed her. In the first few months of the marriage, Charles tried to be the perfect husband and he was for the most part kind and considerate to Diana, for he desperately wanted the marriage to be 'hugely successful'. Diana later came to believe that Charles realised that he was no passionate lover and so he tried to keep her happy and contented by giving her whatever material objects she desired. He was keen to indulge her every wish and whim as though trying to compensate for his performances in the bedroom. He was totally generous with money, happily paying all her credit card bills which, with some of her designer clothes, would sometimes amount to hundreds of thousands of pounds a year. He gave her total and complete freedom to do whatever she wanted, go anywhere she wanted, buy anything she wanted as long as she went along with her unspecified and unspoken side of the bargain – to be his wife, his consort, and the mother of his children.

Of course, this bargain included some pretty tedious extras which came under the heading 'duty'. Diana was expected to not only attend boring, dull functions and dinners that he knew she found tiresome, but she was expected to appear relaxed, happy and smiling as well as feigning interest and fascination with the unknown, unnamed official guests whom Charles knew bored her rigid. Charles knew that the great majority of people Diana would meet at such functions were nearly always grey and colourless. Frequently, while driving to such functions Diana would tell Charles how much she would prefer to be at home, sitting in bed watching TV and sipping a mug of hot cocoa.

As the world knows, Diana's interests were high fashion clothes, friends, keeping fit, ballet and watching TV soaps and, of course, caring for her beloved Wills and Harry. It was unfortunate for Diana that her parents seemed to take no great interest in her education, nor was she encouraged to read books. As a result, she arrived in London at the age of seventeen painfully immature, with the bare minimum of an education and no idea what she wanted to do with her life. Diana would have loved to study ballet and become a dancer but she was not only too tall but also not up to the required standard. When that avenue closed abruptly, Diana had no idea what she would do with her life. She had no other ambition.

One of the reasons Diana was so painfully shy was because she felt she had little or no conversation that could interest or fascinate a young man and would often find herself sitting alone at dinner parties. She hated the fact that, every time she began a conversation, she would blush furiously. It was no wonder she felt awkward and embarrassed when meeting Charles' guests at formal and informal gatherings.

Unfortunately, Diana seemed to have no wish to

broaden her interests or educate herself. As some critics commented at the time, 'Diana brought very little to the marriage except good breeding, a healthy young body, good legs, lovely face and a radiant smile.'

After her death, however, even those who had never warmed to Diana admitted, 'She matured with age and during her life she brought compassion and tenderness to a rather cold Royal Family which has never learned the meaning of the word compassion.'

After his years at Gordonstoun and his stint in the Royal Navy, Charles came to believe, like his father, that order, obedience, duty and firmness were essential in all matters and no deviation from these rules should be considered or condoned. But, unlike his father, Charles did believe in fairness when dealing with people and their problems. Fairness and duty were his criteria for leading his own life. But they were simply useless and probably counter-productive in cultivating a loving relationship with Diana. To that extent, Charles was responsible for the breakdown of the marriage.

Though the Queen rarely met Diana on a one-to-one basis, she would on occasions try to reach out to Diana and involve her in family dinner conversations, but Diana's response was usually to blush with embarrassment. Knowing the Queen was only trying to be kind to her made her feel worse. After such attempts by the Queen, Diana would be so embarrassed that she would immediately sink back into her shell and say nothing as the rest of the family chatted away, oblivious to her discomfort. And, because Diana paid little attention to what had actually been said, she didn't even catch on to many of the jokes, so that when the rest of the family laughed at some comment, poor Diana would simply blush because she hadn't even heard what was said, let alone understood the joke. Diana put it succinctly to one of her girl friends, 'All they talk about at dinner is f***ing shooting; it makes me sick!'

After her first disastrous winter at Balmoral, Diana hoped that now she was pregnant, all the love that she had so wanted to share with Charles could now be directed towards the child she was carrying. Later, she would confess to Howard, one of her lovers: 'After the birth of William it seemed to me that Charles lost interest in me. I knew that he had been forced into getting married because his parents had badgered him for years to find a 'suitable' girl. I understood he had to provide an heir. It seemed that after William came along, Charles lost interest in the sex side of our marriage. I felt that he believed he had done his duty by his parents and now he could relax and get on with his own life again – playing polo and all that hunting, fishing and shooting stuff. I think he was quite happy with things but he must have known that I wasn't.'

Diana had tasted some of the delights of a sexual relationship with Charles but had not enjoyed the passion and lust of a full, demanding and satisfying sex life, for which she now yearned. In the summer of 1981, however, her life changed when she first saw and chatted to a certain Lt. James Hewitt at a polo match in which he was playing against Prince Charles.

According to Hewitt's autobiography, *Love and War,* published in 1999, he first met Diana by accident in the month of May, 1986, at Buckingham Palace, though he did recall that he had seen her some five years earlier at the Tidworth Park polo club.

Referring to the 1986 meeting, he recalled, 'I wish I could remember the exact words we spoke but I do remember exactly what I was feeling: just completely bowled over by someone so feminine and friendly and captivatingly beautiful.'

In his autobiography, Hewitt boasts in a caption of a photograph of him challenging Prince Charles on the polo field: 'Polo at Windsor with Prince Charles. We met frequently on the field, both being keen players'.Both Prince Charles and James Hewitt were members of the Guards Polo Club and they would have met on many occasions during the polo seasons. Being a keen polo player, this author also frequently attended matches at Windsor during the 1980s, and on numerous occasions I saw Diana watching Prince Charles playing polo. So it seems strange that Hewitt, according to his own autobiography, apparently never saw or met Diana during those five years before 1986. And if he did, it is even more strange that he did not record or mention such meetings or sightings in his own book.

He recalled other meetings with Diana in the mid-1980s – a discussion about horse riding, his offer to teach her to ride and her gushing acceptance, riding lessons at Knightsbridge Barracks, slow horse-riding in Hyde Park, conversations about Hewitt's girlfriends and then, suddenly, Diana's brutally honest and surprising statement one day when she confessed to an astonished Hewitt, 'Charles and I are not in love and the marriage is on the rocks'.

Hewitt claimed in *Love and War* that Diana had initiated their affair, that she had made the first move, grabbing his hand and, with tears in her eyes, telling him, 'I need you. You give me strength. I can't stand it when I'm away from you; I want to be with you; I've come to love you.' And Diana followed that dramatic declaration of love by leaning forward and sealing her love with a kiss on his lips.

Hewitt also wrote that the date of his first meeting and conversation with Diana was May 1986. But that is not borne out by other facts. Hewitt's name was included in the Approved List of people permitted entry to Kensington palace in 1983, and Prince Charles' former baggage master, the late Sergeant Ronald Lewis, confirmed that Hewitt was a regular visitor to the Princess of Wales' apartment at Kensington Palace in 1983 and 1984. This has since been confirmed to me by other advisers who were working on the staff of the Prince and Princess of Wales at Kensington Palace during the early years of their marriage.

As a result of Earl Mountbatten's 1979 assassination, security had been dramatically stepped up at all royal residences. At Kensington Palace were Charles and Diana, as well as four other Royal Family members who had apartments there. Armed police were on duty in the grounds and on the gate 24 hours a day. Everyone was checked on arrival and no one was permitted to pass the vehicle check-point some fifty yards from the entrance to the palace without being stopped, their identities verified. Of course, those people who worked at Kensington Palace, as well as regular, well-known visitors, were waved through with a salute.

For a number of years following the birth of Prince Harry in September 1984, no one ever suggested that Prince Charles was not Harry's biological father, but throughout his teenage years Harry came to look more and more like James Hewitt and less like Prince Charles. Questions were raised, comparisons made. Harry's hair colour was one of the principal reasons why people commented on his resemblance to James Hewitt. His hair, his eyes, his mouth and his demeanour showed that Harry had become increasingly like Hewitt physically, and his personality also seemed more akin to Hewitt's than Prince Charles'.

This allegation of Hewitt's paternity has always been strenuously denied by Hewitt himself whenever the matter has arisen. Of course, there is absolutely no suggestion of such an allegation in either Hewitt's autobiography or, more importantly the book, *Diana: Her True Story,* which Diana helped to write and edit.

Hewitt's latest denial came in September 2002 when he issued a statement in response to gossip about Harry's paternity, which had reached a crescendo after portraits commemorating the prince's eighteenth birthday were released by Buckingham Palace. (It is customary for photographs to be released of the younger royals when they turn 18 and 21.) Comparing Harry's looks with his own, Hewitt said, 'There really is no possibility whatsoever that I am Harry's father. I can absolutely assure you that I am not'.

Putting on record for the first time his denial of the persistent rumours, Hewitt went on, 'I can understand the interest, but Harry was already walking by the time my relationship with Diana began. Admittedly, the red hair is similar to mine and people say we look alike. I have never encouraged these comparisons, and although I was with Diana for five years, I must state once and for all that I am not Harry's father. When I first met Diana, Harry was already a toddler.'

Hewitt, who claims he was drummed out of the British Army because of his affair with Diana, continued, 'Now Harry is a grown man and he has very different features from Prince William. William looks very much like his mother – Harry is rather different. There is still some family resemblance but it is a lot less noticeable. All this talk of Harry is really very unfair. I think he has been through enough without having his parenthood questioned in public. I am hoping to nail this nonsense once and for all.'

One of Diana's former police bodyguards, Ken Wharfe, who published a book *Closely Guarded Secret* in 2002 about his six years as Diana's personal bodyguard, wrote: 'The nonsense should be scotched here and now. Harry was born on September 15, 1984. Diana did not meet James until the summer of 1986, and the red hair comparison that gossips so love to cite as proof is, of course, a Spencer trait.'

However, Inspector Ken Wharfe only became Diana's personal bodyguard in 1988, when Harry was four years of age, though he had previously been employed as one of the four armed police officers in the 'back-up' car, which escorted the Prince of Wales wherever he travelled. After selling his memoirs, Ken Wharfe found himself *persona non grata* with the Establishment for 'betraying' a member of the Royal Family, in this case Diana, by writing about his life with the Princess and revealing certain intimate details of her love life, in exchange for a lucrative publishing contract.

Wharfe may not have known the true facts of Hewitt's first meeting with Diana, or he may simply have chosen to be economical with the truth so as not to embarrass Harry, Prince Charles or the Queen, which would have brought him even more ignominy.

James Hewitt claimed in his book that Diana initiated the affair between them after months of him giving her riding lessons. When the army moved Hewitt to Windsor, Diana would be driven there two or three times a week by her personal bodyguard so that she could go riding with Hewitt in the discreet privacy of Windsor Great Park.

Hewitt claimed that the affair took off some months after they first met in 1986, writing, 'Diana said that one of her problems was that there was absolutely no one to help her. The Palace was against her and she found it hard to know who would be for her. I said that she could rely on me. She turned to me and, without warning, grabbed my hand. And suddenly it all came out, all in a rush. Her eyes were tearful and she spoke with a passion far removed from her usual teasing flirtatiousness'.

Hewitt would write, 'We embarked on an affair which was to continue for most of the next five years. It was wonderful – exhilarating, passionate and intensely loving. We were young – in our twenties – and when we were together life was carefree and full of fun.'

The meeting and that affair would have untold consequences for Diana herself as well as Charles, William and particularly Harry. It would also engulf the Queen and the entire Royal Family. The affair would also lead to a string of lies and falsehoods. The affair that would grip the nation would also lead to Diana's extraordinary bid to sideline the House of Windsor, remove Prince Charles as heir-apparent and put William on the throne in his place. To achieve her ambitions, however, Diana needed the British public's full support and she had to find a way to win and retain their confidence and, if possible, their love and affection. Without the support of the British public, Diana realized that she would stand no chance against the Queen, the Royal Family and, particularly the Establishment – not to mention the political elite, the Church of England and the millions who adored the Royal Family.

It was an extraordinary challenge that Diana set for herself and yet, at the time of her death, she had succeeded to a remarkable degree. The nation came to love and almost worship her and they showed in their adoration that they fully supported her in her battle against Charles, the Queen and the entire Royal House of Windsor.

But the adulation which Diana had sought and gained so completely would ultimately bring about her untimely death in the fatal car crash of August 1997.

Chapter Four
James Hewitt

It was an accident of fate that Diana first met Hewitt. At the beginning she saw him as a cheeky young officer with whom she could relax and share a joke; someone to talk to, a man who made her smile when all around her seemed so deadly serious. Hewitt would entertain her with jokes and stories and, remarkably, he was prepared to help her escape the confines of the palace and live a little in the real world. Diana found him a breath of fresh air in the stuffy royal environment from which she was desperate to escape. In a matter of weeks, she found in Hewitt a young man in whom she could confide and later, a shoulder to cry on. Within a matter of a couple of months, she had come to rely totally on Hewitt as a confidant and close friend.

In his autobiography, Hewitt wrote: *'I was genuinely sorry for her, for both of them. Their marriage was going through a bad patch. I always thought they made a good couple and I didn't really want to hear otherwise. But sometimes she could hardly bring herself to refer to her husband by name.'*

Hewitt is not a bad man, as the newspapers sometimes claimed – calling him 'evil' – but he is weak and suffers from a false understanding of his own character. Within a matter of months of meeting Diana, the irrepressible Hewitt admitted that he was becoming obsessed with the princess. He wrote: *'I lived from week to week. I couldn't wait to see her again. It was just a complete joy... And from her phone calls and her conversation she gave every indication of just wanting to be with me.'*

It was totally understandable that their relationship would become a full-blown affair – Diana desperately needed someone to depend on and to provide a respite from her prison life at Kensington Palace, an escape from the husband she no longer loved or respected.

The affair gave Diana an opportunity to unload all her emotional baggage. Hewitt wrote, *'Diana was emotionally fragile... She was a woman deeply damaged by rejection. Whether it was true or not, she saw herself as being wholly alone in a hostile world, with no one to turn to, share her problems with or give her guidance.'*

In some ways, it was most fortunate that the dashing, flirtatious, confident Hewitt appeared on the scene at that moment in 1983 when Diana was desperate to meet people outside the cloistered confines of Kensington Palace. Hewitt's offer to teach her to ride was a great opportunity to escape from her gilded prison. It was unfortunate, however, that Diana was still a naïve, almost innocent young woman who had never practised birth control and had never needed to. Except for those few months of love with Charles at the time of their engagement, Diana had never really enjoyed a full-blooded, passionate relationship with any man. But Hewitt changed all that and Diana revelled in the passion, the sexual craving, the desire and the all-consuming lust she had never before experienced. She felt deep physical attraction for this man who took her to heights she had never before experienced. In those first two years with Hewitt, Diana believed that she had met the man with whom she wanted to spend the rest of her life, especially after Harry arrived.

But when Diana found herself pregnant with Harry in early 1984, she realized she had put herself in a most difficult situation. Diana wanted her unborn child to have been fathered by Hewitt but she didn't know whether he or Charles was the father. She wasn't sure. She knew she loved Hewitt and she also realised her relationship with Charles was falling apart. However, finding herself unexpectedly pregnant, Diana was overcome by a sudden sense of guilt. She confessed all to Hewitt, telling him how much she wanted his child but to Charles, the royal family, her own family and friends she clung to the possibility that Charles was the father. She felt in her heart, she somehow knew that Hewitt was the child's father but, understandably, to all and sundry, she continued the pretence that Charles was the father. Of course Diana feared that if anyone knew of her affair with Hewitt she would be branded an adulteress, a homewrecker. This weighed heavily on her mind. She couldn't face the prospect of the nation, who now adored her, turning against her in condemnation of her philandering so soon after the fairytale wedding. Diana found great difficulty in ridding herself of her gut-wrenching feeling of guilt which she found increasingly difficult to bear.

These were the real reasons why Diana's health deteriorated so rapidly before Harry was born and continued to decline afterwards. These were the reasons she became bulimic and suffered anorexia. And it wasn't only physical. Mentally, as her lack of educational qualifications illustrate, the young Diana was not a strong woman, and she simply could not cope with the trauma going on in her personal life as well as the fear that at any time her most intimate secret – her affair with Hewitt – might be splashed over the front pages of every newspaper in Britain. Those fears tore her apart and she suffered dreadfully.

Throughout her pregnancy, these thoughts never left her mind and, in some desperation, she decided to banish Hewitt from Kensington Palace, though she knew she was was in love with him. Hewitt agreed to her plan, although he did occasionally visit her there. However, these visits were few and far between and he never stayed more than a couple of hours. Instead, they spoke for hours on the phone but the fact that she had to keep the man she loved at arm's length during the months of pregnancy and afterwards made Diana depressed and miserable.

Throughout these months, of course, Diana had no idea, no idea whatsoever, that Charles knew she had taken a lover. Indeed, it is likely that the Queen had also been informed. Of course, the Royal Protection police officers noted that Hewitt had quit the scene and presumed the affair was at an end. To his credit, Charles continued to play the diligent, happy father-to-be and he was also the first person to visit Diana and see Harry only a couple of hours after the birth.

Diana waited six months before she believed it safe to renew her acquaintance with Hewitt. It seemed that no paparazzi had seen them together, there were no stories about Hewitt in the tabloids and no incriminating photographs. It seemed they had managed to keep their affair a secret. Diana felt confident enough to rekindle their affair and looked forward once again to spending magical moments with the man she loved. However, she did not want to take too many risks and so Hewitt's visits to Kensington Palace were for only for a few hours at a time, with him usually arriving for dinner and disappearing before midnight.

It was after the birth of Harry in September 1984 that Hewitt gave Diana his signet ring to place in safe-keeping for the day Harry reached his eighteenth birthday. At the time, both he and Diana believed they were destined one day to live openly together and maybe even marry.

And so the affair continued happily.

But all those thoughts were put on hold when Hewitt was posted to Germany, unnerving Diana, who felt this was yet another rejection in her tortured life. It was not until the day before he was due to fly to Germany that Hewitt told Diana that he was leaving England and, more importantly, leaving her for a two-year tour of duty. A devastated Diana burst into tears, as she felt fate had intervened to exile the man she loved. Later, she wondered whether Hewitt's posting to Germany was part of a plot to separate her from him and, if that was the case, she felt certain that both Charles and the Queen, as well as senior courtiers like her brother-in-law, Sir Robert Fellowes, must now know of her adultery. She would never know that answer. But she wasn't at all pleased. In his book, Hewitt related how resentful and bitter Diana became at that time, telling him, '*You promised you'd always be here for me and now you've broken that promise.*'

Hewitt left for Germany and did not hear another word from Diana for three months. In fact, he served two tours in Germany and during that time, despite occasional home leaves, Diana saw very little of her lover. She convinced herself that their separation was a deliberate plan to keep the two apart but she wasn't sure who really knew. Of course she hoped and prayed it was simply senior army officers, acting on their own, having heard that Diana and

Hewitt seemed too close to each other.

Fed up, unhappy and needing some new interests in her loveless life, Diana began showing an interest in going out for cocktail evenings or small dinner parties. At these parties she would meet a number of young men who were surprised at how friendly and forward Diana had become. Her renowned shyness had all-but disappeared; she joined in the conversations and quickly earned herself a reputation for telling the dirtiest of dirty jokes – and reveling in the effect such jokes had on the men around her. She began accepting dates from some of these men, enjoying one-on-one dinner dates, going to the cinema and letting people know she was now a true party-girl.

When Hewitt's regiment was transferred to the Gulf in 1990, however, forming The Life Guards Squadron, a part of the 4th Armoured Brigade, Diana's reaction was immediate. She suddenly realized she still loved him and feared for his life. The thought that her former lover, the father of her darling Harry, was going to face real danger sent a chill through her. There was nothing she could do; but she followed every day of the war against Saddam Hussein's Iraqi forces with as much nervousness as any woman with a loved one in that war. She listened to every news bulletin, lit candles for Hewitt and wrote him many letters.

One letter contained the following: *'God the worry is simply dreadful bordering on agony for you all. I do hope that you're home soon...I think of you constantly and I've got the youngest son [Harry] doing the same now and every tank on the news contains you as far as he's concerned.'*

For Hewitt, that war will always serve as a memory of the support he received from Diana. She wrote to him frequently, mailed him presents every week and on occasions he would phone her out of the blue from the desert, one time stupidly borrowing the phone from a tabloid journalist who knew exactly whom he was calling. Diana would sign her love letters 'Julia' and the name on the back of the envelope – which was required by the army – was Evelyn Dagley, the name of Diana's personal dresser.

However, there was little or no passion or declarations of everlasting love in the letters she wrote. And yet, her letters appeared to reveal a new side to Diana's character, showing how caring and supportive she could be in a one-to-one relationship. She wanted Hewitt to understand that there was at least one person back home in Britain who was thinking of him in his hour of danger. Despite that, most of the letters were simply friendly, chatty, sometimes even jokey and flippant. Diana would tease Hewitt, often with obvious sexual connotations and references, asking him, for example, how many women he had laid since arriving in the Gulf, adding 'all chicks look good with a tan'. She also asked after Hewitt's personal wellbeing, writing, 'I'm glad to hear about my friend, let's hope he's okay' (a reference to Hewitt's penis).

Diana would send Hewitt top-shelf sex magazines and would lovingly add, 'Take enormous care, I think of you a great deal and long for you to return. F***ing practice really needed.'

Despite their enforced separation and Diana's fear for Hewitt's life she had reached the conclusion that their relationship had probably run its course. After Harry was born, she knew in her heart there was no future for her with Hewitt. The two had talked of a future together on many occasions. Diana had urged Hewitt to quit the army and for the two of them to find somewhere in the country to live together, to raise a family and get on with life as a couple. She didn't want another marriage, just a loving relationship with their Harry and perhaps one or two other children. But whenever Diana broached the subject Hewitt didn't seem to want to know. She came to the reluctant conclusion that Hewitt hadn't really got the guts to run away with her. It was time to find another man.

It is somewhat remarkable that in his autobiography *Love and War*, Hewitt barely makes mention as to how and why their affair broke down or what Diana's reaction was to its ending. Readers are left to ponder with no suggestions proffered.

In essence, Diana had lost interest in Hewitt because she felt that despite his wartime experiences in the Gulf, he lacked the courage required to take her away from the Royal family. He feared the consequences would be dire in the extreme, with him perhaps even facing the embarrassment and ignominy of a court martial and then being cashiered. Hewitt was no rich man's son. He had no money in the bank and no prospects of a good job in any profession. He was a professional soldier whose only income was the paltry pay of a junior officer. He feared that if he quit the army he would be penniless, homeless and jobless with no prospects. The thought terrified him.

Diana moved on. Before she told Hewitt their affair had run its course, she was already dating and bedding other young bucks and had done so for nearly twelve months. However, Diana wasn't alone in her betrayal. Hewitt betrayed Diana in a rather shameful, caddish way, boasting to journalists and others of her sexual demands and appetite, details of her sex life with Charles and of her intense pleasure when making love to him. It was sickening, stomach-churning stuff and the mark of an old-fashioned English 'bounder', a man guilty of ungentlemanly behaviour, discussing intimate details of a sexual relationship. It wasn't surprising that the tabloids described him variously as 'vermin' and a 'cad'.

There were, in fact, two separate love affairs that Diana enjoyed with Hewitt. The first was fierce, passionate and furtive; the second, beginning some twelve months after Harry's arrival, more convivial and relaxed. At first, Diana wanted the excitement of an illicit extra-marital relationship, and Hewitt provided the heights of ecstasy she craved, while he simply loved the fact that Diana wanted him. But during her second relationship with him, the more worldly-wise Diana happily accepted that he enjoyed bedding other women and she rather enjoyed the nefarious thrill of this. Indeed, Diana would cross-examine him about them, indulging her prurient interest, asking details of the lovemaking, the women's sexual preferences and their intimate kinky demands.

Diana was never absolutely certain that Harry was Hewitt's child, but she was fairly confident that he was and she would compare photographs as young Harry grew from babyhood to childhood and later to adolescence. At one stage she toyed with the idea of a DNA check, but decided against it. She didn't want to remove all doubt, preferring, for Harry's sake, to live with the faint possibility that he might be Charles' son.

Diana confessed some two years after meeting Hewitt that although she had, at first, loved the fact that she and Hewitt would drive down to Devon to their love nest – his mother's small, cramped cottage in the quiet of the Devon countryside – she had come to realize that she could never live in such a place or in such surroundings. She had been brought up in her father's ancestral home in

Norfolk, a grand country mansion, and, except for a brief time living in her London apartment with three other girls, her only other home had been a royal palace. She realized all too soon that Hewitt's parents had very little money, no family wealth and that he was only a young serving officer who couldn't even afford to dress himself on his army pay!

Diana said during one of her breakups with Hewitt, 'I've spent a fortune buying that man all the clothes he owns.' And, according to her bodyguard of ten years, Police Inspector Ken Wharfe, she also generously gave Hewitt £17,000 in cash for a sports car, as well as a tie-pin with a fox's head in diamonds, a gold fob watch with the words *I will love you always* inscribed on it, some cufflinks and a gold cross that bore the inscription, *I shall love you forever.*

Diana had enjoyed being generous to Hewitt, looking after his every need, and, in return, he gave her the love and sexual thrills which she had enjoyed and grown to need. But realising Hewitt's family had no wealth and Hewitt himself had no real guts, she happily walked away from him. By that time there were a number of other suitors on the immediate horizon whom Diana felt she might also share her favours. It must also be remembered that within a year or so of her wedding, Diana had taken to the party life and found she rather enjoyed it, often revelling in the champagne, the chatter, the flirting, the atmosphere of young people happily enjoying a night out.

And Diana was also now enjoying her life at home. She adored her two boys, loved spending time with them, bathing and putting them to bed at night and all with the help of nannies and nurses. And now she had come to realize she rather enjoyed wearing designer clothes and fabulous jewellry with servants at her beck and call and a palace to live in. And, to boost her confidence further, she also noticed the men she met on the social scene were increasingly taken by her smile, her chat, her naughty jokes and her new come-hither approach to these handsome young men who had initially been wary of becoming too friendly with the wife of the Prince of Wales.

When Inspector Wharfe became one of Diana's police bodyguards in 1986, he was briefed by senior officers about her relationship with Captain James Hewitt. He was also informed that Diana had become involved with Hewitt because 'though no one had confirmed the relationship, Diana knew in her heart that Charles was seeing Camilla Parker Bowles'.

Following Harry's arrival with his tell-tale 'rusty hair', Charles turned more and more to Camilla for comfort and advice for he was in the most dreadful quandary. He profoundly believed his mother would never agree to a separation or a divorce and, for the sake of the two children, he had no wish to separate from Diana and cause the boys heartache and pain. Charles had come to realize shortly before Harry's arrival that to all intents and purposes his marriage to Diana was over in all but name. She showed not the slightest interest in him, barely having the time to chat with him. He knew that any separation or divorce might have the most disastrous effect on the monarchy, on the Royal Family and the nation. And Charles had no wish to hurl the country into a crisis similar to that caused by his uncle, King Edward VIII, when in 1937 he chose to marry the love of his life, the American divorcee Mrs. Wallis Simpson, and abdicate the throne of England, all for the woman he loved.

By the mid-1980s, Charles reached the conclusion that there was little chance that he could patch up the marriage

– Diana's actions and words left him in no doubt that she wanted nothing whatsoever to do with him or the Royal Family. He made the decision to move to Highgrove on a more or less permanent basis after discussing the matter with Diana. She jumped at the new living arrangements which would leave her at Kensington Palace with Wills and Harry and give her even more freedom to continue her clandestine night-time activities. As a result of that move, Charles soon began seeing Camilla on a more or less daily basis for now she lived just a few miles away.

This arrangement is verified by Hewitt himself, who commented in his book that it was during the mid-1980s that Camilla came more onto the scene. Charles and Camilla had always got along well together, enjoying the country life of horses, hunting, shooting and dogs, listening to opera and classical music and reading good books. Charles had found in Camilla the type of woman who appealed to him: a country woman, involved in country life but who also possessed intelligence, a keen sense of humor, and a sense of fun.

Camilla told Charles that her marriage to Brigadier Andrew Parker Bowles, one of Charles' polo pals whom he had known for years, was nearing the end of its natural life and eventually Charles and Camilla became lovers.

Andrew Parker-Bowles was a man I came to know during his time serving as *aide-de-camp* to Lord Soames during the 1979 transfer of power in Rhodesia from white minority to black majority rule. During his six-month stint in Rhodesia, I noticed that Andrew seemed to lead a bachelor-style life and did not appear to be pining for his wife back in Britain. He thoroughly enjoyed dinner parties, dances, cocktail parties and was a most sociable member of the Soames set in Rhodesia, and he was frequently accompanied by a young woman. Apparently, the Parker-Bowles' separation and eventual divorce in January 1995 was amicable on both sides after they both agreed the marriage had run its course.

So Diana's claims that Charles had been in love with Camilla throughout his adult life, that he was still madly in love with her at the time of their marriage, that he had kept in contact with her while on honeymoon and that, in effect, he had ditched Diana shortly after the birth of Prince William, are simply not borne out by the facts.

Meanwhile, in London, Diana continued to live the life of a bachelor girl, particularly during term time when Wills and Harry were away at boarding school. And she was *really* living it up, dating a number of men at the same time but still keeping in contact with Hewitt, whom she now referred to as her 'old reliable lover'. However, Diana didn't want Hewitt to know that she was dating other men. The new, adventurous, sexually confident Diana had become increasingly hungry for new male companions and she would take great delight in attracting, seducing and enjoying a number of handsome and all too willing men.

Chapter Five
Diana's Guilty Secret

Prince Harry was born at 4:20 pm on Saturday, September 15, 1984, in the Lindo wing at St. Mary's Hospital, London.

In *Diana: Her True Story,* written by Andrew Morton, the chapter about her life in the months leading up to Harry's birth included these surprising words: '*Charles and Diana enjoyed the happiest period of their married life. The balmy summer months before Harry's birth was a time of contentment and mutual devotion*'.

Presumably, this sentence was intended to encourage the reader to believe that during those nine months, everything in the royal marriage was wonderful and that Diana and Charles were really happy together. In fact that was far from true. Charles had been made aware that Diana had taken James Hewitt as a lover weeks before she told him she was pregnant for the second time. But Diana had no idea that Charles knew she and Hewitt were lovers. Throughout the pregnancy, Charles never let on that he knew of her relationship with Hewitt. Nor did he let her know he was aware that she continued to see Hewitt during her pregnancy. Nonetheless, it was true that during those months before Harry's birth, Charles had noted that Diana had become far more attentive, kind and loving towards him.

But, having informed the reader that the marriage was

'the happiest' she could remember, Diana then wrote in the next sentence: *'But a storm cloud hovered on the horizon. Diana knew that Charles was desperate for their second child to be a girl. A scan had already shown that her baby was a boy. It was a secret she nursed until the moment he was born... Charles' reaction finally closed the door on any love Diana may have felt for him. 'Oh it's a boy,' he said, 'and he's even got rusty hair'... With these dismissive remarks he left to play polo. From that moment, as Diana has told friends: 'Something inside me died.' It was a reaction which marked the beginning of the end of their marriage.'*

For some eight months, Charles had hoped that Diana would enjoy a short fling with Hewitt, and would return to him after their second child was born. Charles had instructed Sir Edward to tell no one of the affair and also to inform the Royal Protection Squad officers to carry on with their duties as usual as though nothing untoward was going on. The officers were also instructed to tell no one, not even their wives.

Prince Charles had hoped and prayed that the baby would not look anything like James Hewitt because he presumed there was some slight possibility that the baby could be Hewitt's. So it was with some trepidation that Charles took the lift to the Lindo Wing that September day and went to see the newborn baby, then just a few hours old. Charles looked at the tiny baby in the cot next to Diana's bed and saw the baby boy had rust-coloured hair. In fact, Charles had steeled himself to say nothing about it to Diana immediately following the birth because he knew that would be totally wrong. Yet, it seems, Charles simply couldn't resist making the remark about the 'rusty hair', though he metaphorically kicked himself for doing so the moment he had spoken those words. Afterwards, Charles was angry at himself for blurting out the statement and not having the patience to keep quiet, for he had no proof whatsoever that he was not the baby's father.

The passage in Diana's book relating to Charles' reaction to Harry's birth illustrates the lengths Diana was prepared to go to convince the world that Charles was an insensitive and awful husband who, within hours of his child's birth, would try to hurt and vilify his wife at such a poignant moment. To critics of Diana's infidelity, that passage in the book also reveals Diana's determination to destroy Charles' reputation as a father and a husband at the same time as protecting her own character.

In essence, Diana's book became the core of a plot in which she hoped to persuade the nation to believe that because Charles wanted a baby girl, and she had produced a boy, his reaction had such an effect on her that it was enough to kill her love for him. The idea that Charles' disappointment that the baby was not a girl should have had such a dramatic impact on Diana's feelings towards her husband after their nine months of 'love and devotion' seems difficult to accept. Yet Diana was asking the world to believe that Charles' admittedly ill-timed remark about the colour of Harry's hair was the reason for the break-up of their marriage. It simply doesn't ring true.

The majority of people reading *Diana: Her True Story* had no reason to disbelieve what they had read. Understandably, the British people came to believe that this vital passage in the book proved beyond reasonable doubt that Charles was a heartless, cold-blooded husband who would speak in such a way to the woman he loved just hours after she had given birth to their son. And yet Diana was asking readers to accept her belief that Charles was just such a man. These stories, passed to Andrew Morton from Diana through a third party, had the effect of damning Charles in the opinion of most who read the book.

It is surprising, however, that Diana risked writing of Charles' remark about 'rusty coloured hair' because Hewitt clearly had just such coloured hair. Yet she must have realised that at some future moment, when the world came to know of her affair with Hewitt, the colour of his hair would become a focal point, as indeed it has. Of course, nowhere in the book did Diana reveal that Hewitt was her lover. She only confessed to the affair some years later during her famous and frank *Panorama* television interview on November 14, 1995 – Prince Charles' 47th birthday. The interview was seen by tens of millions of viewers throughout the world. By then, of course, the world had known for some years that Hewitt had been her lover – but this was the first confirmation from Diana herself.

That sensational TV interview won increasing sympathy for Diana as she explained in a quiet, sombre voice the problems she had to face being married to the Prince of Wales. Her composure and fluency were remarkable; her replies to questions polished and articulate; no question took her by surprise and no answers seemed fluffed. Diana's makeup was subdued and she looked pale and wan, some thought gaunt. Her gut-wrenching honesty was compelling when she spoke movingly of her eating disorders, her post-natal depression and the effect it had on her marriage, her self-mutilation and her love affair with Hewitt. She told the world, 'Yes, I did mutilate myself. I didn't like myself, I was ashamed because I couldn't cope with the pressures…Well, I just hurt my arms and my legs.'

Despite her apparent honesty, which everyone praised, Diana did not mention a word about any suicide attempts, leaving many to believe that she had, in fact, never attempted to kill herself. Perhaps Diana, realizing that she had embellished the stories in the book written with Andrew Morton, decided the best policy was simply not to mention the subject.

Many viewers watching that programme felt they were eavesdropping on a confessional burial of a marriage. More ominously, others highlighted Diana's determination not to obey the wishes of the Queen and her advisers and disappear quietly into the background; instead, it seemed she was preparing to put herself forward as a direct challenge to the Queen's role in the life of the nation.

In the latter part of the interview Diana laid down her plans for her own future saying, 'I would like to be an ambassador for Britain, my country. I would like to offer my talents to serve the victims of society across the world. I would like to be the queen of people's hearts. Someone's got to go out there and love people and show it…The perception that has been given of me for the last three years has been very confusing, turbulent and, in some areas, I'm sure, many, many people doubt me. I want to reassure all those people who have loved me throughout the last fifteen years that I'd never let them down. That is a priority to me. The man on the street matters more than anything else to me.'

Diana would be true to that promise of using her talents to serve the victims of society. But, in outlining her plans for the future, Diana had not only given a description of her new career but, more importantly, she had unwittingly set in motion the chain of events which would lead to her death, less than two years later.

Princess Diana knew exactly what she was doing when she gave that *Panorama* interview. She did not seek permission from the Queen to give such an interview, which she was well aware was breaking the Queen's strict protocol rules. Some thought this courageous, while others considered it foolhardy. Nor did Diana have the courtesy to inform the Queen that she had given the interview, which many considered rash and injudicious. Somehow, Diana even managed to keep the interview secret from her private secretary Patrick Jephson. In doing so, she made him appear incompetent to the senior courtiers, who were absolutely furious that Diana had given such an interview without permission. The first that the Queen, her advisers and Jephson knew of the interview was exactly one week before it was to be broadcast when it was promoted for the following week's *Panorama* program. Diana's choice of programs was brilliant, for *Panorama,* Britain's most prestigious current affairs programme, carried authority and influence, only screening matters of importance to the life of the nation.

In retrospect, Diana's *Panorama* interview marked a major turning point in her life and, significantly, in her relationship with the Queen, as well as most members of the Royal Family. It also affected Diana's relationship with the Queen's close advisers, including her own brother-in-law, Sir Robert Fellowes, the Queen's Private Secretary and most important adviser.

Before giving that interview, Diana must have been aware that she was not only challenging the Queen's authority but also, by publicly damning Charles, she was hastening the end of their marriage. Diana went even further in an obvious attempt to discredit Charles' right of succession to the throne. She could hardly have been more lethal in her efforts to belittle and disparage Charles, suggesting that he really wasn't capable of being a good monarch even if he actually wanted the job, which she doubted. Her comments on Prince Charles were devastating, cruel and pitiless. They were also sensational.

The aftermath of the dramatic programme had the effect of highlighting the problems surrounding the monarchy. Royal commentators and constitutional lawyers recognized that the monarchy was in serious trouble. Crisis meetings were held at the palace, ideas suggested, new policies put forward, but all seemed little more than window dressing in the light of the problem the royals faced. They had hoped Diana would be a fleeting phenomenon – like a butterfly enjoying a few months of summer before falling to earth as the autumn winds turned cold. But they were living in a fool's paradise.

Diana had arrived on the scene in a blaze at the start of the 1980s but had made little impact on the nation until the public began to read in newspapers some six years later of possible cracks in the royal marriage. From then on, Diana's hold on the British people, particularly among women, increased dramatically as they rushed to support her in her public battle against the wayward, adulterous, hard-hearted Charles, whom they knew would be supported by the Queen, Prince Philip and the Establishment.

Indeed, every article about 'Princess Di,' as the media referred to her, was avidly read, every television programme about her watched by millions. Diana, her problems, her marriage and her children had become the major topic in most tabloid newspapers and the principal talking point wherever people gathered. Discussion over the royal marriage was not only conducted in the pubs, clubs and bingo halls of the nation but also at the dinner tables and cocktail parties of the nation's political elite and the chattering classes. Her name was on everyone's lips.

Whenever there was an opportunity to actually see

Diana in the flesh, even if only for a fleeting moment, people would flock from miles around to catch a glimpse. Her life may have been a mess, but to her growing army of loyal women supporters, her failing marriage became an added attraction, for they wanted to show their support. Millions of British women recognized Diana as a fellow victim just like millions of them who had also lived, or were still living, with selfish, philandering, adulterous men. By the early 1990s Diana's magnetism had taken a grip on the nation, which some in the Royal Family and the Establishment found quite frightening. Her faithful supporters, however, marvelled at her courage in standing up to the Royal Family. In their eyes, Diana could do no wrong and her vast army of supporters were prepared to back her to the hilt. Diana loved it.

Behind the scenes, however, plots were afoot. Some courtiers even wondered whether the Queen might one day make the same famous, rash request that King Henry II (1133 –1189) made to his knights when he was having problems with Thomas a Becket, his Archbishop of Canterbury – '*Who will free me from this turbulent priest?*' As the world knows, the King's knights responded by murdering Becket on the altar as he was saying mass in Canterbury Cathedral. The Queen's courtiers knew that she would not have wanted Diana dead, but she may have hoped that someone might come up with an idea that would somehow sideline the errant princess.

During the last few years of Diana's life, it is true to say that she succeeded, without exception, in humiliating every member of the Royal Family, who felt that she was rubbing their noses in the dirt. In the eyes of much of the nation, the Royal Family and even the Queen came to appear inconsequential and unimportant. Diana hurt their pride and their dignity with nonchalant ease.

Monarchs and their extended families aren't used to that type of treatment and the tight-knit House of Windsor certainly didn't like it. All their lives, members of the Royal family had been held in the greatest respect by the nation. In particular, the British people revered the Queen for she was the Head of State, the monarch who signed all the parliamentary bills and to whom everyone, including the Prime Minister, would bow in obeisance.

By the end of the 1980s, however, the Queen was showing signs of stress and, understandably she blamed her daughter-in-law. It was the Queen herself who described 1992 as her *'annus horribilis'*, as her position and authority came under increasing pressure from Diana and she also had to endure the embarrassment of the failed marriages of Princess Anne and Prince Andrew.

She did, however, pay Diana a remarkable if silent tribute when she took a leaf out of her daughter-in-law's book, portraying herself, for the first time ever as 'vulnerable' to the events punctuating her jubilee year, at the celebration of her 40 years on the throne. It was the most remarkable speech the Queen has ever made, and it amounted, in effect, to an extraordinary public confession. The Queen appeared before dignitaries from the city of London, leading politicians from the House of Lords and Commons, members of the Establishment, the cream of Britain's high society as well as leading members of the legal profession and pillars of the nation's financial elite. There were aldermen and councillors in their flamboyant robes and finery and all were gathered in the famous Guildhall for the principal celebration marking the Queen's glorious jubilee.

Most of what the Queen said that day was as a direct

result of the criticism heaped on the Royal Family, which could be traced directly to Princess Diana and the nation's perception that the Royal Family – Charles in particular – were behaving badly and unfairly towards the young Princess. The Queen confessed to the privileged assembled listeners who attended the lunch: 'There can be no doubt, of course, that criticism is good for people and institutions that are part of public life. No institution, city, monarchy, whatever should expect to be free from the scrutiny of those who give it their loyalty and support, not to mention those that don't. But we are all part of the same fabric of our national society and that scrutiny, by one part of another, can be just as effective if it is made with a touch of gentleness, good humour and understanding.'

The Queen was hoping not only to rein in the more harsh press attacks on her and her family over the previous two years, but also to win the moral high ground, going over the heads of critics and the press, appealing directly to the people. Elizabeth was following in her daughter-in-law's footsteps – she had witnessed how well it had worked for Diana.

Since the Queen believed the bulk of the nation was still behind her and her family, she was prepared to take the risk of appealing to them directly. 'I sometimes wonder how future generations will judge the events of this tumultuous year,' she mused. 'I dare say that history will take a slightly more moderate view than some contemporary commentators.'

Of course, the royal soap opera and the plight of Princess Diana had become the talking points of the nation, but they were not Britain's only problem in 1992. The country was in a severe recession – three million unemployed, thousands of families unable to pay their mortgages were thrown out of their homes, a record number of people were being declared bankrupt and thousands of firms and companies were going bust.

Another tragedy befell the Queen that November: a fire erupted at Windsor Castle, where she spent most weekends. It destroyed the famous St. George's Hall, the adjacent Waterloo Chamber – said to be the most beautiful room in the world – as well as many priceless paintings and other works of art. Many were moved as they saw the diminutive, rather pathetic figure of Queen Elizabeth beside the tall, well-built firemen battling the blaze. The fire lent an air of unease to the nation, and the photographs and television shots of the Queen amid the scene of carnage seemed to epitomize the mood of desolation and disaster that had befallen her and her family.

But balanced against this feeling of pity for the Queen was the anger the nation felt towards the way the Royal Family had behaved towards their beloved Diana. It was suggested by the Government that the taxpayer should pay the full cost of the repairs, estimated at £80 million. The nation thought otherwise.

A television poll asked callers to phone in with their answer to the question, 'Who should pay for the repairs to Windsor Castle?' An amazing 95 per cent out of a quick poll of 30,282 people watching the programme said the taxpayer should not pay the bill. The Royal Family were castigated by the tabloid press. The *Daily Mirror* accused the House of Windsor of sowing the seeds of its own destruction, saying 'meanness, greed and blatant disregard for the feelings of the people are the mark of a dying, not lasting, dynasty'.

The Windsor fire became one of the most traumatic events in Elizabeth's long reign – it brought about the realization that the British people's attitude to the monarchy had undergone a dramatic change. With the fire still smouldering, Elizabeth, the Establishment and Parliament were forced to face the unpleasant fact that the British people's total support for the monarch and the Royal Family at any cost had been swept away. And, undeniably, it had been the arrival of Diana on the scene, and the perceived way that she had been treated by the family, which was principally responsible.

It wasn't only the Royal Family that the nation was turning its back on. As monarch, Elizabeth is also Head of the Anglican Church, and throughout her reign the numbers attending church plummeted dramatically. By the mid-1990s, less than 2 per cent of the population attended Sunday services.

Opinion polls at that time made gloomy reading for Elizabeth. The nation wanted a dramatic change from the type of distant, aloof, old-fashioned monarchy Elizabeth had epitomized throughout her reign. According to these polls, people wanted a slimline, Scandanavian-style monarchy with fewer royals involved. They also demanded that all the lesser royals take proper jobs, rather than simply opening the occasional wing of a hospital or throwing local parties for charity. And perhaps most distressing for Elizabeth, they wanted a cut in the cost of the royals' upkeep.

Figures published by the Heritage Department in 1994 showed that 268 members of the Royal Family, relatives and staff were living at the taxpayers' expense. It noted that aunts, uncles and cousins of every member of Elizabeth's family lived rent-free in apartments in royal palaces, all attended by lavish staff. To service the royals, free homes were provided for 13 chauffeurs, 55 private secretaries, 47 domestic servants, 41 stable and farm staff, and six gardeners, along with 42 additional craftsmen, porters and other staff.

In a desperate bid to halt the slide in the popularity of the Royal Family, the Queen finally came to the conclusion she must take some positive action. First, she grudgingly agreed to a suggestion that Prince Charles had been putting forward for some years – that the Royal Family should pay tax on their income. She hated the idea, but with headlines in the tabloid press, screaming 'HM The Tax Dodger' she felt she had no option but to bow to the demands of her subjects and pay tax – just like they did.

The Sunday Times commented, *'By joining the ranks of sovereigns who pay income tax, the Queen has seized the opportunity to sweep away some of the cobwebs that have surrounded the royal finances for centuries. In doing so, she has taken a historic step towards putting the monarchy on a new, more modern footing, which is to be welcomed'.*

Secondly, the Queen decided that those members of her extended family whom the public regarded as 'hangers-on' should quietly retreat out of the limelight and into oblivion. Until the 1990s, the Queen had made it an imperative that the family show they were a family unit on every possible occasion. Now she ordered that the 'lesser' members should adopt a lower profile and fade into the background. At celebrations, when the entire Royal Family would stand on the balcony at Buckingham Palace and wave to the crowds, the numbers were severely curtailed and, from then on, only the Queen's immediate family gathered to greet and wave to the people.

However, Elizabeth's rather desperate efforts to re-establish herself and the family's position as beloved and respected leaders of the nation did not bring back the adoring, cheering crowds. The thousands who had turned out in the earlier decades of her reign had been reduced to a few score, and they were mostly children given a half-day off school to stand by the side of the road and wave little Union Jacks. She did, however, see hundreds of people turning out to cheer Diana whenever and wherever the latter appeared in public. The Queen knew that she was being ignored but had no idea how she could reverse this trend, which she understood could one day sound a death knell for the House of Windsor.

The Queen fully realised that the person responsible for that dramatic change in the nation's respect and affection for the royals was, of course, Princess Diana. But the blame was laid not at Diana's feet but at the feet of the Queen, Prince Philip and Charles for what the nation believed was their disgraceful, abhorrent and cynical treatment of Diana. One year after her divorce from Charles in 1996, Diana had virtually swept away the nation's interest in any other members of the Royal Family, usurping their place in the affections and respect of the great majority of the British people. To many, Diana had become the angel of hope, visiting the sick in hospitals and retirement homes throughout London and the world.

In 1997 – the year of her death – Diana had all but eclipsed the Royal Family. On one occasion, Charles was away on a four-day, high-profile official royal visit to Germany, and yet only one reporter and photographer from the entire British media went along to record the event. Five days later, Diana flew to Asia and 400 reporters, photographers and television personnel accompanied her. The game was over for the Royal Family. Single-handedly, Diana had undermined the prestige and primacy of the monarchy, and there was seemingly nothing whatsoever they could do to counter the situation.

Six months later, Diana, Princess of Wales, the one person the House of Windsor believed was responsible for the plunge in the Royal Family's popularity, was dead.

Chapter Six
'They Want to Kill Me'

Within twelve months of giving birth to Prince Harry in September 1984, Diana became convinced that some members of the Royal Family wanted her dead or, at the very least, out of the way. Quite openly, she would discuss the matter with close friends who visited her at Kensington Palace telling them in a melancholy, resigned voice that the Royal Family no longer needed her services. She had carried out her duty, providing an heir and a spare for the House of Windsor and now they wanted rid of her.

She would relate this startling and extraordinary opinion as though it was a simple matter of fact; as though it was perfectly normal for the Queen and the rest of the Royal Family to want to be rid of the wife to the heir to the throne – the mother of the next generation of royals – simply because she had carried out her duty and produced two offspring. She would give no other reason behind her belief that the Royal Family wanted her out of the way.

Some would laugh at the suggestion, as though Diana was simply making a self-deprecating joke, but one glance at Diana's anguished face and tear-filled eyes would reveal to the listener that she believed it to be true. Other friends would try to humor her, suggesting that it was 'preposterous' or 'nonsense' for her to even think for one moment that the Queen and other members of the family wanted her dead. But Diana could not be persuaded otherwise, and she would continue to tell friends of her certainty that there were members of the Royal Family, senior courtiers and members of the Establishment who thought it might be better for them if she were dead!

Sometimes, Diana would suggest that the reason the Royal Family wanted her removed from the scene was because of her close relationship with 'her darlings', Wills and Harry. Diana believed that those opposed to her thought she had too powerful an influence on the young princes and that one day she might persuade her sons to act in some way that might be detrimental, or even disastrous, to the House of Windsor.

On occasions, Diana would go further, telling friends that 'they' – the unnamed royal flunkies whom Diana despised and sometimes loathed – feared that her independence, her anti-royal views and her determination to hog the limelight to the exclusion of the Queen and Prince Charles might have a serious effect on William and even one day lead to the demise of the House of Windsor.

Of course Diana could not let on that she was talking in this vein because she was suffering a massive guilt complex. She knew full well that she should never have committed adultery with James Hewitt, despite her unhappiness with her marriage. She also knew that the world would turn against her if it became known that she had taken Hewitt as a lover so early in her marriage.

Diana may have joked publicly about her lack of intelligence but she certainly had natural mental ability, a sharp, astute intelligence that she often used to good effect. Some thought her more cunning than intelligent, full of guile and artfulness. She was most certainly clever enough to understand that she had to find a way of explaining herself when news that she had taken a lover finally hit the headlines.

And Charles' lifelong friend, Camilla Parker Bowles, gave Diana the perfect opportunity to weave the plot she needed. All she needed to do was make the allegation that Charles and Camilla had been lovers from the very beginning of Diana's marriage and she believed, rightly, that the world would then condemn Charles and forgive Diana for any indiscretions she may have indulged in. That was the primary reason Diana wrote such allegations in *Diana: Her True Story*. Before that book landed like a thunderbolt on an awe-struck nation, there had been no suggestion from any quarter that Charles and Camilla were lovers.

At that time, Diana was also concerned for her future because she knew that the Queen and other members of the Royal Family knew the truth. They knew that Charles and Camilla had been friends for years but there had been no question of an affair between them. That worry remained with Diana from the moment her book was published because she realized the Royal Family and their courtiers would dismiss it out of hand as they did most royal books, which they knew were frequently full of false stories. Diana took every precaution possible to ensure that no one knew of her involvement in the book. She intended that to be her life-long secret.

On some occasions, Diana seemed to accept that it was possible that the Royal Family might be happy enough if she simply agreed to divorce Charles and slip away to live quietly in the country, far from the glare of cameras and publicity. Of course, Diana was right that the royals would be happy if she removed herself from public life, resigned from her charities and led a life of quiet obscurity somewhere in the country. She accepted that the Queen would let her see Wills and Harry but only in the privacy of her country home, far from the cameras and the public. On some occasions, however, Diana would add as a joke, 'From their viewpoint, of course, the best of all conclusions would be for me to disappear, have an accident, die.'

During a private chat in 1992 with Max Hastings, the former editor of *The Daily Telegraph,* Diana told him, 'I know of a scheme that has been funded by a Canadian gold tycoon, Peter Munk of Barrack Mining, to hire the public relations man David Wynne-Morgan to get rid of me at any price.' Hastings was taken aback by the suggestion and assured Diana that he had never heard of such a plot. To him the idea seemed preposterous. It didn't matter to Diana that Hastings denied hearing any such suggestion – nothing would dissuade her from her firmly held conviction.

Since Prince Harry's birth in September 1984, Diana believed that there were a number of plots to remove her by various means and strategies, and she continued to believe that right up to the moment of her death. Sometimes it felt to Diana that some members of the Royal Family wanted her dead while, at other times, they just wanted her 'to go away, get married to someone, anyone, and disappear from the royal scene.'

In his biography of Princess Diana, *Diana: Closely Guarded Secret,* Police Inspector Ken Wharfe, who was her personal police bodyguard for six years, told of another occasion in May 1992 when Diana was visiting Egypt. She had taken a swim in the British Ambassador's private pool at his official residence in Cairo. Photographers were perched on the flat roof of a house in the near distance, but the glint of reflected light from their camera lenses betrayed their presence to Diana and she fled the scene.

Wharfe recounted: '*As Diana wrapped a towel around her shoulders she said, "Ken, if anything happens to me you'll let people know what I was really like, won't you?"*' Later that morning Diana, speaking of her feeling of total isolation within the Royal Family, revealed, '*Ken, I want out of this once and for all*'.

When visiting the United States during the 1990s, Diana chanced upon a book I had written, *Queen Elizabeth II: A Woman Who Is Not Amused.* She bought the book because she found the title amusing and I understand she found the book fascinating, providing her with knowledge of the Royal Family that she had never before known. However, one passage in particular that alarmed her concerned the late Prince John. Although it occurred many years ago, it proved to Diana how harsh the Royal Family can be when preserving their image.

Born in 1905, the youngest son of King George V and Queen Mary of Teck, Prince John developed epilepsy at the age of seven, possibly as a result of the harsh treatment and beatings meted out to him by his father. Embarrassed that a son of theirs should have epilepsy, the family removed poor John and locked him away in a small house on the Sandringham Estate, ironically, only a few miles from where Diana spent her childhood.

One night at dinner, Queen Mary announced to their other five children, 'John is unwell and has gone away to be cared for. It is very unlikely that we will ever see him again.' John, who was being cared for in his 'prison' by a single nurse was indeed never seen again by any of his brothers or sisters. And, to their everlasting shame, neither his mother nor his father ever visited him or set eyes on him again. John died in 1919 unloved, unnoticed and unmourned. He was fourteen.

This story shook Diana, for it proved to her how heartless and ruthless Britain's Royal Family can be in their determination to protect their public image. Prince John was ill and they wanted him removed from their presence because he was an inconvenience and a poor advertisement for the Royal Family. Diana convinced herself that if it were possible, both the Queen and Prince Philip would deal with her in the same way.

It was in the 1990s that Diana decided she had to rewrite her Last Will and Testament, not just because she had recently divorced Charles, but mainly because she feared something terrible might happen to her. She always believed, as she illustrated when chatting to the *Daily Telegraph* editor Max Hastings, that she did have this 'gut feeling' that there was a plot against her, to remove her from the royal scene once and for all. Diana would have serious conversations with a number of friends telling them she believed the Royal Family were 'out to get her', as she put it, and she would leave no doubt in anyone's mind that she had this 'suspicion' this 'feeling' this 'premonition' that they wanted her dead.

But there was another reason for Diana rewriting her will. Not only did she believe she might be 'removed from the scene' at an early age but, more importantly, she wanted to ensure that Prince Harry would have substantial funds available for him to lead an independent life as a wealthy man in his own right without necessarily having to go out to work to support a wife and family. She also wanted to ensure he would have the means to run a large country house and maintain an apartment in London. Diana feared for Harry in case the Royal Family turned against him as they had turned against her. Towards the end of her life, she trusted no one in the Royal Family. She knew that if the Queen and Philip decided something should happen, it did not matter a damn whether Charles, the heir to the throne, agreed or not.

Diana's fear that she might meet a sudden end, though she was only in her thirties, was also the reason that she put so much faith in Paul Burrell, her loyal butler, telling him many of her secrets and entrusting him with access to many of her private papers. This was one of the reasons why Burrell, who had been her butler, friend and confidant for ten years, took three hundred items from Kensington Palace to his home following Diana's death. He admitted taking papers, Diana's private correspondence, private tapes of her conversations, knick-knacks and other personal items – a total of 310 separate items which he secreted at his home in Cheshire, 120 miles from Kensington Palace. He explained that the removal of the items was solely to keep them safe for Princes William and Harry for when they were older.

In reality, Paul Burrell took them because he knew that Diana would have wanted him to hide them for fear that, if she did meet her death when still a young woman, many of her private papers, some damaging to the Royal Family, would conveniently disappear from her Kensington Palace apartment. She knew that MI5 would have been quite capable of removing such items following her death without arousing any suspicion, ensuring they would never enter the public domain.

In October 2002, Paul Burrell stood trial in London on three theft charges relating to the 310 items that had belonged to Princess Diana. Sensationally, the trial was stopped after the personal intervention of the Queen herself, who suddenly and inexplicably remembered that during her conversation with Paul Burrell after Diana's death, he had told her that he was removing some of Diana's 'things' for safekeeping.

Many people, including politicians and establishment figures, believed it was strange, and so unlike the Queen to forget then suddenly recall the now-famous conversation with Paul Burrell immediately following Diana's death in 1997. Even more extraordinary was that Burrell stated that the interview with the Queen had lasted for three hours. Those with knowledge of the Queen know that she not only has a remarkable memory but that she never has private conversations with people for three hours, not even Prime Ministers! And she certainly would not have had such a lengthy interview with a lowly servant, even one she wanted to impress upon the necessity of not revealing anything that might be embarrassing to the monarchy. According to senior courtiers, Burrell's conversation with the Queen lasted about fifteen minutes.

However, the Queen was not certain that Burrell would keep his side of the secret bargain. So, in an extraordinary last-minute move to ensure he revealed no embarrassing royal secrets, the Queen stepped in to stop the trial only days before Paul Burrell was to give evidence in court for his own defence. The Queen, Prince Philip, Prince Charles and all her courtiers were aware that Paul Burrell knew nearly all of Diana's most intimate secrets. He also knew how the Royal Family had treated her since the birth of Prince Harry and since the family had 'persuaded' – forced would be a more accurate word – Diana to agree to a divorce. Burrell knew about the incredible legal haggles over the details of the divorce settlement, the pressure put on Diana by the Royal Family to force her to leave

Britain, and he knew the contents of the secret letters from Philip to Diana which would have shocked the nation.

Indeed, the revelations Burrell would have been able to describe to the jury, and the world, would have shown the Royal Family in such a pitiless light that there might have been serious repercussions for the monarchy. The Queen simply could not take the chance of Burrell giving testimony in court for she had no idea what royal secrets he might reveal.

The arrest and trial of Burrell took place as a result of a request from both Prince Philip and Diana's sister, Lady Sarah McCorquodale – Charles' former mistress. They approached the police and asked them to obtain private letters they had written to Diana in the final years of her life and which they understood were in Paul Burrell's possession. Apparently, they were worried that these letters might fall into the wrong hands and would end up splashed across the front pages of the nation's newspapers.

The letters from Prince Philip were described as 'cruel and insulting' – no wonder Philip was worried that the contents of his letters might reach the press. They apparently contained strong suggestions that Diana should remove herself from the Royal Family, or face the consequences; that Diana's behaviour was a disgrace to the Royal Family; that she should be ashamed of herself for leading an adulterous life; that her now-famous book was a catalogue of lies and deceit that she should never have written. Allegedly, in one devastating letter Philip called Diana 'a harlot'. It is widely believed that the letters from Sarah to Diana mainly concerned Prince Harry and Diana's estrangement from her brother Charles and the Spencer family.

With such a lack of trust and deep suspicion between

Diana and senior members of the Royal Family, it was no wonder that Diana felt under constant threat. From Diana's viewpoint, her nagging fears were exactly why she never wanted a divorce from Charles. She reasoned that, once she was divorced, her removal from London – or worse, her sudden, mysterious death – might be the next logical step. Because of this deep conviction, Diana refused requests from the Queen to even consider the matter of a formal separation or divorce for almost a decade – until the early 1990s, when she was subjected to so much pressure from so many different sources and so-called friends that she felt forced to agree to the separation and later the divorce. In agreeing to a divorce, Diana recognized that she now had a strong hand to play. And her terms were tough indeed.

The Diana that the royals were dealing with in the 1990s was a far stronger, more confident woman than the nervous, docile Lady Di of the late 1970s. She had developed a remarkably steely character and showed that no one, not even the Queen, was going to push her around. This tough, more mature Diana proved to be quite a shock, not only to Prince Charles, but also to the Queen, Prince Philip and the courtiers who had to deal with her on a day-to-day basis. To a number of senior courtiers the quiet, innocent, vulnerable Diana, who seemed almost angelic to the general public, was in reality, so some courtiers claimed, a determined, duplicitous, scheming woman who loved to flirt with everyone in a bid to gain their support.

Following the Queen's demand for a quick divorce, Diana took legal advice and gave her lawyer a list of settlement demands. She was determined to keep the title 'Princess' and though she recognized that she could not continue to be 'Her Royal Highness, the Princess of Wales', she still wished to be known officially as 'Her Royal Highness, Princess Diana'. In the final settlement it was agreed she would be known as 'Diana, Princess of Wales'. In addition she demanded either a substantial London mansion, or the massive apartment she was occupying at Kensington Palace, rent-free. For all concerned, and especially from a security viewpoint, Kensington Palace was a far preferable home. Diana also demanded a personal annual income of £750,000 after expenses, on the understanding that the upkeep of her home, staff salaries, cars and all ancillary expenses should be met by the Duchy of Cornwall, Prince Charles' private estate. She also demanded that all costs relating to Wills and Harry, including their education, clothing and holidays, should be met by Charles. More importantly, she demanded the settlement be guaranteed for her lifetime, whether she remarried or not.

Diana accepted that the question of custody of Wills and Harry was quite different from any other British children caught up in their parents' divorce settlement as they were both heirs to the throne. In English law, the princes are the responsibility of the monarch who has jurisdiction over them. However, Charles and Diana agreed that the arrangement for access to the children, which had been in effect since their 1992 separation, should continue.

The Queen forced through the divorce in a bid to sideline Diana by removing her from the House of Windsor, hoping this would result in the full focus of attention being trained on Prince Charles, as it had been before Diana entered the scene in 1980. The Queen was well aware that Diana was stealing the headlines not only from Prince Charles but also from herself.

It was a tough decision for the Queen to make. She recognized that since Diana's arrival, there had been a remarkable surge of pride and passion in the Royal Family not only in Britain, but across the world. On the other hand, the Queen also recognized that since her public break from Charles, Diana had inflicted untold damage on the monarchy. At the time of Diana's divorce from Charles in 1994, only one third of British voters believed the monarchy was relevant, and more than half demanded less pomp, ceremony and lavish lifestyles from the monarch and the Royal Family.

For almost six years, the raging stand-off between Charles and Diana and their respective advisers had played out beneath the surface in Buckingham Palace, Kensington Palace, St. James's Palace and Charles' country residence, Highgrove. Both the press and the general public knew that something was mighty wrong with the royal marriage, but they had no concrete evidence that such a dramatic guerrilla war was going on.

On one side, there were the massed ranks of the House of Windsor, the most powerful and wealthy Royal Family in the world, whose determination that their family should remain Head of State of Great Britain was of paramount importance. As allies, the Royal Family could rightly claim the Establishment, the Church of England, the Government and the Armed Forces. Ranged against this phalanx of power, prestige, position and wealth was one person – Diana, Princess of Wales, who had no power, no wealth, no influence and no allies.

It was around this time, however, that Diana began formulating plans to ensure her future. It was a brilliant idea which, if it succeeded, would cement her growing popularity with the British public.

It was in the late 1980s that Diana considered writing a book. Every day, the tabloids, and sometimes the more reputable newspapers, were writing stories about her and the number one topic was the state of the royal marriage. Whether the original idea to write a book was Diana's, a friend's, an adviser's or a publisher's is not known, but Diana thought long and hard about it before deciding to go ahead. The more she thought of the plan, the more she liked it because she could then tell her story exclusively from her viewpoint, which she was certain her loyal supporters would love. Of course, she would need to write this book in secret, away from the prying eyes of her advisers, her staff, Prince Charles or anyone employed by the Royal Family. Diana knew that if even one of them had an inkling that she was writing a book about the royal marriage, she would be stopped dead in her tracks and forbidden to continue.

But what if someone else wrote it?

For some months, Diana considered the possibility of hiring a writer, but she realized that could never work. She knew that she couldn't ask someone to write her autobiography because that would seem like it was all her idea. But if the book was seen to be written by another individual, always referring to Diana in the third person, and never quoting her, there was a real possibility that the public would accept the book as authentic and she would escape censure from the Royal Family.

One of her close friends, Dr. James Colthurst, a consultant at London's St. Thomas's Hospital, was seen by *The News of The World* royal reporter, Andrew Morton, chatting amicably to Diana when she toured the hospital on an official royal visit. Morton played squash at the same club as Dr. Colthurst. One thing led to another, and

Colthurst agreed to become the secret go-between, providing Morton with tapes and written material given to him by Diana, which he passed to Morton, who would write the book about Diana's life within the Royal Family. In other words, it would indeed be Diana's own true story.

During this time, Diana was feeling particularly low. As she put it, 'I felt demons in my head'. Her marriage to Charles had been over in all but name for nearly nine years; her serious love affair with James Hewitt had run its course and Diana ended that relationship shortly after he returned from the Gulf War; her dear, beloved father was near death and her mother was living on a remote island off the north of Scotland. Diana felt lonely and miserable, unwanted and unloved. But she also felt anger. She was convinced that the Queen and the Royal Family were about to move against her, but in what way she wasn't sure. That gave her sleepless nights. Diana wondered to what lengths the Royal Family would go to be rid of her once and for all.

Diana knew that the book she was planning would cause Charles and the Royal Family untold harm. But she also knew that she had little or nothing to lose. She hoped and suspected that by revealing so much of her marriage, detailing the way she was treated by Charles and his family, she would not only win the support of the nation but she might also make it difficult, if not impossible, for the family to move against her. In moments of deep anxiety, Diana came to believe that publishing the book might be the difference between life and death.

When *Diana: Her True Story* went on sale, the bookstores ran out of copies within days. And the more the people read of Diana's plight, her anorexia and the details of her miserable marriage, the more they warmed to her. The book also turned the great mass of the British people against Charles, in particular, but also against the Royal Family as an entity.

Within weeks Diana realized that she now had the nation on her side. And, more importantly, that inner feeling gave Diana a sense of security. She was convinced that publishing the book in such a subtle manner by using Morton had been the right decision for she witnessed its effect every time she made a public appearance. The numbers of people who turned out to see, cheer and demonstrate their support for her grew to an extraordinary degree. 'We love you Diana!' they shouted whenever she stepped from her official car. 'We're with you, darling!' some screamed while others joined in shouting, 'You can trust us!' Many simply shouted, 'God Bless you Diana!' whenever the Princess made an appearance. Some even wept openly, so concerned had they become for Diana's future and what they perceived as her intolerable treatment at the hands of the Royal Family. It was mainly the women who rushed to her support, showing their love and affection for her at every opportunity.

In contrast, shortly after the book's publication, some people actually booed Prince Charles when he made public appearances – which no member of the Royal Family in modern times had ever before experienced. The Queen's courtiers were becoming concerned, some alarmed, by the dramatic change in the mood of the nation towards the Royal Family. The situation had sunk to such a worrying degree that the Royal Family seemed to have no idea what they could do to counteract the nation's extraordinary love affair with Diana.

In the late 1980s, I was approached by two senior courtiers and asked to write a book about the royal couple. As a polo player like Prince Charles, I had long been accepted in the polo set and I knew some of their friends and one or two royal courtiers whose job it was to advise and counsel Charles and Diana. I was asked to write a straight, honest, objective book about their life together, the real facts about their marriage in an effort to put an end to some of the wild speculation and ill-informed gossip that the tabloids were writing day in, day out. I readily agreed. When I had completed the book, my agent took the manuscript to five or six British publishers during 1989, but not one would publish it.

The publishers were simply incredulous, refusing to believe that the Prince of Wales was having an affair with an old flame Camilla Parker Bowles, the wife of Brigadier Andrew Parker Bowles and a woman of whom they had never heard. They accused me of fabricating an affair between the chaste Diana and some unheard of young Guards Officer by the name of James Hewitt. They considered my allegation that the royal marriage was nothing more than a sham to be libellous against both Charles and Diana, and they branded the manuscript 'a bunch of lies' which they had no intention of publishing. After spending a year trying to sell the book in Britain, my agent went to New York where the manuscript was snapped up. *Diana: A Princess and Her Troubled Marriage* finally reached the bookshelves two years later in the spring of 1992.

At exactly the same time, Morton's book *Diana, Her True Story* hit the stores and instantly became a bestseller with its stories of suicide attempts and marital violence which unnerved the British Establishment. The book told Diana's extraordinary story: behind her public smiles and glamorous image was a young woman who was enduring a loveless marriage, living on her own in London while

Prince Charles had been enjoying a raging affair with his former girlfriend Camilla almost since their wedding day.

The world knows that *Diana, Her True Story* was written by Andrew Morton, but what the nation did not know was that most of the contents relating to Diana and Charles had been provided, and in some cases actually written and edited by Diana herself. And the level of hate Diana felt towards Charles is revealed in the writing. Diana must have realized that such intimate details of Charles' alleged involvement and adultery with Camilla from the beginning of the marriage could ruin his life and, destroy his relationship with Camilla. As a by-product, Diana understood that such revelations would seriously embarrass the Queen and further undermine the nation's love and respect for the Royal Family. Diana also hoped that her revelations might drive a wedge between Charles and their two sons.

The book would pull no punches and would allegedly reveal the true story of her life, her marriage, her husband's indiscretions and the dramatic effect the failed marriage and Charles' extra-marital affair had on her health, driving her in desperation to undertake seven separate suicide attempts.

The publication of the Morton book was greeted with a hail of abuse by the Establishment. They wanted the public to believe that it flagrantly exaggerated the facts. But the great majority of the British public was convinced the facts revealed in the book were true. It was an instant bestseller, and the public voraciously read every juicy detail – and believed every word.

Chapter Seven
A Book of Truth, Exaggerations and Porky Pies

The book that so upset the House of Windsor and won the hearts of the nation, *Diana: Her True Story,* was no objective appraisal of the royal marriage but a one-sided account of a relationship between an angel of a bride and a cad of a husband who allegedly had turned his back on his wife so that he could continue his affair with a married woman who had been his mistress for years.

However, over the years, facts have emerged to cast doubt on much of what Diana wrote in her book. Much can now be revealed as invention, fabrication, gross exaggeration and even lies. Perhaps the most dramatic and shocking revelation for most readers were the stories of Diana's alleged suicide attempts. The British public had no idea whatsoever that her life had been such hell that she had actually tried to take her own life on seven separate occasions over a number of years. Understandably, this piece of information sent shock waves through Britain, not only winning the nation to Diana's cause but also helping to destroying Charles' reputation.

The nation believed those horrendous suicide bids. They did not attempt to scrutinize or examine the details of those suicide attempts for they believed the title of the book, *Diana: Her True Story,* was accurate.

111

It was only some time later that those suicide attempts came under further scrutiny. On closer examination, the details of her seven separate suicide attempts revealed that they had not been very convincing; indeed, some sounded improbable, others downright unbelievable.

No one had ever heard of someone attempting suicide by walking into a display cabinet; no one had heard of a suicide attempt using a lemon grater; and the alleged efforts to kill herself by slashing her wrists on two occasions were so half-hearted that, apparently, there were no visible marks. The book alleged that in one dramatic suicide bid, Diana had picked up a penknife in Charles' presence and repeatedly stabbed herself in the chest and thighs. But there was no blood and no one ever saw a scratch on her body.

In another heart-rending claim, Diana was said to have tried to kill herself by 'hurling herself down a wooden staircase'. That surprised even Diana's most ardent supporters because at the time she was three months pregnant with William. The book revealed that *'Diana felt absolutely wretched...Charles seemed incapable of understanding or wishing to comprehend the turmoil in Diana's life. She was suffering dreadfully from morning sickness, she was haunted by Camilla Parker Bowles and she was desperately trying to accommodate herself to her new position and new family...On that January day in 1982, her first New Year with the Royal Family, she now threatened to take her own life. He accused her of crying wolf and prepared to go riding on the Sandringham estate. She was as good as her word. Standing on top of the wooden staircase she hurled herself to the ground, landing in a heap at the bottom.'*

To all intents and purposes, this dramatic description of that particular suicide attempt was a fabrication. In fact, on that occasion Diana accidentally slipped on the last step of a three-step wooden staircase and half-stumbled to the floor. Slightly shaken but unhurt, her immediate concern was for her unborn baby, but the fall was so insignificant that she insisted there was no need to call a doctor or visit hospital for a check-up. She didn't even want to lie down and rest, saying she felt fine.

It seems extraordinary that Diana should have included that suicide bid in the book. It is incredible that the pregnant Diana would have risked killing her own unborn baby by deliberately throwing herself down the stairs. And yet, this possibly deadly consequence of her suicide attempt was not mentioned or even referred to in the book – despite the fact that during her pregnancy, Diana was so concerned for the wellbeing of her unborn baby that she refused to take any drugs, fearing that the child might be born with a deformity. Any act of self-harm whilst pregnant was also totally out of character for a woman like Diana, who loved babies and wanted a large family.

I had been told that on one occasion, Diana claimed she had taken an overdose of tablets. A doctor was called and, after talking to her in private, came back to report to Prince Charles that there was no need to pump her stomach or take her to hospital for observation. It was his opinion that it was most unlikely that she had taken an overdose. He deduced that this alleged attempt had simply been a cry for help, a craving for attention.

It is this closer examination of the Morton book's reports surrounding Diana's alleged suicide attempts that not only tend to negate her suicide claims but, unfortunately for her, raised many other questions which should have been examined and answered at the time of publication. However, people were so carried away by the horror of what they read, and the anxiety they felt for poor Diana, that they took everything as gospel. Even those who doubted that she would ever intentionally commit suicide interpreted the events as a desperate cry for help by a young woman who had been severely wronged by her adulterous husband and treated disgracefully by her royal in-laws.

In writing the book, Diana revealed a shrewd, innate intelligence, for the facts she revealed to the reader were cleverly and skillfully managed. Many events described in the book had, in fact, occurred, but Diana showed them in a different light. In some cases she grossly exaggerated, portrayed a fact dishonestly, or lied about particular events, sometimes turning them around completely to suit her dramatic storyline.

She wrote, for example, how the weight 'dropped off her' after moving to Buckingham Palace before the wedding 'because she was so miserable'. The fact that she lost weight was accurate – but not the reason she gave for losing it. In reality, on the advice of her friends at Vogue Magazine, who were helping to re-invent the plump, rather dowdy Diana, she enthusiastically and deliberately dieted like crazy, reducing her waistline from 29 inches to 23 inches in four months to make sure she would look slim and beautiful for her wedding day. Indeed, immediately before the wedding, Diana proudly told her friends of her weight loss. She was justifiably proud of the achievement of losing so much weight in such a short time.

There was also the heartrending story of the gift Charles sent to Camilla a week before the wedding. In the book, Diana made much of that gift because she claimed the highly personal present – a gold chain bracelet with a blue enamel disc with the initials G and F entwined – proved that only seven days before the wedding, Charles was still deeply involved with his beloved Camilla. Diana claimed the initials stood for 'Fred' and 'Gladys' – the nicknames Charles and Camilla called each other.

The book claimed that an angry and upset Diana immediately ran to the Prince's Office and the office staff stopped work as she 'confronted her husband-to-be about his proposed gift'.

The book continues, *'In spite of her angry and tearful protests Charles insisted on giving the token to the woman who had haunted their courtship and has since cast a long shadow over their married life'.*

Again, Diana's story was inaccurate. Diana had indeed gone to see Charles about the gift, but the meeting was in private, not in front of staff. And instead of a 'confrontation', Charles put her mind at rest by explaining that the initials G and F stood for 'Girl Friday', the nickname Charles had always called Camilla because of the number of errands and little jobs she had carried out on his behalf during his bachelor days. The book also failed to mention that at the same time Charles presented Camilla with the bracelet, he had also given identical gold bracelets – with initials – as presents to nine other women who had helped and supported him during his bachelor years, some of whom had been former girlfriends with whom he had enjoyed full-blown affairs.

On the same subject, Diana claimed in the book that one week before the wedding, she was seriously thinking of calling a halt to the whole affair because at that precise moment she knew that Charles was personally handing over the gold bracelet to Camilla. He wasn't. All ten bracelets were sent by post to the ten women.

Prince Charles was rather unusual, if not remarkable, in that he invariably liked to keep in contact with many of his former girlfriends and still does so today. He hardly ever seemed to become involved with girls for purely sexual pleasure, but once he had met and enjoyed the company of a young woman he would want her as a friend, a confidant with whom he could relax – whether they went to bed together or not. Even today, for example, one of Charles' great friends is the actress Susan George, star of the movie *Straw Dogs*, who remains close to him some twenty-seven years or so after they first met. Today, they correspond regularly and sometimes meet as friends for a coffee, a meal or simply to chat.

Within a week or so of the book being published, Diana began to back-pedal on the many allegations made in the book, telling her close friends a rather different story about her suicide attempts. She told one, 'My suicide attempts were really only cries for help. I didn't really mean to do anything silly. I knew that I just needed time to adjust to my new role as a princess but I didn't receive any help or advice from anyone at the palace. I was just expected to get on with the job'.

That statement, which Diana repeated over and over to most of her friends, was also untrue. In fact, the opposite was true. Diana had been given considerable help to adjust to her new role as the Princess of Wales and future Queen. Unusual in royal circles, the Queen gave Diana permission to ask her own close friends from her bachelor-girl days if they would like to be her ladies-in-waiting. Their job was not only to accompany the princess whenever she went on official royal visits, but also to advise and befriend her, if necessary on a daily basis.

Diana also had guidance on form and etiquette from

the Queen's own ladies-in-waiting, including Lady Susan Hussey, the Queen's most experienced senior lady-in-waiting. She was advised on protocol by courtiers and advisers and received advice from fashion designers as well as gurus from Vogue magazine. And when her unhappiness and personal problems, her black moods and doubts, her bulimia, anorexia and eating problems arose, she had London's most respected doctors, analysts, psychiatrists and professional counselors at her beck and call, only too willing to help her.

Indeed, Michael Colborne, an old navy colleague of Prince Charles' in the early 1970s, who also served as Personal Secretary to Diana for two years in the 1980s, commented, 'At one time and another, the doors of Kensington Palace were busier than Christmas shopping in a West End store, with the number of professional medical people coming in and out to see the Princess'.

And, to her credit, Diana, who called Colborne her 'surrogate uncle' because of the help and advice he gave her, also admitted that during the early days of the marriage Charles was helpful and kind, advising her on what to do and what not to do on royal visits, at royal banquets, at cocktail and dinner parties and even when out walking in public.

On occasions, Diana would publicly confess to official duties being 'a nightmare', primarily because she was so painfully shy and feared she might say the wrong thing. But advisers like Colborne were always on hand to tell her how to behave, what to say to strangers, how to dress for the varied occasions and what protocol to follow. Diana received a personal briefing before every royal event, was informed who she would be meeting or chatting to, what their jobs were and the importance of each person. She was advised about what topics to discuss with the people sitting on either side of her at official dinners or banquets and what topics to steer clear of. And, according to Colborne and other advisers, to her great credit, Diana never did say the wrong thing. Indeed, she was soon recognized by courtiers as a 'fast learner', who had picked up the technique of going about visits and meeting people as though born a royal. That was praise, indeed.

Much of the book ran contrary to what was in fact going on in private in Kensington Palace, even during those first tentative years. Diana revealed she was not only a quick learner but also no shy violet. She showed not an ounce of nervousness or weakness when dealing with the staff running her affairs or working in their 28-room palace apartment. Indeed, she quickly showed a surprisingly tough aspect to her character when dealing with the staff responsible for looking after her and Prince Charles.

In retrospect, it was extraordinary that Diana should have such strength of character that she even fired some of Prince Charles' most loyal and highly respected members of staff. Charles was the Prince of Wales, heir to the throne, but that didn't matter to Diana once she decided that, come what may, she was going to get rid of many of those people on whom Charles had relied ever since leaving the Royal Navy, some four years before.

During his bachelor years, Charles had gathered a team of people around him, those he liked and respected, for he wanted his key staff and senior advisers to be men who were not only efficient and pleasant but who understood him. Charles acted like the captain of the ship and his officers and men understood that every one of them had a role to play to make the ship efficient, well-run and basically a happy place in which to work. They all respected him and he respected the work they carried out.

Understandably, when Diana arrived on the scene she wanted some changes in the staff organizing and running Charles' household. Over the years, his staff had all come to know exactly what Charles liked and disliked, what was important to him and what was not. There was, naturally, apprehension among the staff at the arrival of a young wife into the household. None of them was certain what changes she might request or demand. None of them knew whether or not they would get along with their new boss, who also happened to be an enchanting and beautiful young woman. Initially, they all felt confident that things would, more or less, continue as before because Diana seemed delightful, charming and friendly. Little did they know what trouble lay ahead.

From the start, Diana was not happy with the staff. She felt some of them treated her as a young, inexperienced interloper who didn't know how to handle royal servants or behave in the best traditions of the Royal Family. To a great extent, of course, that was true, but Diana didn't like the fact that some staff continued to organize everything the way they had always done without consulting her or asking if she wanted any changes.

After a few weeks, Diana demanded things be done differently, and some of the staff rebelled. They wanted to keep the cosy existence they had always enjoyed. It was unfortunate, to say the least, that Diana did not get along, either, with the most important royal servant in the household – Charles' highly intelligent private secretary, Edward Adeane. From the start, there was enmity between the two. Adeane, whose great-grandfather had been private secretary to Queen Victoria and whose father, Lord

Michael Adeane, had been private secretary to the Queen for many years, believed that Charles' duty to the nation must always come first, before his personal life, his family life and, on occasions, even before his wife.

Diana and Adeane clashed from the first moment. Shortly after Diana and Charles returned from their honeymoon, Diana entered Sir Edward's office and headed toward Charles' study beyond. Sir Edward jumped to his feet, walked briskly towards the study door, turned towards Diana and said politely, 'Can I help you, Ma'am?'

'No thank you,' replied Diana. 'I'm just going to see my husband for a moment.'

'I'm afraid he's busy,' replied Sir Edward. 'Is it urgent? If not, shall I phone you when he's free?'

Diana glared at Sir Edward but made no reply. She turned on her heel and walked quickly out of his office.

This initial confrontation persuaded Diana that there would need to be changes in the staff. She had no intention of permitting any flunky, no matter how important he thought he was, to stand between her and her husband. An hour later, still smarting from the rebuke from Sir Edward, Diana went to see Charles and demanded that Sir Edward be fired immediately for 'gross insubordination'. Charles asked Diana what had happened and then said to her, 'I'm afraid that wouldn't be possible. I can't fire him for simply carrying out my orders'. Diana immediately formed the impression that Charles was taking Sir Edward's side against her. His wife of just seven weeks was very put out.

After further clashes with Sir Edward, Charles had to explain to Diana that he would certainly have a word with Sir Edward but he explained to her that on some occasions it might not be possible for him to talk to her at a moment's notice because he might be involved in a meeting. To Diana's annoyance, Charles then said that some meetings were very important and he could not be seen breaking off discussions simply because his wife wanted a word. Diana felt Charles was putting his work before her – and she didn't like that one jot.

Later, Charles organized a chat between the three of them in a bid to clarify the situation and clear the air. Diana told Sir Edward that as the Princess of Wales she should have immediate access to Charles at all times. Adeane disagreed. Whether Diana was simply trying to see how far her power extended or whether, as a newlywed wife, she just wanted to be around her new husband is unknown. Whatever the case, Diana did not like the outcome of the meeting, as Charles ruled that she simply could not have immediate access to him at any time, but that his study door was open to her 'nearly all the time'.

As one of Diana's friends commented later, 'When Sir Edward and Diana were in a room together you could cut the atmosphere with a knife. It seemed there was mutual distrust.'

Whether it caused tension or not, Diana continued to push the point home that she was in command of her husband and not Sir Edward. When William was a baby, Diana insisted that both she and Charles should spend an hour together with William in his nursery most mornings, feeding and playing with their first born. Sometimes, when urgent matters arose, Sir Edward would knock at the nursery door, saying he needed to speak to His Royal Highness. Diana would open the door and say, 'His Royal Highness cannot see you at the moment; you will have to wait until we are finished'.

Sir Edward would hold his ground, explaining, 'But

Ma'am, this is a most important matter. I really do need to speak to him urgently'.

Diana would reply, 'Well, it will just have to wait'. And, without another word, she would close the door in his face.

Charles was in a quandary and didn't know what to do. But he was certain that this state of affairs could not continue. Diana believed that if Charles gave in to Sir Edward it would be a dereliction of his duty as a father to young William and as a husband to her. Sir Edward, on the other hand, believed Charles was showing a dereliction of his royal duties. It appeared to be a stand-off – the last thing Charles wanted between his new wife and his most important royal adviser.

Charles asked Adeane to be patient, believing that, in time, things would calm down. He thought maybe it would take a year or two. Adeane said he was prepared to be patient, but it seemed to him that Diana was trying his patience on purpose. Of course, the arrival of William had given Diana a privileged place within the royal establishment as the mother of a future king. It had also given her a determination and a strong will that she had never realized she possessed. Almost overnight, Diana had matured.

It was this new-found determination that enabled Diana to push for the changes she wanted. Staff began leaving at an alarming rate. The first to go was Stephen Barry, Charles' gay valet, who knew many of his secrets and had known most of Charles' former lovers and girlfriends. Diana believed that Stephen was too close to Charles – closer than she would ever be – so she decided he must go. She told Barry that now that they were married, she would be carrying out many of the little tasks he had done over the years and that his services would no longer be required.

It was, of course, untrue. And Stephen Barry knew it. He would say later, 'Diana was just jealous of me. I knew far more about Charles than she would ever know and she didn't like that. I knew exactly what clothes Charles wanted and needed for every occasion. I would only need to look at his schedule for the following day and I could lay out all his clothes, including the ties he would want to wear with each suit. I knew Diana had little or no idea what Charles liked to wear for all the different functions and occasions he had to attend. In reality, of course, she wanted total control over Charles and was prepared to do everything to maintain that position of power'.

Diana was pushing her luck, saying that she could replace a valet at a moment's notice if necessary. Someone in Charles' position, who sometimes needs to change his clothes four times a day, really does need a full-time valet – not simply to arrange his clothes for the day and the week ahead but also to keep them pressed and in immaculate order, down to the last detail. And that, of course, would include all his various uniforms for the Royal Navy, for different Regiments of the Army and the Royal Air Force which in total numbered some twenty different forms of dress.

Barry realized that the arrival of a wife on the scene had also fundamentally altered his relationship with Charles, and it was better if he quietly slipped away to find another job. Diana felt that she had won a major victory – a valet was closer to Charles than any other member of his staff. Now that position was hers. Diana's next goal was to remove as many members of staff that had been with Charles during his bachelor days.

In the first six years of their marriage, Diana got rid of twenty-four members of staff – not just the old royal retainers, which she called 'fuddy-duddies', but also some of the young, less experienced staff whom Diana herself had hired and later fell out with. Understandably, these dismissals did not improve her standing or popularity with the royal courtiers and servants at any level. The House of Windsor has always prided itself on caring for its staff, being kind to them and keeping them for decades. The fact that it paid them dreadfully low wages didn't seem to bother the Royal Family and never had. The royals liked to think that courtiers and servants were privileged to work for them and to be accepted inside their palaces and homes; in comparison, wages were of little importance. As a result of Diana's firing and hiring policy, the talk amongst both the lower servants as well as the privileged, titled courtiers was of Diana being unable to cope with her position as the Princess of Wales.

At first, Charles would ask Diana why she wanted to be rid of whoever she was planning to fire, but in the end, he just went along with her wishes, hoping for a more peaceful, less abrasive atmosphere. From her wedding to the time of her death in 1997, Diana had arranged for the removal, or had personally fired, some forty members of staff. It was not a record to be proud of, yet those decisions to fire staff – some of whom had become almost close friends with Charles – never appeared to worry her or even cause her to lose a moment's sleep. It also meant, of course, that no adviser or royal servant who worked with Charles or Diana felt secure in their jobs. One mistake or simply a wrong gesture could end in a firing. As a result, of course, none of the advisers, staff or servants trusted Diana. And yet she either didn't realize how important such people could be in a royal household, or she simply didn't care.

Those figures reveal what a remarkable change had come over Diana during the first few months of her marriage. Staff at her family home in Norfolk, where she spent her childhood, always remembered the young Diana being kind and thoughtful to staff, even giving them little presents on their birthdays. She loved visiting the kitchens – helping the cook and the maids prepare food, helping to make cakes and biscuits. As a teenager, Diana would inquire about their families and sit and chat with them, sometimes eating lunch or taking tea with them. All that changed the moment she became Princess of Wales. It seemed that Diana's natural warmth, friendliness, kindliness and endearing qualities had disappeared overnight.

Indeed, her life had, to a great extent, changed overnight and she came to that realization in a flash. Later, Diana was able to pinpoint the exact moment when life became too much for her, something from which she would never be able to recover until she had split irrevocably from Charles. It was the moment she came down to dinner at Balmoral, following her sunshine honeymoon sailing and swimming in the warm blue waters of the Mediterranean. As her mother-in-law the Queen greeted her with a wan smile, and Prince Philip cracked a joke, she sat down and looked around the table at her new family.

During various chats with her friend Caroline Fraser, a single woman of her own age, Diana said that at that moment her heart froze as she realized what she had let herself in for by marrying Charles. She told Caroline how she looked around the table and everyone was starchy, straight-laced and boring.

Dining that evening were the Queen and Prince Philip,

Princess Anne, Prince Andrew and Prince Edward and, of course, Charles as well as six older guests she had never met and didn't recognize. She told how she looked at the expressions on their faces and saw false smiles and heard weak jokes... They treated the Queen as though she was unreal, even the children behaving as though they had to be on their very best behaviour because she was sitting amongst them... There was no joy, no fun, no *joie de vivre*, just boring people of all ages making polite, tedious small talk. Diana told how she sat there and the realization hit her that this would now be her existence for the rest of her life. She told her friend, 'I just wanted to scream, leave the table and walk out of the dining room, the castle and the family. I just knew that it wasn't me and never would be... I wasn't royal and I didn't want to be royal but stupidly, stupidly I had been carried along with the thrill and pride of being Prince Charles' girlfriend, something that I had dreamed of since I was ten years old. I simply hadn't thought it through properly, what it would really mean being his wife'.

Diana went on to tell of the conversation that night which revolved around shooting and riding, subjects she detested. She told how she sat there and realized she had made the most awful, terrible mistake and she panicked, not knowing how she could escape. Diana told how she had glanced at Charles, being so correct and dutiful to the Queen as though she wasn't really his mother; and in that instant she felt a fit of the horrors, knowing this was to be her life, and it would continue like that till the day she died.

Michael Colborne, the adviser to whom Diana frequently turned for advice and guidance, would say later, 'Charles and Diana should never have gone to Balmoral for that dreadful initiation following their return from honeymoon. It was a terrible mistake. Diana wasn't ready for it; she couldn't cope with the strict observance of royal protocol which dictates how everyone must behave when in the presence of the Queen, even when they are all supposedly on holiday. It never alters, and the realization of her future life in the Royal Family must have frightened the wits out of poor Diana. It is totally understandable that she should have reacted in such a negative way. Any young woman would have done the same in such a fraught situation. The formality of dinner at Balmoral is always strict and precise and never varies. For Diana, more used to eating a snack on her knees while sitting in front of the television, those dinners must have been hellish.'

From that first dinner at Balmoral, Diana's marriage went downhill. Her interest in Charles and his family began to wane, the fear of her future life alarmed her and as a result her relationship with Charles went downhill. She was never to fully recover her love and admiration for Charles because she had seen how he behaved when in the presence of his own mother, simply because she was the Queen. Diana could never rationalize that and never did. To her straightforward, no-nonsense, down-to-earth approach to life it seemed unbelievable that the man she married should treat his mother with such reverence and respect as though he was a mere servant in her presence. And, understandably, the young princess would become angry with Charles when he sided with his mother in any discussion, when Diana knew full well that Charles actually held the contrary opinion.

This loss of respect was perhaps the most crucial and fundamental reason for the collapse of the marriage for, until those two weeks in Scotland, Diana had held Charles in the highest esteem. She would tell her friend Caroline, 'I can recall looking across the table at Charles during that first week at Balmoral and seeing not the man of action that I thought I had married, but a bumbling, weak, sorrowful excuse for a man who buckled at the knees whenever in the presence of his mother'.

On one occasion, she heard Charles and Sir Edward Adeane discussing the merits of employing some members of staff on a contract basis – hiring them for a specific time to carry out a specific task. Sir Edward was advocating this more modern approach to save money and avoid the problem of hiring and firing staff. Charles argued that he preferred to employ people on a permanent basis because he could then rely on their loyalty and, he believed, he could thus exercise greater control.

Some time later, Diana was present when the same subject was being discussed at Balmoral during dinner. The Queen advocated the same proposal as Sir Edward and, much to her surprise, Charles totally agreed with his mother, never putting forward his loyalty argument, as he had done only a few weeks earlier. To Diana, this showed a fundamental flaw in Charles' character, and it was another reason why she found herself losing confidence in him. It seemed to her that her husband had no backbone when it came to holding any conversations with the family, as though he was scared of disagreeing with his mother for fear she would be angry or disappointed with him. Diana simply couldn't understand it. She had never been like that with her own parents and she had never known her friends to behave in such an obsequious, groveling way towards their parents.

Almost overnight, Diana found herself reacting to Charles in a negative way. Until then, she had looked forward to making love when they went to bed but now, she found herself less interested, even drawing back. Almost immediately, Charles realized that Diana seemed less than interested and so he too held back, in deference to what he thought were her wishes. The physical side of the marriage was already beginning to disintegrate, and they had only been married a few weeks.

Of course, Charles brought some of his own personal problems to the marriage, problems of which Diana was totally unaware. To a great extent, his first seven years seemed more like the life of a child growing up in the Victorian days rather than the 1950s. He suffered feelings of inadequacy and inferiority caused by his strict upbringing and his disastrous relationship with his father. Undoubtedly, as head of the family, Prince Philip bears a major responsibility for the part he played in creating a dysfunctional family and for the lamentable, sad relationships his four children endured. Because of the Queen's role as Head of State, Philip had taken over total responsibility for the upbringing of the four children and, unfortunately, he seems to have made a poor fist of it.

Prince Philip is regarded by many as a rude, selfish, arrogant man. Indeed, even the quiet, amiable and highly respected former Archbishop of Canterbury, Dr. Michael Ramsey, summed up Prince Philip with a withering comment: 'When I met Prince Philip, I thought he was very boorish, and he is'.

To the Queen, Prince Charles and his two brothers, Andrew and Edward, the loud-mouthed Philip was always seen as a bully. And he was. From the beginning of their marriage Philip assumed the role of the archetypal Victorian husband who believed that a man was the more important in any marriage and that the woman must love, honor and, importantly, obey her husband. It never seemed to occur to Philip that because his wife was the Queen, he would forever be second in importance to her. The fact that he walked two paces behind her made no difference whatsoever when they were alone together or with friends or relations.

Philip's treatment of Charles, in particular, verged on the brutish. Philip beat Charles for the most minor misdemeanors, such as forgetting to say 'please' or 'thank you', and always if he did not obey his father in an instant. The frequent beatings became a ritual, with Philip ordering Charles to his study, making him bend over and then administering the punishment, usually six smacks on the backside with a tennis shoe or a slipper. This was before he was six years old.

Prince Philip continued to bully his eldest son at every opportunity. Earl Louis Mountbatten believed Philip's behaviour towards Charles was driven by jealousy because, of course, from the moment of his birth, Charles was a far more important person than his father ever would be. Philip knew that and didn't like it – he always wanted to be top dog. Philip was also tough on Andrew and the more frail Edward but not to the same degree. However, despite his macho tendencies, he seemed to admire his daughter Anne and doted on her.

It was little surprise, then, that Charles became a nervous little boy, frightened of his father. As Charles' first governess, Miss Catherine Peebles, observed, 'Charles was nervous of coming forward, afraid to say anything for fear of retribution he would receive from his father. If you raised your voice to Charles he would draw back into his shell and for a time you would be able to do nothing with him'.

Such treatment from his father was not conducive to Charles enjoying easygoing relationships with others throughout his formative years. It also meant that he was nervous and hesitant when dealing with young women, which made life very difficult not only for Charles but also for the girls he dated. They were never sure that he had sufficient self-confidence to enjoy a natural, loving relationship.

John Barratt was Earl Mountbatten's personal and private secretary for twenty years and Mountbatten would talk to him about the various relationships within the Royal Family, particularly, what he described as the 'difficult' relationship between the Queen and Philip. Barratt told me, 'Elizabeth would frequently want to see Mountbatten privately and she would seek his advice as to how best to deal with her authoritarian husband.

'I witnessed Philip telling the Queen to shut up during conversations in a rude and abrupt manner; telling her when it was time for her to go to bed, and on occasions dictating what she should and should not eat during a meal. In discussions, Philip would always insist on silence while he made a point, interrupt the Queen when she was speaking and rubbish her arguments and points of view, sometimes telling her "not to behave like a silly woman".

Barratt went on, 'Philip had a rather unpleasant way of putting down his wife, making her feel small, and such comments were often made in front of the family. It was as if he got some pleasure from treating his wife like that, deriding her, telling her she didn't know what she was talking about, ridiculing her views and her opinions. He intimidated her. He always did. And most of the time she accepted the admonishments he threw at her. As far as I can recall, she always did as he said.'

Charles also found settling down to married life far more difficult than he had imagined. Since leaving Cambridge, aged 23, with a respectable B.A. honors degree, he had enjoyed his bachelorhood and his freedom. He enjoyed the six months he spent learning to fly with the Royal Air Force and loved his six years in the Royal Navy, where he achieved his ambition of captaining his own ship. Life after the Royal Navy was very different, but Charles knew that he had a duty to the nation and to his mother, removing some of the burden from her shoulders and carrying out his share of royal engagements. During the next few years Charles was happy playing the bachelor prince, enjoyed being a man's man, playing polo, and skiing, hunting, shooting, fishing, sailing and piloting his own plane and helicopter and earning the nickname 'Action Man', though he hated the sobriquet. He also enjoyed a string of girlfriends.

Charles first met Camilla Parker Bowles in 1972, only a few months before he was to go to sea with the Royal Navy. Her name then was Camilla Shand, and she was twenty-three, but so very different from Charles' customary girlfriends, who tended to be tall, leggy blondes. Camilla was dark, animated and bright. She had a quick mind and, more importantly, she understood Charles. She quickly came to know what made him smile or laugh, and she encouraged him to open his mind to her and talk without constraint. Whenever they met they enjoyed lively discussions, chatting as if they had known each other for years. Camilla quickly became a real *friend* to Charles, a woman with whom he discovered he could relax and be himself. He had never before felt like that with any other young woman.

But Camilla was no girlfriend in the accepted sense of

the word; they enjoyed a few lunches together in those few months but they never dated as such; never kissed passionately, never made love. And, as Charles admitted later, though he felt there was chemistry between them, he hadn't really fancied her. Indeed, Camilla's friendship with Charles began some nine months after she began dating Andrew Parker Bowles, whom Charles also knew. In February 1973, Camilla and Charles said a fond farewell to each other at a private dinner in Charles' apartment at Buckingham Palace with champagne and much laughter. Then he went to sea for the next six years. One month later, the engagement of Camilla Shand to Major Andrew Parker Bowles of the Household Cavalry was announced in *The Times.*

Charles kept in touch with Camilla, as she had offered to become his pen-pal while he was at sea and they kept up a steady stream of apparently chatty letters throughout the next six years. In 1975, Charles was thrilled to be asked to be the godfather of Camilla and Andrew's firstborn, a son, Thomas.

Unfortunately, Charles never found that deep affection, that meeting of minds, with any other woman, certainly not with Diana. In many respects, Diana was the antithesis of Camilla, despite the fact that she had a great sense of fun and, on occasion, a wonderful and wicked sense of humor that Charles admired and often enjoyed.

Diana had felt excited, exhilarated, overcome with love and devotion to Charles even before their first date. She had always felt that way about him and had secretly been quite jealous of her sister Sarah during her twelve-month intimate relationship with Charles. But Diana's sense of exhilaration and love toward Charles didn't even last until the wedding day. The gloss had vanished from the romance, and Charles was having difficulty balancing his duty to the Crown and his mother and his duty to his young fiancée. From there, unfortunately, it was nearly all downhill.

The deep regard and esteem which had so attracted Diana to Charles all but disappeared within the first weeks of marriage. She discovered to her chagrin that she had married a man whose duty was first and foremost to his country, then his mother the Queen, then to the Crown and the job that came with it. Last on Charles' list of priorities came duty to his wife and, understandably, Diana didn't like that. The omens were not good – but things would become far worse.

Chapter Eight
Diana Unmasked

The marriage of Charles and Diana was the result of a well-intentioned conspiracy by the Queen, the Queen Mother and Diana's grandmother, Lady Fermoy. During Christmas week of 1979, out of the blue, Diana received an invitation to join a shooting party at Sandringham that was to take place two months later. The invitation surprised and thrilled her. The conspirsacy was organized by the three ladies, who had decided that if Charles couldn't find a suitable bride for himself then they had better find one for him. They knew that Charles had taken out some 20 or 30 girls during the previous few years and yet he hadn't wanted to settle down with any of them.

The pressure was also mounting from Prince Philip, who would frequently upbraid Charles for being selfish in remaining single, for it was his duty to make certain that there were at least one or two heirs to the throne in case Charles met with an accident. This pressure from his father annoyed Charles because he believed it was none of Philip's business to urge him to find a bride until he felt ready to settle down. 'All in good time,' Charles would tell his father who would then walk away making comments such as, 'You'd better get a move on', 'Your mother is becoming concerned', or 'Stop being selfish and find somone'.

In fact, Charles' foot-dragging had become a matter of real concern inside the Royal Family. By the late 1970s, everyone except Lord Mountbatten wanted Charles to set about finding the 'right' young woman, marry her and produce a few children to make certain the House of Windsor would not simply fade away. Indeed, a 'find a wife for Charles' quest had become almost a national pastime, with the popular press forever trying to find suitable royal brides. The Queen and the Queen Mother were concerned that Charles was so enjoying his bachelor life with his select coterie of advisers and courtiers, his polo mates, his hunting, shooting and fishing that he felt no urgency to marry.

Lord Mountbatten, however, advised Charles to do nothing hasty unless he was certain he had found the right girl. Charles had always turned to Mountbatten for advice throughout his adult life, until fate had cruelly intervened and the IRA had killed Mountbatten and other members of his family in August 1979 by bombing his fishing smack as he holidayed in Ireland.

Mountbatten's abhorrent, violent death shocked the British people and devastated Prince Charles. Indeed, Charles was so angry that the IRA could have committed such an evil act against an innocent man and his family that he went so far as to suggest in a strongly worded letter to the British Government that he wanted to raise an army which he would lead, hell bent on hunting down and capturing or killing as many Provos as his army could unearth. Unbelievably, Charles was deadly serious. Tactfully, the Government replied that they did not think that would be a good idea.

But Mountbatten's death also gave Charles a massive wake-up call, for he suddenly realized that he too could be taken out by the IRA at any time without leaving any heirs to the throne. Now that the IRA were targeting and killing members of the Royal Family, the Queen and Prince Charles were the most likely targets, according to MI5 and the Special Branch in Northern Ireland.

Within months, Charles believed he had found the woman he wanted to marry. Out hunting in November 1979, he met a dashing, attractive young blonde woman named Anna Wallace, a good horsewoman and the daughter of a Scottish landowner. Charles fell for her almost overnight. Never had he experienced such a fiery, passionate young woman in the bedroom and she took his breath away. Known as 'Whiplash Wallace', a nickname she was proud of, Anna was so different from every other girl Charles had ever met, let alone bedded. Swept off his feet, he asked her to marry him. She refused, but Charles was not deterred and he continued to woo her.

At a ball celebrating the Queen Mother's 80th birthday, Charles invited Anna as his girlfriend and she felt honoured and flattered. On such occasions, of course, Charles is bound by duty and protocol to dance with the majority of the women, married and unmarried, as he did on that occasion. But Anna failed to understand Charles' role as Prince of Wales and the protocol that meant he had no alternative but to dance with most of the women present. Towards the end of the ball, the fiery Anna exploded in anger, yelling at him in front of guests, 'Don't ignore me like that again. I've never been treated so badly in my entire life. No one treats me like that, not even you.' Charles was stunned. No one had ever spoken like that to him before; and for Anna to do so in front of so many friends and VIPs was an appalling insult to the heir to the throne. It was, of course, the end of the affair, for Charles could not be seen dating a woman, even one as stunning as Anna Wallace, who spoke to him like that. The brush-off didn't seem to worry Anna, however, for within a month she had married another member of the aristocracy, Johnny Hesketh.

Charles licked his wounds and wondered if he would ever find a suitable woman to marry him. He looked at his rapidly balding pate and wondered if it was already too late. With the beautiful but demanding Anna Wallace having burned her boats, the three conspirators – the Queen, her mother and Diana's godmother – set about their task with renewed urgency. They wanted to find a girl of good breeding, preferably from an aristocratic family, who, naturally, had to appeal to Charles' preferences, meaning she should be tall but not too tall, blonde with long legs, good-looking and fun.

Despite the fact that their original choice, Diana's elder sister Sarah, had ended in disaster, Lady Fermoy believed that the younger sister Diana might make an ideal royal spouse. They knew Diana was quieter and less of a handful than the feisty Sarah. After numerous discussions, Lady Fermoy persuaded the two others to push for Diana Spencer. She matched the physical criteria, but they didn't really know about her character or personality. They knew she was shy, not very intelligent but kind and sensitive, nothing like her more red-blooded sister Sarah, whom Charles had recently dumped after eating problems caused her to become irrational and over-emotional.

The matrons watched from a distance to see how the two would get along. None of them was too concerned about Diana – Charles was the important one in these marriage stakes. They hoped the two of them would be compatible enough to settle down together in a happy marriage, but they were realists. They knew that the majority of aristocratic marriages ended in failure, but only after the birth of two or three children, ensuring the family name would continue for at least another generation. Frequently, instead of protracted hard-fought divorces, which were damaging to the children and to their estates, many aristocratic couples continued to live in the same house but carried on separate lives while purporting to be happily married. Occasionally, they would appear together at church and attend local fetes. They stayed married, but made separate friends and, more often than not, took lovers. Such goings-on were always conducted discreetly and never in front of the children or the staff. It had come to be accepted practice and considered rather civilized. As evidenced by so many other aristocratic marriages in Britain, most couples were able to enjoy relatively happy relationships while living virtually separate lives.

The ladies could tell from the very beginning that Charles was quite taken with the immature, teenage Diana, despite the fact that she was somewhat plump and lacked sophistication. They noted that he seemed attracted to her especially when she laughed or smiled broadly. The Queen Mother, whom Charles always respected and admired, broached the subject of Diana with Charles, and received quite a positive reply. Invitations to informal royal gatherings took off. That summer, Diana was invited to informal lunches at Windsor Castle, and she would accompany the family to watch Charles play polo in the afternoon. Soon, Charles asked Diana for a date – dinner in his private quarters at Buckingham Palace. That dinner date was so successful that within a few weeks it had become obvious that the couple were happy together.

The three ladies congratulated themselves and, as the

world knows, Charles and Diana's wedding was one of the most extravagant royal events for a generation, the first royal wedding watched live by millions around the world. And yet within only a couple of years, the three women acknowledged that their conspiracy had failed. Charles and Diana were simply not suited. They weren't happy; indeed Diana was so miserable that shortly after the birth of William she had taken a lover. And Charles had become sullen and angry. It hadn't worked – failure was staring them squarely in the eye.

The three wise matrons laid the blame for this failure at Diana's feet, conceding that it was Diana's immaturity, desire for independence and lack of discipline that were causing the rift. They sensed that without a mother at home to guide and discipline her, Diana had grown up almost running wild with no one, including her father, prepared to take on such responsibilities. Instead, all four children were packed off to boarding schools and during school holidays ran wild at home.

The three conspirators were now faced with the problem of how to put the marriage back on track. This was the 1980s, and young women were becoming more independent by the day. To their surprise, it seemed English women's new-found independence had spread to the Royal Family. New divorce laws had been introduced with 'no blame' clauses and women were divorcing their husbands in far greater numbers than ever, some refusing to live with a man who treated them badly while others simply wanted the freedom of living on their own. Diana belonged to that generation.

In royal circles, it was hoped that Charles and Diana would understand that they had to stay together for the sake of the children, the Royal Family, the Crown, the

Church and the nation. When the marriage irretrievably broke down and Charles turned to Camilla for solace and love, the three women hoped Charles had decided to get on with the next episode of his life. The marriage hadn't worked but so what? Diana had done her duty, bearing two sons, famously commenting that she had produced 'an heir and a spare'.

But Diana didn't want to acknowledge that the failure of the marriage had anything whatsoever to do with her or her behaviour. Like tens of thousands of other women wanting to escape from unhappy marriages in the latter half of the 20th century, she wanted to tell the world that she was the wronged party and the blame fell fair and square on the adulterous Charles and his long-time mistress Camilla.

But that was *not* how it happened.

When the marriage fell apart, Charles tried to placate Diana, tried to please her, help her, guide her and, in his strange way, to love her. But Charles simply had no idea how to handle Diana. With every other girl he had ever dated, Charles had done whatever he wanted when he wanted and the girl had been happy to go along with his wishes. Some girls hadn't enjoyed playing that role and had gone their own way. But this time it was different – Charles was married and he was at a loss to know how to handle his wife's demands. Sadly, there was no Mountbatten to advise him now.

Charles desperately needed advice. He turned to his friend Camilla, a woman his own age. If Lord Mountbatten had been alive, Charles would have gone straight to him, not to Camilla. Indeed, Charles would have taken Diana to Mountbatten to seek his opinion on whether he considered her a suitable bride before even thinking about marriage. Charles had enjoyed a remarkable relationship with Mountbatten, who had become the father figure he had so sorely needed.

Following the assassination of Mountbatten, Charles renewed his friendship with Camilla and her husband Andrew. Godfather to their firstborn, Charles would drive down to their Gloucestershire home to see young Tom and have a meal with the Parker Bowles. Their house in the country had become a second home to him, a place where he was welcome, where he could relax and chat with a real family, so different from a lonely room in a cold, uninviting, palace or castle with long, dark passages, vast rooms, flunkies and outdated plumbing.

It was Camilla who told Charles that Highgrove was for sale and she thought it might be suitable for him as his country estae not too far from polo grounds, hunts and London. After Charles had made his decision to buy the mansion, Camilla offered to decorate and furnish Highgrove for him. He jumped at the offer, telling her he wanted a simple but well-furnished country house, a friendly, comfortable home where he could relax at weekends away from London, invite friends to stay, and entertain informally.

Of course, Charles would frequently drive to Gloucestershire to see how his 'new' home was progressing and Camilla and Charles saw more of each other. Charles would frequently dine with Camilla, Andrew and their family; go for walks together with their dogs. Charles and Camilla saw more and more of each other and he came to rely on her as a friend who would offer sound, down-to-earth advice and sort out his new home.

It must be recalled that, famously, Charles took Diana to see Camilla before he made the decision to marry her.

He so valued Camilla's sound, sensible advice that he asked her whether she thought Diana would make a suitable wife and companion for him. It seems extraordinary that if Charles and Camilla had been lovers, and were still lovers, he should take the young woman he intended to marry to meet his current mistress. And it was actually in the cabbage patch at the Parker Bowles' home some months later that Charles asked Diana to marry him. That too would be extraordinary if Charles and Camilla were still lovers. Indeed, Diana rather took to Camilla and would see her whenever she visited Highgrove in the early part of their marriage.

Now, as his marriage seemed to be falling apart, Charles turned to Camilla in the hope that as a woman who knew Diana a little, she might be able to advise him where he had gone wrong and what he could do to save the marriage. Charles poured out his problems while they sat around the kitchen table drinking tea. He told Camilla everything including the fact that Diana had taken a lover and that, to all intents and purposes, it seemed their marriage was over. He wanted to know how he could win back Diana and mend his broken marriage. He revealed that they no longer shared a bed, made love, kissed or even held hands and they barely talked except to fight and argue over petty, ridiculous things.

Camilla gave Charles the only piece of advice she could, knowing there was not the slightest possibility of Charles and Diana being given permission by the Queen to separate or divorce: that he had no other choice but to put on a brave face, find out why Diana had turned to another man, and try to mend the broken fences.

Charles returned to Kensington Palace and tried to carry out Camilla's advice, but it didn't work. Nothing seemed to work. Diana made it plain to him that she just didn't want to know. She wanted out of the marriage, out of the Royal Family and she never wanted to carry out any more royal duties, never wanted to attend any more boring dinners, and she wanted the freedom to go wherever she wanted, when she wanted, with no questions asked, just like every other young married woman of the 1980s.

Charles explained time and again to Diana that there was no question of separation or divorce because the Queen would simply not permit it, under any circumstances. During these discussions, which nearly always turned into arguments and frequently deteriorated into swearing matches, Charles often became angry and Diana would erupt in tears. It was during these early years of the marriage that Charles became increasingly frustrated and that frustration would, invariably, turn to anger. And when in such a fury, Charles would lose his cool; kick chairs and tables, knock things off tables, thump walls and doors with his bare fists, all the time shouting abuse at Diana. On occasions, Diana was genuinely terrified that he would hit her, but he never did. On one occasion, he picked up a wooden boot-jack and hurled it at the wall – just missing Diana's head and frightening the wits out of her.

During another furious row, Diana threw a heavy glass paperweight at Charles' head and it hit the back of his head as he turned away, felling him. Silence followed as Charles collapsed on the floor. Diana stared down at his prone figure lying inert at her feet and turned white with terror, fearing that she had killed him. Seconds later Charles stirred, sat up and wondered what had happened. He was all right. But the incident had given Diana a real shock.

Charles has had problems coming to terms with his

bursts of incredible anger, and those ferocious moments when he loses control of himself alarm him. This author has seen Charles at polo matches become angry at something that went wrong on the field of play. He would jump off his pony, throw the reins towards his groom, hurl his helmet, his whip and his stick to the ground and stand in front of a large, mature tree, thumping away at the trunk with his fists and swearing. Then suddenly he would stop, shake his head and go and pick everything up.

There have been many other incidents. On one occasion, a new Range Rover was delivered to Balmoral. Charles had asked that no carpet should be fitted in the back because the vehicle would be used for throwing recently shot carcasses of deer in the back and the carpet would soon be bloodstained and ruined. Instead, the Rover car company put in a carpet with press-studs so it could easily be taken out whenever necessary.

Charles walked out of the Castle and looked around the new vehicle admiringly, then he looked through the rear window and saw the carpet on the floor.

'Does no one take any f***ing notice of what I say?' he screamed at the five or six members of staff standing around him. Still yelling, his face puce with fury, he shouted, 'I told them I didn't want any f***ing carpet in the back and there it is… What the hell do I have to do to make my words understood? Jesus Christ; will no one obey an order any more?'

For the best part of an hour, Charles continued in this vein, sometimes stopping for breath, at other times remaining silent for a minute or so before launching into a fresh attack on all, swearing and hurling abuse at everyone and anyone for not carrying out his request. Time and again, those around him tried to point out that the carpet could be removed in a minute or so by simply releasing the press-studs. But he wouldn't listen. Those around him were amazed at the extraordinary outburst and many thought that Charles had lost all control.

After such an abusive outburst, Charles would calm down and then worry that he had lost his temper so badly, it was tantamount to a complete loss of self-control. It was in the late 1970s that Charles came across a book entitled *George III and the Mad Business,* a serious, intelligent work published in 1969, written by Ida MacAlpine and Richard Hunter. Together, they had researched the nature of George III's mental illness and the possible causes for his deranged mind.

George III's madness was well known during the latter part of his long reign (1760 to 1820). His problematic behaviour was discussed in private, in public, in Parliament, in the press, by doctors, laymen and indeed by the King himself. It was of course King George III who famously 'lost' the North American colonies in 1789. However, after his death at the age of 82, a conspiracy of silence descended on the subject in deference to Queen Victoria, who was sensitive about her grandfather's derangement.

The lore of the 'mad King' later gained in popularity and became something of a legend. George had his first attack at the age of 26 and although he was suffering a debilitating illness at the time, there was no evidence that his mind was affected during that illness. In fact, it is now accepted that King George was 50 years of age when he first became deranged, and all the periods of derangement added together hardly amounted to six months in all. In his final illness from 1810 to 1820, when the Regency was established, it was said at the time that permanent madness had closed in on him. But that was a convenient fable. In reality, he suffered a series of accessions and remissions before he was overtaken by senility, then blindness and ultimately deafness.

MacAlpine and Hunter scoured all the medical records of the King's illnesses and derangement, the published letters between the King and his Prime Ministers and physicians about his illnesses, faithfully recording them in their account and investigation of the reasons behind the alleged madness. They concluded from their research, from the King's medical history records and examining the symptoms of his illnesses that George III suffered from a recurrent, widespread and severe disorder of the nervous system, now called porphyria. In extreme cases, as the King experienced, such effects attacked the central nervous system and eventually the brain, causing giddiness, mounting agitation, non-stop rambling, persistent sleeplessness and confusion which, in turn, produced delirium, tremors, stupor and convulsions.

Prince Charles was even more interested in the research carried out by MacAlpine and Hunter in tracing any subsequent family history of the disease in the second part of the book, for porphyria can be handed down through the generations. The condition may also be latent for a generation or two and transmitted by someone who shows no symptoms, or only inconspicuous ones. The research confirmed that close and distant relations of King George III had probably suffered porphyria at one time or another during the previous four hundred years. They discovered the likelihood of the disease in James I of England (1566-1625) and through his daughter Sophia to both the English and German royal blood lines.

Research also showed that George III's son, George

IV (1762 to 1830), and Frederick the Great of Prussia, (1712 to 1786), suffered from the disease, as well as other family members. And within the present British Royal Family, the Queen is descended from Queen Victoria through both the bloodline of George III and the German bloodline. Prince Philip, of course, is German and his distant relations reach back to Frederick the Great. Recent medical research has shown that porphyria is basically an inborn error of metabolism and it can most certainly be inherited.

For more than 20 years, Prince Charles was seriously obsessed with porphyria, reading a number of books on the subject and discussing with Lord Mountbatten the possibility that he might have inherited the disease. And every time Charles lost his temper and resorted to violent language or violent behaviour, he would wonder whether he was suffering from similar disorders that other porphyria victims suffer.

Even today, Charles occasionally loses his temper. He still kicks chairs and tables, smashes things on the floor and swears. He knows he loses control but he doesn't know why. Two recent explosions of anger involved his young brother Prince Edward and the second was a moment of fury at a dinner party he was hosting at Highgrove.

The first outburst occurred in the autumn of 2001 when Prince Edward ordered a camera team from his film production company to make a film of Prince William's first days at St. Andrews University. In an effort to protect William's privacy all film, TV cameramen and photographers, as well as journalists, were banned from entry to the university campus. But Edward ordered his team to go onto the campus and film William, explaining to those in charge that this venture had been agreed upon by St. James's Palace. When Charles heard what had happened he immediately phoned Edward and went berserk, shouting, swearing and using a string of four-letter words in his fury at his brother's stupidity. Charles could not understand how Edward could have given such an instruction when every effort was being made to protect William from film crews and the paparazzi.

In January of 2003, Charles was enjoying a private dinner party at Highgrove when a joke was made by one of the male guests about the BBC's poll of listeners that had voted Charles as the fourth person they would most like to boot out of Britain. Charles leapt to his feet in a fury, picked up a piece of china and hurled it to the floor in front of the astonished dozen guests at the table, shouting that the poll was a 'bloody stupid stunt' by the BBC.

However, the servants in attendance hardly blinked an eye at Charles' furious outburst because during the past few years, he had shown all the appearances of a troubled man, losing his temper at the slightest provocation. This was one of the demons Charles was battling, as Diana was realizing that she would never fit in with the Royal Family.

When Diana returned from her honeymoon and discovered to her horror how her life had changed for ever, she wrote that she was drowning in a world turned upside down.

She eventually sought solace in her children while she continued her affairs with Hewitt and others. Through Andrew Morton in *Diana, Her True Story,* she made clear that the children were a point of stability and sanity in a topsy-turvy world: '*She loved them unconditionally and absolutely working with a singleness of purpose to ensure that they did not suffer the same kind of childhood that she did'.*

According to the book, it was Diana who chose their schools, their clothes and planned their outings. They came first and foremost throughout her life. But to those friends who had known the young Diana, it was surprising that she made the decision to send both William and Harry away to boarding school at such a young age. As a single girl, Diana had taken work as a kindergarten assistant because of her love for children. She herself did not attend boarding school until she was a teenager and she wasn't happy at being sent away even then. Wills and Harry were only eight years of age when Diana sent them to board at Ludgrove Preparatory School in Berskhire, some 30 miles from Kensington Palace. She did so even when there were many first-class day schools in London where Wills and Harry could have been educated while living at Kensington Palace with her.

When Harry began boarding in September 1990, Diana had discovered a new-found freedom in London. She was all but single, fancy-free and enjoying a number of lovers while Charles, as before, spent most of his time undertaking royal duties. When not on royal duty, Charles would drive to the country, enjoying life with Camilla and what Diana dismissively referred to as 'the Highgrove Set'. Some of her friends said that Diana was happy to have her days, evenings and nights free to do whatever she wanted with no children around.

According to *Diana: Her True Story*, the Highgrove Set centered around Camilla, whom Diana maintained was never simply a confidante of Charles', the two having fallen in love with each other when they met in 1972, just a few months before Camilla married Andrew Parker Bowles. Of course, such a course of events suited Diana because it laid the blame on Charles for the break-up of their marriage. As a result of her book, the great majority of people came to believe Diana's version of events. However, she was being distinctly unfair because it wasn't true.

Michael Colborne, who served in the Royal Navy with Charles in 1972, has said, 'The suggestion that Charles was in love with Camilla at that time is plain wrong. At the time, he was on leave from the Royal Navy. They met perhaps a dozen times at the most, usually when other people were around, got on well and became good friends. But in 1972 Camilla was engaged to Andrew and very happy. Camilla married Andrew just six months after she met Charles and, as I understand it, the two were very happy together for many years'.

Princess Diana fully realized that her book, with all its inaccuracies, half-truths and deceptions, would attract the wrath of the Royal Establishment, including the Queen and Prince Philip, so she was careful to portray her relationship with the Queen as being cordial and friendly. Diana wrote that her relationship with the Queen became 'much friendlier in 1990 and 1991', and that they 'developed a more relaxed and cordial relationship'. Diana went further, suggesting that the Queen was becoming more critical of Charles, finding 'the direction of his life unfocused and his behaviour odd and erratic'. Diana kept her fingers crossed that no one would ever discover her guilty secret – that to all intents and purposes, she was the book's author.

In a bid to ensure she did not engage the Queen's anger, Diana wrote, 'Diana had a deep respect for the manner in which the Queen had conducted herself during her reign', and claimed she told the Queen 'I will never let you down'.

In fact, Diana and the Queen rarely met from the moment they were introduced in 1980 until Diana's death. Indeed, Diana admitted to being 'simply quite terrified' in the presence of the Queen and remained so most of her life.

Diana assumed that the Queen would have been informed of her affair with Hewitt at the same time Charles learned of it. As a result, Diana always found it embarrassing and awkward talking to the Queen about any subject because she felt guilty. And she knew the Queen would have expected her to keep up the pretence of a happy marriage rather than engage in a campaign of vilification against Charles, which the Queen felt was grossly unfair on William and Harry. On occasions, the Queen commented that taking tea with Diana was always difficult because the conversation usually dried up within minutes of pleasantries being exchanged and they would often sit in silence, discreetly looking around the room but making sure their eyes never met. That was the main reason why the Queen hardly ever invited her daughter-in-law to take tea with her on a one-to-one basis. The Queen understood Diana's predicament, knew that she was nervous whenever they met but the Queen was of the opinion that Diana's actions in taking a lover so early in her marriage were both disreputable and contemptible. She never forgave her.

After Diana began her affair with Hewitt, she realized immediately that the Queen would hear of it sooner rather than later and that caused her a problem. She hoped that the Queen would understand that she was miserable and unhappy and was trying to be discreet. Diana had already come to understand that she had brought a touch of glamour and fresh life to the Royal Family and that her being a part of the Royal Family would be of great benefit to the House of Windsor in its on-going public relations campaign with the British people.

Within weeks of the wedding Diana came to realize that she had, almost overnight, become the darling of the media and the great majority of the British people. She would look at newspapers and magazines and would, more often than not, find pictures of herself splashed across the covers and the clothes she wore discussed on the fashion pages. Her immense and immediate popularity also earned her sympathy from the Queen. When Diana was first recognized as a possible future bride for Prince Charles in 1980, until the moment of her death in 1997, she was the prime target of innumerable photographers, cameramen and film-makers. For seventeen years Diana was subjected to the most incredible onslaught by photographers keen to make their mark in the cut-throat world of royal snappers. To the great majority of these photographers it didn't matter whether Diana sought their attention or not. They wanted a picture come what may, and any pleas by Diana for restraint were invariably ignored.

One must wonder whether the great mass of the public, who loved seeing pictures of Diana whether laughing or crying, looking glamorous or rain-soaked, ever stopped to think of her feelings at being bombarded, chased and frequently insulted by the men and women taking those pictures. Following the marriage break-up, photographers came to realize that a picture of Diana in tears earned them more money than a happy, smiling picture of the princess. As a result, Diana became subjected to heavy-handed aggravation, cursing and threatening behaviour by the paparazzi the longer she remained the centre of world attention. At times it wasn't a pretty sight.

This author can recall one such incident on a dark, wet winter afternoon in London in 1994. Diana had dispensed with her police bodyguards, had come out of her London gym and was making her way to her car dressed in tracksuit, trainers, a ski jacket and a baseball cap. Two paparazzi photographers stood in her way as she walked along the footpath to her car, while two others took up positions in the road. Diana walked with her face down to stop them getting any face shots. She tried to squeeze past the two men but they stood shoulder to shoulder. 'Please,' she said. 'I want to pass.'

The two men stood still, refusing to move and, as Diana attempted to walk into the road to pass them, one flicked her baseball cap off her head. With her face now exposed, the cameras immediately began to flash. As she bent down to retrieve her cap, pictures were taken of her backside.

'You bastards!' she said and as she spoke the flashes fired and the cameras clicked madly. Their planned ruse had worked for they had obtained a photograph of an unglamorous, unhappy, tearful Diana. Those pictures sold around the world.

'Come on, give us a smile, lady!' one shouted and she looked at him in anger.

'Now may I pass?' she asked, after picking up her cap.

'Not till you smile,' he replied.

'F**k off!' she said loudly.

I had seen enough. I told the photographers to let Diana through. They looked at me disdainfully, not sure who I was or what authority I might have, and Diana took the opportunity to push past them and run to her car. 'Thanks, thanks very much,' she said to me as she got into her car.

On occasions, however, Diana also used the press and the photographers to her own advantage. She knew that for the most part the press, the photographers and the public were on her side in the great marital battle of the late twentieth century which often seemed to be fought out on the pages of the tabloid press.

One of Diana's favourite tricks was to telephone national newspapers – mostly the tabloids – speak in a Cockney accent, and tip them off that 'Princess Di' would be at a particular place at a particular time. Diana was a good mimic. She famously mimicked the Queen one evening as she and guests were waiting for the monarch to arrive in the dining room. Unfortunately, Diana hadn't noticed the Queen's arrival, and she blushed bright red as her audience of guests fell silent and all looked to see the Queen standing, staring at Diana. She must have heard everything but made no comment. Diana never made that mistake again.

Diana rather enjoyed giving tips of her whereabouts to the press, but it wasn't long before the photographers realized that the person giving these fantastic and accurate tips was Diana herself, though she never admitted it. She also had some contacts in the tabloid press and, without doubt, her favourite was Richard Kay, the highly-rated royal correspondent of the *Daily Mail*, to whom Diana gave many a first-rate exclusive story, much to the annoyance of royal reporters on rival papers.

So, understandably, there were numerous occasions when Diana was very happy that the 'rat-pack,' as she nicknamed the photographers, were around: the famous Taj Mahal photograph; the royal kiss that 'missed' because Diana turned her head away at the moment Charles went to kiss her cheek; and the summer evening in June 1994 when Charles was on television giving the fullest and frankest two-hour interview of his life, and Diana nevertheless stole the next day's front pages by appearing in a sensational, breathtaking off-the-shoulder black chiffon Valentino dress at a gala banquet in Kensington Gardens.

Those paparazzi photographers and the British tabloid press only received their comeuppance at the moment of Diana's death. Many millions were convinced that Diana would not have died if she hadn't been chased and hounded so frequently and aggressively by the paparazzi. Perhaps it was only right that following the chase through the streets of Paris by a large gang of photographers on motorcycles and scooters, a share of the blame for the tragic car crash should have been shouldered by the tabloid press and the paparazzi. The *Daily Telegraph* wrote in a leading article that some tabloids had treated Diana 'with bestial cruelty'. It was scathing. 'The fact that they also published many articles of slavish adoration of the Princess makes their cruelty only more refined, more cynical. It is almost past belief that organs which harried her and defiled her now claim to be guardians of her flame'.

Diana's brother, Earl Charles Spencer, was so angry at the press that he withdrew the editors' invitations to her funeral, believing that Diana would not have wanted them there. Reluctantly, they all agreed and stayed away. They had little option but to stay away, for the great mass of the British public held the tabloid press and the paparazzi partly responsible for her death.

In an interview with the French newspaper *Le Monde* only months before her death, Diana had said, 'The press in Britain has always misrepresented me in my attempts to help people. I can think of any number of occasions when I have been attacked by the Press because I dared to help other people. They attacked me for hugging AIDS victims, for my visits to Imran Khan's [the Pakistani cricket captain turned politician] cancer hospital in Lahore, and for wearing make-up during a visit to a hospital operating room during a heart transplant operation.

'The British Press is ferocious. It gives nothing, it only hunts for mistakes. Every good intention is twisted, every gesture criticized. I believe that abroad it is different. I'm welcomed with kindness when I'm overseas. I'm taken for what I am, without prior judgements, without looking for blunders. In Britain, it's the opposite. And I believe in my position, anyone sane would have left a long time ago.

'Over the years, I've had to learn to rise above criticism. But the irony is that it's been useful to me in giving me strength which I did not think I had. That's not to say the criticism hasn't hurt me. It has. But it has given me the strength to continue along the path I've chosen.'

And yet, ironically, it would be the photographers, and in particular the paparazzi, feeding the demands of the tabloid press, who would be crucially instrumental in creating the scenario that led directly to Diana's death.

It was Diana herself who had unwittingly and naively made the task so much more simple and straightforward for those planning to take her life, by making the rash decision in the summer of 1994 to dispense with her police bodyguards, except at public engagements. Even at that time this was a dangerous move for Diana to make, and it was against the advice of everyone. Diana had her reasons but they were not very well thought through. She wanted more personal privacy and she wanted to operate without the fear that what she did in her private life would automatically be reported back to Buckingham Palace. She knew that from the moment she became engaged to Prince Charles, every move she made, every person she met, every tiny part of her private life would be probed and examined and, if it was considered necessary, referred to senior police officers and palace courtiers. Diana had always been a very private person, but since her marriage she felt she had no private life whatsoever. She hated that and felt uneasy that her entire life was an open book, constantly probed by the media, the police or palace apparatchiks.

There were two other reasons. Diana wished to appear different from her in-laws and other members of the extended Royal Family, who often retained their personal bodyguards as status symbols, even though they were under very little threat. She wanted to demonstrate that she was the one high-profile royal who didn't need police protection for she had the protection of the entire British people. 'Nobody's going to hurt me,' she would say.

Her faithful private secretary, Patrick Jephson, wrote in his book *Shadows of a Princess:* 'She seemed to be indulging her death wish. I could think of no other explanation for the whole series of decisions which marked her descent into self-destruction.' Jephson went on, 'This apparent appetite for self-destruction was inextricably linked with a craving to be noticed. When – as was inevitable in the absence of a police protection officer – photographers got too close, crowds too insistent or even parking wardens too zealous, the inconvenience and occasional alarm she suffered could be borne as something akin to the wounds of martyrdom. The experience was painful but somehow holy, and suffered in the cause of reminding the world not only that she was there but also that she was defenceless and occasionally at least potentially in danger.'

Chapter Nine
The Magical Princess

It seems the world will never forget Princess Diana. Her engaging, sunny appearance, the spring in her step, the joy in her eyes – her sheer presence will be remembered for a generation. Those who never met Diana speak of her natural attraction and her devastating smile; those fortunate people who knew Diana well also speak of her sense of fun, her mischievous nature, her spontaneous laughter and her naughty dirty jokes.

To many, Diana, Princess of Wales, was a remarkable young woman. To some she was a ministering angel, to others a comforter in their time of need, to still more she was the person who gave them hope in times of despair. To all of these people, she brought something special into their lives.

When she died, Diana left behind her an extraordinary sense of communal loss. As day dawned that autumn morning in 1997 and people heard the tragic news, mothers wept openly as though they had lost a daughter; fathers felt they had failed her; young women felt they had lost a best friend who understood them. People wept openly at the realization that someone they had grown to love should have been snatched from them so abruptly, so tragically, so finally. Yet her death brought together millions of people in shared compassion and heartrending grief, which circled the globe. Hundreds of thousands of people from across Britain headed for London in the days following her death, wanting to be close to where Diana had lived and breathed; and there resided a deep-seated yearning to share their sense of loss and despair with total strangers who shared a common love for one remarkable person.

Throughout that long period of mourning, people's thoughts turned to William and Harry, the teenage lads who would now grow up without the mother who had so openly adored them. Those thoughts brought forth more heartbreak, more pain and more tears and yet most of those who mourned had never set eyes on Diana or the boys, let alone met them.

But for all the pain and heartache that Diana suffered from childhood till her untimely death, it is not why she is remembered. It is everything else that she did, frequently against the will of the Queen and her phalanx of advisers, for which people will long remember her. Her heroic AIDS campaign, as much against prejudice as the disease itself, transformed the way many people came to understand this killer disease. Indisputably, it was Diana who was responsible for people becoming far more compassionate and sympathetic to those suffering and dying from AIDS.

Diana's decision to throw her full weight behind an AIDS campaign in Britain began as a direct result of a friend of hers, Adrian Ward-Jackson, an art dealer and a Governor of the Royal Ballet, who had contracted the disease. In the late 1980s, Ward-Jackson, who became deputy Chairman of the AIDS Crisis Trust in Britain, persuaded Diana to join the Trust and help their efforts to 'de-demonise' the disease to the public. Ward-Jackson was responsible for helping Diana launch her public crusade for a better understanding of the disease he had contracted. Indeed, it was the rapidly worsening condition of the dying Ward-Jackson that gave Diana the incentive to wake up Britain and the world to the AIDS crisis.

Diana's determination to highlight the needs of those people unfortunate enough to contract HIV and AIDS was both brave and bold. In her single-minded decision to face down the Queen and her courtiers, and at the same time display her compassion, Diana showed a side of her character that most had no idea she possessed.

Let there be no mistake. Diana was 'invited' – in royal parlance that means 'ordered' – to see Sir Robert Fellowes, then the Queen's private secretary and, of course, Diana's brother-in-law, and he tried, in a smooth and gentle way, to persuade Diana to drop her support for AIDS victims, although he knew there was no point in simply ordering her to do anything – Diana wasn't going to be bullied. He knew she would have left the room immediately and held him in contempt for even suggesting such a thing. So Fellowes 'suggested' that an AIDS organisation 'might not be suitable' charitable work befitting the Princess of Wales because the 'image' wasn't positive for her or the Royal Family.

During that conversation, Diana became increasingly angry, but somehow managed to contain herself throughout most of her brother-in-law's diplomatic attempts at persuasion. Finally, after some ten minutes, she could contain herself no longer and, as she said later, 'I was raging inside at what he was saying. In effect, I was being told that the Royal Family considered AIDS a "dirty" disease and that those suffering from its effect were not deserving of royal patronage. I was told that I should concentrate on other charities that would be more acceptable to the family.'

At the end of the discussion, Diana said to Sir Robert, 'So you are telling me that the Royal Family should take no notice of people dying from a particular disease and should have nothing to do with charities involved with killer diseases. Well, I will decide what charities I shall support and I fully intend to continue supporting those people dying from AIDS, come what may.'

To her great credit, Diana did just that. Until that moment in her life, she didn't realize that she had such determination, inner strength and courage to defy the wishes of the Royal Family so openly and ignore their bureaucrat messengers. She did it and it made her feel good. Now, she would go about her charitable work with greater gusto then ever. The royals didn't like her sudden streak of independence, however – it worried them.

Diana set about breaking down the prejudice that surrounded AIDS and her personal commitment to the task was primarily responsible for ordinary people, charities and the British Government adopting a more relaxed and understanding attitude to the disease.

That was one reason behind Diana's decision to open Britain's first ward for AIDS patients at London's Middlesex Hospital. Newspaper columnists were amazed that a royal such as the pristine Princess Diana, the mother of two young sons, would take such an enormous risk as meeting AIDS patients 'without wearing protective clothing'. Shocked and dismayed, many people thought that Diana's decision to shake the hand of a man who was dying of AIDS was foolhardy at best and stupid at worst.

As Pamela Harlech, a British AIDS fundraiser said, 'One cannot overestimate the importance of what Diana did the day she touched an AIDS patient with her bare hand. At a stroke, it changed people's conception of the disease'.

When in New York during a visit to an AIDS clinic, Diana picked up a baby with AIDS and cuddled her. By doing this, she took the stigma out of the dreaded disease, changing people's perception of its dangers. For months and years doctors and clinicians had been searching in vain for a way to lift the taboo that many ordinary people held against AIDS patients. Diana did it in an instant and earned the heartfelt and sincere admiration of not only everyone suffering from AIDS, but of all their relatives and friends.

AIDS was one of the diseases that remained at the forefront of Diana's charitable work until the end of her life. Nick Partridge, Director of the Terence Higgins Trust, a major British AIDS charity, has revealed that Diana asked to be kept abreast of the scientific and medical advances being made in the search for a cure. Every two or three months Partridge would brief her, informing her of the progress medical investigations were making and of the latest up-to-the-minute treatments for sufferers. She never lost interest.

One of the principal reasons Diana became involved in the cause was not only because of her concern to help those who had contracted the disease, but also because of her subconscious need to be closely involved with sufferers, particularly those whose diseases made them outcasts from society. Diana wanted to help these people because they were victims rejected by society, and she shared their feeling of rejection because she had been cast aside by her mother, her husband and the Royal Family. Diana felt strongly that the more involved she became with those rejected by society, the more appreciated and loved she felt in return.

This feeling of rejection remained with Diana all her adult life. As she told patients at an AIDS clinic in London in 1987, when the subject was almost taboo in many social circles in Britain, 'I understand the rejection you feel because I feel the same rejection'.

Pamela Harlech explained Diana's remarkable empathy with AIDS sufferers, saying, 'Diana really does believe that she understands the rejection they feel better than anyone because she feels she is one of them'.

But her AIDS work was only one example of the way in which Diana acted as an agent of compassion to those in need and, at the same time, forced people to face unpalatable and fearsome truths. To Diana, it was paramount to help the sufferers and she wanted to bring some peace and understanding to the victims and their families. She also wanted to get a better deal for the sufferers, many of whom were feeling ostracised and rejected by society.

There was also leprosy, the highly infectious bacterial disease which results in severe physical deformities. Diana realised that, like AIDS victims, lepers were being shunned across the world, rejected by the societies in which they lived by people who were frightened of coming into contact with them or even touching them. She understood that, unlike AIDS, this was no new disease, but something poverty-stricken societies had lived with for centuries.

Baptist Minister Tony Lloyd, executive director of the Leprosy Mission in Britain, accompanied Diana on trips to Africa. 'Our first trip was to Harare in Zimbabwe in 1993 and I noticed that Diana was looking at a woman with no fingers. After a short while, Diana went behind a partition in the hospital and I saw she was crying, unable to control her sobbing. When she had composed herself, she told me that she wasn't only crying for the woman but the fact that she was now getting proper treatment.

'Diana was without racial prejudice. She would talk to blacks and whites in the same way and was completely fearless for herself in the middle of a leper colony,' said Tony Lloyd.

Before she left Britain, some tabloid newspapers exhorted Diana with headlines screaming, 'Don't Do It!' and doctors wrote articles curdling the readers' blood with details of disfigurement and loss of limbs that might occur if Diana shook hands with a leper patient. Little did the public know that Diana not only shook hands with AIDS patients and lepers but, when out of view of the cameras, she would take the opportunity to cuddle babies, hold AIDS sufferers in her arms and hug anyone that she believed needed to be hugged by another human being.

Tony Lloyd related another story: 'We flew to a refugee camp near the Mozambique border and she shook hands with everyone, and those people who had no hands, she shook their wrists instead as though that was perfectly normal. With all of them she laughed and joked and chatted, listening to whatever they had to say.

'But what I noticed was that when Diana walked into the tent where they were all sitting, she simply looked around the room at everyone and smiled to them all, as though she was really happy to be among them. It was like a ray of sunshine coming to visit them for she had this incredible charisma and, I have to say, I was in awe of it.

'I believe she sympathized with lepers because she realized they had been rejected and cast out from society, forced to live like outsiders forever, until they eventually died – alone, unloved and often despised. It seemed to me that in her care for lepers, Diana was searching for a spiritual dimension. The more I came to know her and work with her the more I felt, in the last couple of years, that she had found her place in the world, helping and inspiring the outcasts of the world and this brought a sort of peace to her life. As a result, she seemed much clearer in her life's work. She had found herself.'

Lloyd explained that Diana had brought three things to the leprosy cause: 'Firstly, a high profile; secondly, money, including tens of thousands of pounds from her own back account which no one ever knew about; and thirdly, she helped people around the world to overcome the stigma of leprosy as she had with AIDS. Diana touched lepers, cradled children dying of leprosy in her arms, kissed them and joked with them. No one in her position had ever done anything like that before and, even today, we thank God for what Diana brought to those suffering from leprosy. I can understand why some people called her a saint.'

And though some people disparaged the charity work Diana did with AIDS victims and lepers, suggesting she only involved herself with these charities for publicity or headline grabbing photo-opportunities, much of the work she carried out with victims of both those diseases she carried out in secret with no photographers or media people in attendance. Indeed, for most of the time, the media had no idea what she was doing.

During another African visit, Diana found herself deep in the Southern African bush at the Mazerera Red Cross centre feeding hundreds of children who had walked for hours in the hope they would be given a bowl of bean soup. With tears in her eyes, Diana personally ladled out the soup from a huge iron cooking pot to the children of the Karanga tribe, many of them suffering from severe malnutrition. She stood for three hours in intense heat handing out the soup, until every child had been fed. With sweat pouring down her face, neck and arms and her dress soaked with perspiration, Diana managed a smile for every child who stood in line waiting for the food. As she flew back from the bush she sat in the helicopter with tears streaming down her face because she knew she was returning to a life of luxury and plenty and the children were returning home on foot with no idea where their next meal would come from.

As a result, Diana determined to do far, far more to help alleviate the suffering of lepers and, as she had done with AIDS sufferers, make lepers feel a part of the social fabric rather than having to face life as outcasts whom very few people wanted to help and care for. On her return home she contacted experts who came to the palace to brief her, explaining the best ways she could help the cause of lepers worldwide. She not only admired and applauded the extraordinary courage of the victims, but also the nurses and helpers who defied so much prejudice to help them. She would confess, 'Whenever I think of those poor, deprived lepers, particularly the children, I can't stop the tears because I feel so ashamed that the world turns its back on these desperate, lonely, helpless people and does virtually nothing to help them.'

Patrick Jephson, Diana's private secretary and her most influential adviser from 1988 to 1996, wrote in his memoirs, *Shadows of a Princess*: 'To me, the Princess's work with lepers stands out as her greatest monument. It would be impossible to find a better example of her ability to transform attitudes, to help the ignorant accept the untouchable. There were no moral overtones to distract from the central message, as there sometimes were in the case of AIDS. This was goodness in a rare form, and if it also made a good photo opportunity, I should really only have been glad.'

Diana had become an angel of hope and not only in championing major, high-profile diseases. She never forgot those at home. Every so often, the postman delivered a letter from Kensington Palace to the home in Copthorne, West Sussex, of one Emma May. The postman knew they were personal letters from Diana. He also knew that Emma May was a girl of quite exceptional courage. She had been born with a rare chromosome disorder called Turner's Syndrome, which not only causes heart and kidney problems in young children but also stunts their growth. As a result, Emma had to make regular visits to Great Ormond Street Hospital for Children in London, staying there while she underwent difficult and painful stretching surgery. Doctors and nurses see many brave youngsters, but even in their experience Emma May was exceptional.

Bright, blue-eyed Emma would lie in hospital for months at a time, wondering what the future held for her. She had always been a sickly child, unable to enjoy the normal rigours and rough-and-tumble of childhood. Whenever she went into hospital, she knew it would mean pain, sometimes extreme, and always physical discomfort. When she was ten years old, the doctors and nurses at the hospital had become so overwhelmed by her courage that, in 1992, she was awarded the annual bravery prize for children who had triumphed over adversity.

As always, Diana, Princess of Wales, the hospital's patron, came to present the award and it was then that she first met Emma. After that first meeting, she asked the doctors, 'Her eyes are so bright; she seems a remarkable child. How can she take such pain and still smile? She makes me feel ashamed'. Until the day of her death, some five years later, Diana never forgot the courageous young girl.

Emma, now 21, recalls their meetings through the years. 'Diana told me that I was her special friend. She would come and sit on my bed and talk to me. After a while I didn't call her "Princess", just Diana, and she called me Emma. That's because Diana told me we were friends.

'So much of what happened to me is down to Diana. She was my inspiration throughout some traumatic times when I would lie in bed feeling rotten with the continuous pain. I would think of her and smile. During the first meeting Diana told me to keep in touch and write to her, telling her how I was getting on. I felt a bit silly writing to her because I knew I would never get a letter back. But she wrote back immediately, telling me how lovely it was to hear from me and asked me to keep writing. She seemed really interested.

'Diana gave me hope. She gave me the courage to face all my operations and the strength to face the future. She kept telling me that one day everything would be fine and because she told me I believed her. She was such a wonderful, extraordinary person and she was right. Now, basically I'm fine and never a day goes by without me thinking of her.'

Emma May was not the only child to have faith in Diana. All over the world there are children who have met Diana in similar, disturbing situations and, somehow, she would encourage them to believe in themselves and

169

have faith in the future. She gave them hope, which they never forgot.

On many occasions when Diana carried out her charity work, it was a high profile event, meaning headline-grabbing photo opportunities. The photographers and television crews needed their pictures, and the journalists wrote their pieces, encouraging people who saw the good works the charities were carrying out to contribute desperately needed money. As patron of these charities, Diana was only too happy to pose for such activities. Towards the end of her life, however, some journalists began to carp, exclaiming that she only appeared at such charitable functions when she knew the cameras would be present. That was a slur on Diana's good name and totally untrue.

In fact, Diana saw far more ill, sick and dying patients, particularly children, when there were no cameras present to record the scene. And she preferred it that way because she discovered that on a one-to-one basis, particularly with children, they would relax more easily and become more open and confident with her.

The case of Bonnie Hendel was typical. Diana had met Bonnie at St. Mary's Hospital, Paddington, London, where she was lying desperately ill from AIDS. Doctors warned Diana that they feared Bonnie was close to death. When Diana arrived at her bedside she could see the child had eaten no food so, slowly and patiently, Diana fed her the food until she had eaten every morsel.

After Diana had left, having chatted to Bonnie's parents and asking to be kept informed of her progress, Bonnie told the doctors, 'I don't need any more medicine, just lunch with Diana every day. She makes me feel better'.

A few days later, Diana sent Bonnie a letter wishing

her well and enclosing a photograph of herself for Bonnie to keep by her bed and kiss every morning and every night. Within a matter of weeks, doctors at St. Mary's phoned Kensington palace to tell Diana that Bonnie was only hours away from death. Diana immediately cancelled her next engagement, jumped in her car and raced to the hospital. But she arrived too late; Bonnie was dead.

Diana joined Bonnie's grieving parents, and for fifteen minutes the three stood together clasping each other, tears running down their cheeks. When Diana left the hospital she was still holding a handkerchief to her eyes, trying to stem the tears. There was not a photographer or journalist in sight. Diana had not taken the trouble to rush to Bonnie's bedside because she thought it might provide a photo for the next day's papers but simply out of her love and concern for a helpless child.

In the great majority of her private visits to hospitals, Diana would arrive alone, usually driving herself. Unlike any other member of the Royal Family, she preferred to arrive with no police protection, no armed bodyguard, lady-in-waiting or secretary. She preferred to chat with patients one-on-one, especially with children, when there was no one else standing around the bed. She wanted the occasion to be personal, intimate and totally informal, which is why she usually dressed in jeans and a sweater.

As Anne Houston, director of ChildLine Scotland, commented, 'We were all struck by Diana's understanding of children's problems when she visited us in Glasgow. She had an amazing empathy with children.'

Eleven-year-old Joy Bradbury woke up in London's Royal Brompton Hospital after open-heart surgery. She was critically ill, hovering between life and death, and doctors weren't sure whether she would survive the trauma of the operation. Still on a ventilator and unable to speak, she had drifted in and out of consciousness, watched by doctors and nurses who kept her under constant supervision. Then she awoke and looked up to see a woman with blonde hair, dressed in a sweater and jeans, smiling down at her. Instantly, Joy recognized Diana. A smile crossed her lips and her eyes lit up.

'It was a wonderful, magical moment,' said her mother Doreen who was also at the bedside. 'Diana gave her the will to live because she showed she cared for Joy. Diana's presence made Joy feel special. And Diana never lost contact. The following Christmas, Joy received a card from Diana wishing her well. That's the sort of person she was, always thinking of other people, putting ordinary people first, caring for them. That's why everyone was so distraught at her death.'

In a similar story, Diana met Paul and Jo Thompson during one of hundreds of private visits to the Paediatric Intensive Care Unit at St. Mary's Hospital, London. Their son Harry, only twelve months old, was suffering from a rare disease which destroys the lungs.

Jo explained, 'Diana came to comfort us shortly after she heard it was Harry's first birthday. We were sitting by his cot praying he would recover when, to our surprise, Diana walked into the ward, came over to the bed and began to chat to us about Harry. She held his hand and chatted as though she was one of the family. She was so sincere – you could tell she was genuine. She had a compassionate aura about her.'

A month later, Harry's condition began to deteriorate and he was given only days to live. As Diana had requested, the doctors wrote a letter to her informing her that young Harry was at the point of death. An hour later, she had handwritten a note to Harry's parents expressing her concern and sympathy. And she had immediately sent the letter by car to the hospital. Jo said later, 'She had no need to write – no one knew about what was going on – and yet she took the trouble to do so.'

Amazingly, within 24 hours after receiving Diana's letter, Harry began to improve. Jo said, 'It is a miracle that Harry is still here. That's what the doctors say. They thought he only had days to live but somehow he pulled though. I just wish that Diana could see him now. Sometimes I really do believe that Diana was an angel of mercy.'

Dr. Parviz Habibi, director of the Paediatric Intensive Care Unit, said, 'Harry was just one example of Diana's caring nature. Once she had pledged her support to a patient, she did so in style. We knew she was a genuine and honest person – she proved it time and again. Harry's parents had gone through hell with worry and she gave them moral support when they so desperately needed it. That was why she was such a remarkable person.'

However, there were few people who realized the extraordinary toll those secret hospital visits took on Diana. Frequently, she would arrive back at Kensington Palace, walk up to her bedroom on the second floor, throw herself on her bed and lie there, face down, crying and distraught at the suffering of the children she had seen that day. She felt their pain and wretchedness and would frequently castigate herself for living such an indulgent life and having the nerve to complain about her lot. But throughout her visits Diana would always be the smiling, upbeat, happy Princess, though the distress she witnessed week in and week out drained her and left her physically exhausted.

An example of the pressure Diana was under and the trauma of her marriage problems was illustrated in yet another secret initiative that Diana undertook when she was alerted that an 18-year-old girl, Louise Woolcock from Poulton-le-Fylde, Lancashire, was dying from terminal cancer.

Social worker Philip Woolcock told the story of the remarkable friendship that grew up out of the relationship Diana began with his daughter Louise in 1992: 'Louise was looking forward to university when she was diagnosed as having a virulent form of cancer. My wife Judy and I took the decision to protect her from the knowledge that she was dying, trying instead to help through a traumatic course of chemotherapy.

'But Louise was so wonderfully brave that she began raising money for a cancer charity to help others. Diana heard of her efforts and came to see her. That first meeting was magic. They had lunch together, talking for an hour and both giggling like schoolgirls. Louise was always incredibly loquacious and bubbly and I think Diana was moved because she felt Louise should have her whole life ahead of her.'

At the end of that first meeting, Philip Woolcock asked Diana if she would open the local day hospice in honour of his daughter. Diana told him to write, but could promise nothing. Diana did eventually come to open the hospice but Louise had not come out of remission and was close to death.

Philip continued, 'By any normal scale Louise should not have been alive for that visit but the thought of meeting the Princess again instilled in her a new-found strength and determination. Even though she was full of morphine, Louise forced herself into a wheelchair and out into the reception area. When Diana arrived she almost bounded up to Louise, hugging her, and soon they were giggling and laughing as they had a year before. It was wonderful to see. But one week later Louise was dead.'

Diana was informed of her death by the hospital, and the Woolcocks received a letter of condolence from her. Shortly afterwards, Diana phoned and asked if she could come and see them. She arrived at their house at the appointed time. Philip told the story: 'We spent quite a time just sitting and chatting. It was about this time that the newspapers were full of Diana's marriage problems and she looked pale and distraught. Her knuckles were white, her eyes full of tears.

'Eventually, I asked her how she was about everything and suddenly it all came spilling out... about her marriage, her distress, her loneliness. "I've had eleven years of this," Diana said, "and I'm getting out. I can't take any more".'

From 1992 until a few days before her death, Diana kept in touch with the Woolcocks, primarily through long phone calls. Judy recalls, 'My son Sam had had his navel pierced and his hair bleached and I told Diana about it and she laughed, saying, "Gosh, I don't know what my mother-in-law would do if William did that!"

'She also told me that she didn't know how she would cope with the situation when William found his first girlfriend. She said, "I don't think there's anyone on the scene at the moment... I hope!"'

During her last phone call to the Woolcocks in August 1997, Diana sounded bubbly and happy. Philip said, 'She spent fifteen minutes chatting away to us about everything – children, holidays, work. She sounded so happy and we both felt happy for her. When we woke on that Sunday morning and heard the news of her death, we were devastated, speechless. Now we are over the pain of her death we feel we were privileged to have known Diana so well but we do miss her. I just want people to know what a wonderful difference Diana made to our lives and to countless others.'

Diana relied on the teams of doctors, surgeons, consultants and nurses at various hospitals to keep her informed if there was a child whom they believed would benefit from one of her personal visits. And she never forgot that it was those teams who carried out the day-to-day work that really mattered and not a quick visit from her. She simply hoped that her visits might provide something memorable to cheer up a child, often after weeks and months of hospitalisation. To Diana, it did not matter whether the child was black or white, rich or poor, British or foreign; only that there was a possibility that her presence might prove positive to the youngster concerned.

Robert Creighton, chief executive of the Great Ormond Street Hospital, gave an example. 'For 18 months we had cared for a poor little Bosnian girl, Irma, aged eight, who had been seriously injured when a bomb exploded near her during the fighting in 1993. Irma was paralyzed from the head down and we tried to make her life easier. Diana came to visit her once or twice and she would sit and stroke her forehead and encourage the little girl to smile, trying to give some encouragement to this child who for so long hovered between life and death. And then, on March 31, 1995, little Irma died and all of us who had fought long and hard to save her life were truly devastated. We felt we had failed her, all of us.

'We phoned Diana and told her of Irma's death and she asked me if I could gather the team who had looked after Irma throughout her long illness so that she could meet and chat to us. There was probably a core of about a dozen doctors and nurses who had been closely involved with Irma and Diana came, chatted to us all and thanked every one of us for the effort and devotion that we had all put in for Irma. It was a sad, moving experience for all of us, including Diana, and I think that on that day there were tears in all our eyes, including Diana's. But the team really appreciated that Diana wanted to come and say thank you to them for all the care and nursing of the little Bosnian girl that no one in England knew anything about.

'There were no cameras, no journalists present. There was only Diana and us. It was typical of her. She felt for people, understood them like no one ever had before. I often witnessed Diana meeting parents and sick children, and I must tell you it was always a remarkably moving experience. Both parents and children seemed to trust her instantly, to gravitate towards her as though they had known her for ages. Usually, in hospitals, children take time to adapt to a stranger, but not to Diana. She had an instant rapport with them that was warm and natural, and children responded to her. It was wonderful to see. I can honestly say that Diana's presence will be impossible to replace. She was simply unique.'

Diana also found great benefit in her hospital visits. She confessed to Dr. Habibi, 'It's not only one way. I believe that I gain from these visits too. These visits to the children give me a warm feeling of wellbeing, that I'm giving something of myself to others far less fortunate than me. I know that I'm living a privileged life and I feel that visiting the sick and disadvantaged children is a personal duty which I have grown to love.'

Later, Diana would tell her friend Sarah Ferguson, 'I

began these hospital visits after years of feeling sorry for myself, wallowing in my own misery because of what I believed was a pointless existence in a failed, loveless marriage. I believe that for some unknown reason I had an extraordinary capacity for unhappiness which is why I wanted to encourage others to overcome their sadness. Fortunately, it seemed to work and that brought me great inner happiness.

'When I began visiting children in hospitals, it was a form of therapy for myself. And when I saw them suffering, often fighting for their very lives, it hit me hard and made me realise that my troubles were as nothing compared to theirs. The more private hospital visits I made, the more I realised that my own unhappiness was of little or no consequence. It also stopped me returning to the dark days when I was unable to control my eating habits because I was so wrapped up in my own wretchedness. Those poor children gave me a feeling that my life could be useful and I found the children responded to me no matter how ill they were. Finally, I was doing something positive and it made me feel a different person. I could hold my head up.'

Diana also understood that she had a very important public role, getting people to dig deep into their pockets and contribute to worthy causes. She recognized that the charities needed the money to carry on their wonderful work and Diana was of the mind that if her presence would give their coffers a boost, she was happy to take part. That was the reason she was only too happy to make high-profile visits to hospitals in front of ranks of photographers and television crews, but she didn't enjoy these occasions half as much as her private visits.

As a result, Diana came to wonder whether she might

actually possess a form of healing power. This developed in her mind because some people came to believe that she enjoyed a form of saintliness and, as a result, she became only too happy to touch, hold or shake hands with people not only suffering from AIDS or leprosy but other ailments as well. So many matrons and doctors in hospital wards all over the world would tell Diana that her mere presence in a ward full of patients had a more beneficial effect on the patients than any amount of medicine. It is accepted that so much healing of patients, particularly in Third World hospitals, takes place in the mind of the patient and Diana came to believe that perhaps she was actually capable of making people recover faster than if she had not visited them.

Her private secretary Patrick Jephson wrote in his autobiography: '*The idea that Diana had some kind of gift of healing remains very much an open question, of course. If she did possess such a gift, then it was completely unrefined, undisciplined and undirected. Had it been recognized and developed as the talent it sometimes seemed to be, I believe that her round of compassionate visiting would not have taken the toll it did on her emotional stamina. Sadly, the lack of any appropriate direction and discipline forfeited for her any chance to explore or use a gift for which she seemed otherwise so eminently qualified. After all, as many believe, it is a gift which requires a level of personal spiritual development that I do not think she would ever have claimed to have reached.*'

Jephson, who studied Diana closely for nearly a decade, noticed that the more charity work, both private and public, that Diana undertook, the more desperate she became for personal fulfillment. He wrote in his book: '*However cynical, manipulative or self-indulgent her motives might sometimes have been for doing some of the good things for which she received such credit, in the act of doing them there was no cynicism at all... People who had no knowledge of her other than as recipients of her concern or gratitude were in no doubt about what they felt she gave to them. It is the same quality we can see now, years later, in contemporary news photographs of the Princess doing her routine work of bringing hope and comfort to people in need. It was given and received at a level beyond speech and I do not think it can ever be explained properly in simply human terms.*

'In my time with her, however, she never found the faith that might have given her strength in moments of real doubt and loneliness. It was probably the only way in which she could have gained genuine satisfaction and happiness from the good that was so often laid at her door... In the absence of a solid faith that could comfort her, she took refuge in impulsive bouts of mysticism and psychology. Without a reliable framework of knowledge and support, or wise guidance she was prepared to trust, these too were bound to fail her.'

But in the last few years of Diana's life, the public image which the press had created for her – a cross between Mother Teresa and a supermodel – faded as she preferred to direct her energies toward her secret, more private visits to young hospital patients. She preferred that work – she was tired of the cameras and TV crews. She had also become angry and upset at the cruel sniping by some in the media who had come to the conclusion, incorrectly as it happened, that she only undertook her hospital visits for the publicity it gave her.

When Diana was invited to become involved in high-profile matters of major international importance, such as the campaign to rid the world of anti-personnel mines, she was only too happy to help. The new Diana wanted to become more involved in humanitarian issues on an international level. AP mines was the first cause for which she earned praise for her contributions and, at the time of her death, she was planning her next major international campaign, fighting for the rights of refugees.

Chapter Ten
Power and Glory

Princess Diana made one of the most important decisions of her life some months before Prime Minister John Major officially announced her separation from Prince Charles in December 1992. She determined that she would branch out on her own and decide her own fate independent of Prince Charles and the rest of the Royal Family. She reached that conclusion as a result of the tremendous upsurge of public love and affection towards her following the revelations in *Diana: Her True Story*, which portrayed her life as so miserable and unbearable that she had resorted to numerous suicide attempts.

The tide of public opinion had been flowing strongly in Diana's favour for some years, and her book cemented the bond between her and the great mass of the British public, particularly amongst women with young families. They had seen what a loving, good mother she had proved to be to Wills and Harry, and they knew that being married to a man who kept a mistress caused stress and despair, triggering other health problems like bulimia and anorexia. Diana's star burned brightly while Charles' reputation continued to plummet.

She would further cement her relationship with the ordinary mums and dads of Britain by showing that she was one of them, taking Wills and Harry to public amusement parks, where newspaper photographers would be waiting to snap away. It was, however, no accident that the photographers were on hand – pretending to be a palace maid, Diana would phone tabloid picture editors, tipping them off about the next day's royal visit. In these theme parks, Diana would enjoy some of the rides with her lads, putting on a wonderful display of unstuffy modern motherhood so very different from the traditional way royals were expected to behave with their children in public. Nothing like it had ever been seen before and the nation loved it. In 1993 Diana went further, taking Wills and Harry on holiday to Disney World in Florida. And once again the 'snappers' were on hand.

There was, however, a perceived negative element to such ordinary family entertainment. Patrick Jephson, her secretary, would write, '*Such actions however also reinforced the contempt in which she was held by many of those who would never have dreamt of setting foot in such a place.*' To her eternal credit, Diana didn't care a damn what those 'stuck-up old fossils' – the palace courtiers – thought of such outings. She would raise her children in the way she considered best for them.

Such excursions were signs that Diana was indeed no empty-headed numbskull, but someone with a carefully thought-out strategy. Having secured her base at home, Diana could now target her true ambition – to capture the hearts and minds of people across the world so that she would be seen as the new embodiment of the British Crown, at the same time casting Prince Charles and even the Queen deeper into the shadows.

After much debate at the highest level in the palace, and after discussing the matter with Prime Minister John Major, the Queen finally agreed that Diana could conduct her first solo overseas visit in September, 1991. Diana was thrilled. A royal tour to Pakistan had been planned for some years, but members of the Royal Family had not been keen to undertake such a trip because some members of the Pakistani political elite still remembered the days of the Raj when Britain ruled the entire sub-continent. That fear didn't worry Diana one bit. She was different from every other member of the Royal Family because she carried with her no historical or political baggage and she was also confident of her ability to step into the Queen's shoes.

She had been given the golden opportunity to prove herself, and she was determined to show the doubters in the British Foreign Office that she was not only a capable ambassador for Britain, but someone who would show the world that the Royal Family had changed and that she embodied that new change. Now she faced her moment of truth.

Diana knew that if she failed, she would never again be permitted to travel alone overseas as the Queen's royal ambassador. But if the tour was a success, her future as a representative of the Royal Family was bright indeed. She was playing for high stakes and she knew it.

Back home in Britain, even Diana's private secretary and principal adviser Jephson knew the potential danger of this solo trip, recording in his diaries, *'Opinion on the visit on the royal home front was at least neutral, if, I felt, rather watchful. Not too many tears would be shed if this ground-breaking solo tour disappeared in the inside pages of the tabloids.'*

In fact, Diana's first solo foreign tour was a triumph, far surpassing the critics who believed that she wasn't 'royal enough' to carry out such a visit without the odd diplomatic gaffe or two. Her ground-breaking overseas visit even surprised the pro-Diana tabloid editors back in

London. The tour was splashed over the front pages of both the tabloids and even the sceptical broadsheets. Finally, after ten years as a member of the Royal Family, Diana had earned her spurs.

In *Shadows of A Princess,* Jephson's account of life as Diana's private secretary, he noted that after Diana's speech at the Pakistan Prime Minister's dinner, *'the Princess proposed a toast and made a speech...with an assurance that would have brought sorrow to all – and there were not a few – who would have liked her to be portrayed on her solo mission as an empty-headed lightweight, more accustomed to pop concerts and clothes shops than the volatile politics of the subcontinent.'*

Diana returned in a blaze of glory and secretly wondered if she would be permitted to represent the Queen on any future foreign tours. She knew that one day the Queen would be forced to permit Charles a divorce, but right now she was enjoying living in the limelight, revelling in the escalating adoration of the nation. Whenever the media examined any aspect of her life the verdict was always high praise, whether it was for her lifestyle, her fashion sense, her fitness, her beauty, her charitable work or the obvious love she showered on her two boys.

Diana did, however, have one frightening concern. She knew that one day the question which she so feared would be raised. As young Harry grew older and became a teenager, and then an adult, there was every probability that he would look more and more like James Hewitt.

She believed she was living on borrowed time. She was certain that the Queen and the entire Royal Family had been led to believe that Harry was not Charles' son, but she was keeping her fingers crossed that they would never want that fact revealed for fear of the damage it might cause, not only to poor Harry but also to the House of Windsor. Diana understood she was conducting a high-risk strategy but rather enjoyed being able to live an entirely free life, taking as many lovers as she wished, while still being legally married to Charles. She was fully aware that the Queen and the Queen Mother were adamantly opposed to divorce – particularly in their own family. She rather hoped that she would be permitted to continue with her married status as long as she kept her nose clean, didn't flaunt her lovers and didn't embarrass the Royal Family. Diana reasoned that the Royal Family had more reason to let the status quo continue rather than push for a divorce and cut her off, permitting her to pursue a life over which they would then have no control whatsoever.

For a decade, the Queen and the Queen Mother had closely followed Diana's path from quiet, subservient, shy teenager to a woman who seemed to revel in her ability to win the hearts and souls of the British public. And it worried them. After the breakdown of the marriage their initial thought had been to force through a quick divorce and rid the Royal Family of Diana. But that moment passed as they witnessed the nation's remarkable love affair with the princess. They came to believe if they forced through a divorce in the early 1990s there was a real possibility that the monarchy itself might be put in jeopardy and the deep-seated cause to which they had both dedicated their lives – the preservation of the House of Windsor – might collapse. They couldn't take that risk, so they decided to wait and see.

The 'War of the Wales' continued in print. The media were constantly on the watch to report any problems or difficulties between Charles and Diana. My book, *Diana: A Princess and Her Troubled Marriage*, and *Diana: Her True*

Story had both been avidly read and, it seemed, the entire nation was now riveted by this classic royal soap opera unfolding before their very eyes in the national press. The vast majority of the ordinary British people took Diana's side while the traditionalists, the monarchists, the Establishment and the wealthy classes supported Charles and the monarchy.

Throughout the ten years of their separate lives within their marriage – 1982 to 1992 – many attempts were made to repair their relationship but all came to naught. Charles believed that Diana showed so much ill-temper and spite towards him that he could never forgive her. He could also never forgive the fact that Diana had gone out of her way to lie to the world that it was he who had quit the marriage bed for another woman when, in fact, both he and Diana knew that she had been the one who fled into her lovers' arms a full two years before he and Camilla made the decision to become lovers.

Charles could not comprehend why Diana had become so vitriolic towards him, seemingly more so since they had been living separate lives. He never understood why Diana, who had so obviously loved him in their pre-marriage days, had so completely turned against him, venting her rage, blighting his reputation and insulting him in front of friends, relatives and even servants.

One such occasion was the death of her beloved father, Earl Spencer, in March 1992, when she and Charles were skiing together in Austria. On that trip, however, there was no pretence whatsoever as the royal couple illustrated to the world that they were living separate lives, Diana insisting that she stay in a separate suite in the hotel – a fact known to all the journalists who accompanied them. In fact, the couple not only resided in separate hotel suites, they also dined separately and skied on different mountains. Throughout that holiday they were rarely seen together. Diana wanted to make a public statement and did so in style.

When her bodyguard broke the news to Diana of her father's death, anticipated since he had been in ill health for some months, Inspector Wharfe reported that she broke down in a state of 'terrible distress'. She told him that she wanted to return to her dead father and the Spencer family – without Prince Charles at her side.

He quoted a vitriolic Diana as saying, *'I mean it, Ken. I don't want him with me. He doesn't love me – he loves that woman. Why should I save his face? Why the bloody hell should I? It's my father who's gone. It's a bit bloody late for Charles to start playing the caring husband, don't you think?'*

Charles had always been his own worst enemy and was hopeless in such a situation. He had little idea how to comfort women in distress and virtually no idea how to humour, charm or cajole them. He was too gauche, too artless. Throughout his life, he had been in the company of only boys and men, from his schooldays to the armed services and beyond. He generally felt awkward with women, even his mother or his sister Anne. And when Diana made it plain that her love for him was fading, he did little to persuade her otherwise. He simply had no idea what to say, what to do or how to act. So he froze her out, turned his back and walked away.

In private, Diana retaliated by freezing him out of her life. She was happy when Charles moved to Highgrove in the mid-1980s, leaving her alone at Kensington Palace with the boys. She preferred to be left alone to carry on her own life in her own way and let Charles carry out his royal duties without her. She simply wished to turn her back on the entire Windsor family but was proud to be the mother of the heirs to the throne. She also reveled in her title of HRH the Princess of Wales and the life she was permitted to lead doing precisely what she wanted, when she wanted, with no holds barred – and everything paid for by Charles.

Occasionally, Diana felt guilty for what she had done to blacken Charles' name in her bid to conceal the reasons for her own adultery, but she had no wish for a divorce. She had grown up in a family where her parents' acrimonious divorce had cast a blight on her life and the lives of her siblings. She hated the very idea of divorce because of the effect it had on children. Indeed, *Relate,* a British charity of which she was patron, studied the effects of broken marriages on children and she recognised it could be catastrophic for them. On a number of occasions, Diana would sit-in during interviews when young women would pour out their problems to trained counselors who would offer advice. And, time and again, Diana would hear the professional advisers tell couples of the distress caused to children when their parents divorced.

This knowledge of the ill effects of divorce on children was one of the reasons Diana wanted to keep her marriage legally intact – she had somehow convinced herself that if she remained married to Charles, though living a totally separate life in separate homes, in places seventy miles apart, it was far better for the children than the agonies and embarrassment of a very public divorce. It was, of course, an intellectually defenceless argument, yet she clung to it. Throughout her life, Diana had always turned her back and run away from problems; from her Swiss finishing school, from dance lessons and from jobs, and now she was running away from marriage. Though counselled and urged by family, friends and advisers to give the marriage another try, not once did Diana ever consider such a move.

She even refused to go on holiday with Charles and the boys, despite marriage counsellors urging her to do so for the children's sake. One of their last suggestions to which she reluctantly agreed, after great pressure from the Queen, was a ten-day Mediterranean cruise in the summer of 1992. Wills and Harry joined their mother and father. But Diana, unhappy at the idea, adamantly refused to enjoy herself and spent the holiday feeling miserable, deliberately ruining what should have been a happy holiday atmosphere for Wills and Harry.

She demanded separate cabins, and insisted she ate at different time to Charles and the boys. Throughout, the atmosphere was tense. After four days at sea, Diana disappeared and could not be found. After the captain consulted Charles a complete search of the entire boat was ordered with all hands taking part. Many feared that Diana had somehow fallen into the sea; others feared she might have jumped overboard. Those that knew of the royal marital problems and Diana's penchant for drawing attention to her unhappiness, believed she had probably jumped overboard, not to commit suicide, but to draw attention to her unhappiness. After two hours of sustained searching by the entire crew, she was discovered hiding in a lifeboat under a tarpaulin, crying her eyes out.

When her hiding place was discovered Diana quickly dabbed her eyes, clambered out of the lifeboat and ran crying to her cabin, without saying a word. But no one knew why she had gone into hiding and what was the purpose of the public demonstration of self-pity. More importantly, why would she want to make such a public display of her unhappiness in front of her beloved sons and the entire ship's company? That conundrum was never solved.

Those histrionics were surprising at that time because Diana was seemingly enjoying her new found freedom and most of her women friends thought she had come to enjoy her life as a single mum, particularly after she had solved her bulimia and anorexia problems, not to mention her new sexual confidence. The display on the cruise, however, that though was telling all and sundry how happy she was as a single mum perhaps deep down she was not so confident as she appeared in public.

At that time Diana was wallowing in a seemingly constant stream of media stories about her eating disorders and played up her suffering – making sure that the causes of these alleged disorders were always focused on her unhappy marriage and unfaithful husband. But there were some people who knew the truth.

Hewitt himself alleged that Diana consistently over-played her bulimia, continually exaggerated her miserable, unhappy life. He would tell how, around that time, the two of them enjoyed many wonderful meals together without any sign of her eating problems. He also knew, better than Charles of course, that by the mid-1980s Diana's body was slim, her muscles well-toned, her skin and hair in perfect condition which would not have been the case if she was still suffering from major eating disordersv that had gone on for some years.

Diana had found herself, and she was reaping the benefits with lovers at her beck and call, with the world's press salivating over her every deed, her every dress, her every appearance, and the mass of the civilized world accepting that she was one of the most popular people in the entire world. She was a person who could persuade others to part with their cash for charities, sway governments, make grown men go weak at the knees and all with a stunning smile or a mischievous glance.

But despite her interesting love life and various affairs, Diana did not always enjoy success with all the men whom she targeted. There were two or three men who spurned her attentions, preferring closer, more fulfilling relationships in which they called the shots. Those rebuttals really upset her, and she found it hard to cope and very difficult to recover from being spurned by a man with whom she had fallen in love.

Her staff at Kensington Palace would frequently note the unhappy Princess wondering around the place looking depressed. For no known reason, Diana would burst into tears, run to her bedroom, throw herself on the bed and stay there for an hour or more until she had composed herself. She would then return and chat away as though nothing whatsoever had occurred. Sometimes at small parties of 30 or so people, most of whom Diana knew, she looked like a lost and unhappy figure. She only seemed happy when there was a gaggle of people around her, smiling, giving her compliments, enjoying the chit-chat and laughing at her jokes. It was at these times that Diana would tell her very risqué jokes. Some of these jokes were so sexually oriented, and so coarse that many listening didn't know whether to laugh or pretend they hadn't understood the punch line. Most of the women would blush and cover their faces in embarrassment, amazed that someone like Diana could crack such jokes. Diana took a delight in shocking these people, whom she thought were just being priggish or prudish.

In the autumn of 1992, Diana learned that the Queen

would finally permit Charles to seek a legal separation from Diana, though not a divorce. She had been given no warning that the Queen was planning such a decision, nor had her Secretary or any of her staff. Presumably, the Buckingham Palace senior advisers and the Queen hoped the news would shock and intimidate Diana into fearing that she was about to be exiled entirely from the Royal Family, thrown out alone into the cold. In the words of one senior courtier, the Queen and the Queen Mother hoped such a move might 'knock some sense' into her. On the other hand, they wondered whether such a move against her might encourage her to move away and begin a life of her own, far removed from the Royal Family. The Queen believed exiling Diana might only lead to more trouble for the Royal Family. She already had experienced enough trouble with other members of the family without wanting further possible embarrassments.

The Queen was fully aware that the close relationship between Charles and Camilla Parker Bowles had entered a more serious phase in the early 1990s but, nevertheless, she was adamant that divorce was out of the question. She discussed the matter with the Archbishop of Canterbury and other senior clergy as well as with her mother. All had reinforced her intention of never permitting the heir to the throne to divorce for the message it would send to the churchgoers of Britain could be disastrous to the few faithful Church of England congregations still attending church every Sunday. The Queen informed Charles in a letter that, if it was his wish, a legal separation could go ahead but she would not permit divorce. Within 24 hours Charles issued a statement agreeing with his mother's suggestion.

Charles' immediate acquiescence surprised Diana, for

Charles never once mentioned to her the possibility that they should divorce, although they had discussed the possibility of a legal separation. It also unnerved her. However, Diana's reaction was more furious than nervous as she exclaimed to a friend, 'If that's what he wants, he'll get everything he deserves. He behaved like a s**t to me during our marriage and I will never forgive him, nor will I forgive that bitch Camilla.'

That was typical Diana when she had worked herself into one of her rages. Sometimes in a loud voice Diana would say, 'Charles has never said no to his mother in his entire life and hardly ever said no to me either. It's typical of his character that even now he gets his mother to carry out his dirty work because he hasn't got the balls to do it himself.'

Diana wondered why the Queen had suddenly permitted the separation because during one of their few chats together in the late 1980s the Queen said that there should be no question of a separation or divorce for many years because of the affect it might have on Wills and Harry. Diana agreed. Now, it seemed, for some unknown reason, the Queen had changed mind. That worried Diana.

One of the reasons the Queen made the decision was to placate the bishops of the Church of England on the point that the heir to the throne and the next titular head of the Church, by being formally separated from his wife, was not breaking church law by living with another woman. It was in many ways a pathetic and empty gesture, but it had to suffice in the present delicate situation.

Her next solo trip, to Paris in November 1992, was another very important tour for Diana. She selected her wardrobe for those few days with meticulous care and much advice. She knew that Parisiennes were convinced that France was still the capital of *haute couture* and she was determined to show them that the Princess of Wales knew how to dress and, if necessary, dazzle her hosts. Diana understood that this trip could make or break her wish to become accepted by the Royal Family that she was capable of doing a first-class job representing the family abroad and that she would never let the House of Windsor down. Before leaving Britain she told numerous people, including close friends and her officials, 'I'm going to show them. I'll bloody well show that family.'

The French people and the all-important French media took Diana to their hearts, newspapers proclaiming, '*Courage Princesse!*' – they had also followed the *travails* of the Princess and her marriage problems. Diana glowed throughout the trip, giving her best, captivating the *paparazzi* and winning the hearts and minds of the French nation. More importantly, back home in Britain, the media reported the tour a triumph.

Her Private Secretary, Patrick Jephson wrote in his account of their life together, '*For me, her Paris tour marked the Princess's apogee ... To my eyes, knowing what she had already endured and what lay ahead in the immediate future, there was something heroic in her. Like much heroism, it was not without its flaws and may even have been the compensating flip side of some deep fear. Nonetheless, that night in Paris it sprang from a strength of spirit momentarily freed from accumulations of false sentiment in a simple bid for survival.*'

Back in London, Diana knew from the newspapers she avidly scoured, that her solo trip had been a huge success and that she had won the laurels she so desperately wanted. Now she could represent the Royal Family and do a job that many of them would be envious of. Challenging them on their terms and on their turf she had scored a resounding victory. Now she would plan more trips and would hope to conquer more hearts and minds in the process. There was no stopping her. Her adrenalin was coursing through her veins. She felt fantastic. For the first time she had tasted power and she revelled in the confidence it gave her.

Six months later, in March 1993, Diana secured another foreign tour for herself – a working visit to see British aid projects in Nepal, accompanied by Lynda Chalker, the Minister of the Crown responsible for overseas aid. Once again it was a triumph. She not only looked stunning in designer dresses when pictured dining with the King of Nepal in the splendour of his palace in Katmandu but she also won praise for visiting the poverty-stricken peasants living in ramshackle huts in a rural village high in the Himalayas and sympathizing, in her inimitable way, with the squalid life they were leading.

Diana continued with her work with the British charities, winning praise from all. Her disarming, engaging charm captured the hearts and genuine admiration of all she met and, at the same time, secured approval from the all-important media that she was doing a wonderful job. The more headlines proclaimed her endeavours, the more charities asked for her assistance. The more success Diana achieved the more she was usurping the power and prestige of not only Prince Charles but also the Queen herself. And she knew it.

Diana sought private, informal chats with Prime Minister John Major at 10 Downing Street, which were happily granted. Diana understood that if she could make the Prime Minister an ally, he would be very useful in persuading the Queen that it was important for Britain that Diana conduct more foreign tours because of the prestige and popularity it would bring the nation.

During her visits with the Prime Minister, Diana flattered him in her inimitable way. He was charmed and thrilled that this beautiful princess would come to see him for advice and to seek his help in organizing her life and realizing her ambitions. John Major revelled in his new role, and Diana came to trust him, confident that he would support her new, unofficial role as a roving ambassador for Britain.

At first, the Prime Minister tried to persuade Diana to concentrate her energies on British charities, suggesting that she consider promoting a national scheme of recognition for carers and helpers which would bear her name and of which she would be the patron and guiding light. Diana told John Major that she would consider the project most seriously but in reality she didn't want that. She wanted to target the wider world. She finally persuaded the Prime Minister to support her plan of action.

Having the support of the Prime Minister gave her planned tours the added impetus of political legitimacy. Diana then moved on to plan where she should visit to gain maximum publicity. As patron of British Red Cross Youth, she suggested that she would like to carry out overseas tours on behalf of the International Red Cross. Such high-profile, high-minded and serious work on the international stage was exactly the type of work that Diana needed to propel her from being seen as a lightweight, empty-headed clothes horse to being accepted as a serious-minded woman whose work for and on behalf of world-class humanitarian organizations was valued by governments.

She was convinced that she would get worldwide coverage for the International Red Cross, and the Red

Cross agreed. They were only too happy to have the celebrated Princess of Wales carrying out overseas trips on their behalf – such visits not only received press and TV coverage in Britain, but news organizations around the world reported the princess' activities wherever they took place. Diana was exactly the type of apolitical high-profile celebrity the IRC needed to conduct such tours, sometimes in highly sensitive political areas. She had become the world's most photographed and celebrated person – it seemed that everyone wanted to see her, meet her and read about her life, her problems, her children and her charity work. Diana was only too happy to oblige.

As Patrick Jephson wrote, *'In due course it became evident that the Princess had only to express an interest in any of the Red Cross's activities for them to be made available for her patronage.'*

But Princess Diana's ambition to become a celebrated and famous ambassador of world humanitarian organizations by undertaking headline-grabbing visits to the world's trouble spots would lead – in a few years – to her own tragic death. Unwittingly and unknowingly, Diana had ventured into political arenas where her work was not wanted or respected. The politicians and powers-that-be had different political agendas and ambitions they did not want usurped or swept aside by some trumped-up princess who, in their eyes, was someone of no importance.

Diana, however, had come to believe her own sought-after publicity. Was she not the crowned angel of mercy, the title bestowed on her by the media? Was she not the natural successor to the acclaimed octogenarian Mother Teresa? Was there nothing that Diana could not achieve with her personality, charm and effortless manner? She was about to find out.

Her first major trip on behalf of the International Red Cross was to Zimbabwe in May 1993. She was happy to carry out numerous inspecting projects in the depths of the African bush on behalf of the Red Cross, the Leprosy Mission and Help the Aged. That visit also gave fresh impetus to Africa's major emerging problem, the AIDS plight, which was threatening to engulf an entire generation of young Africans and their children.

Patrick Jephson, who accompanied Diana on the trip, wrote, '*Late one evening we visited a hospice for orphaned children with AIDS. None was over five. None was expected to reach the age of six. The Princess wept.*'

Once again, Diana's trip was greeted with great applause from the travelling press, and the photographs showed a quiet, introspective, concerned Princess carrying out some harrowing, meaningful duties – not riding around in the back of an open limousine waving to masses of cheering, flag-waving children and their parents. She loved the image the television and the newspapers were portraying.

Diana also wanted to go solo on the overseas political stage to show that she wasn't just some mindless woman who was only capable of touchy-feely charitable work, but someone who had a brain. In September 1993, she enthusiastically carried out an official engagement in Luxembourg intended to boost British interests. Diana was informed that the Luxembourg Royal Family was connected to the House of Windsor through Europe's interrelated royal families. Officially, Diana was the guest of the Grand Duke, but she also attended a dinner hosted by Jacques Santer, Luxembourg's Prime Minister who, shortly afterwards, became President of the European Union. Diana was happy that the Prime Minister wished her to attend the dinner – it proved to her that her endeavours to portray herself as a woman of intelligence and substance were paying off.

In November, Diana flew to Brussels, as patron of the Help the Aged charity, to promote the work of the international charity HelpAge. Once again, there was a political bonus in the trip, for she was invited to give her views about organizing aid and projects for elderly people with the European Union's Commissioner for Social Affairs.

Patrick Jephson, who accompanied Diana on all of these overseas trips, wrote, *'Diana's formidable combination of talents had the potential to be a vehicle for far greater causes – the grand, global welfare crusades for which she seemed outwardly so suited. As events were to show, however, in the end she was tragically unable to prove herself a reliable standard-bearer for many of these.'*

Diana now sought more high-level relationships with the powerful and influential. During these years, she entertained the United States Ambassador to Britain at Kensington Palace as well as the Russian, Chinese, Hungarian, Pakistani and Argentine ambassadors. It was obvious that these ambassadors believed the Princess to be a serious-minded young woman of some powerful, even political potential otherwise they would not have wasted their time attending informal private meetings over tea or lunch.

The Queen and her advisers were becoming increasingly worried about the power and prestige that Diana was wielding as her popularity escalated throughout the 1990s. British Ambassadors discovered that they might wait months for an invitation to see a Head of State, but when Princess Diana even hinted at a possible visit, the red carpet was laid out immediately and she was given direct access. This was becoming hard for the Queen and her advisers, as well as senior advisers at Downing Street, to bear – they all saw that Diana was being invited to fly the flag for Britain over and above any other member of the Royal Family, including the Queen. Diana had achieved her greatest ambition. She had become the world's most sought-after personality whom Kings, Presidents and even Emperors wanted to meet and be seen with on a personal level. Prince Charles wasn't even in the picture and Diana loved that. The taste of victory was sweet indeed.

The time had come to clip Diana's wings, according to the men and women of influence who rule the corridors of power in both Buckingham Palace and 10 Downing Street. The Queen gave instructions that Princess Diana must never be permitted to represent her abroad but it did not stop the invitations arriving each and every week at Kensington Palace.

A whispering campaign began throughout Buckingham Palace – aimed, it seemed, at undermining and belittling Diana's overseas trips and suggesting that the only reason she was accepted by Kings and Presidents was because she was still, technically, a member of the House of Windsor since she was only separated from Prince Charles and not divorced from him.

It seemed that Diana would not be permitted to go overseas again as a representative of the House of Windsor, but there was little or nothing Buckingham Palace could do to prevent her accepting overseas invitations to whatever was offered. As a result, when foreign governments, organizations or charities wanted her to attend a function in their country, they would simply write a formal letter of invitation. And Diana would reply in the affirmative.

In an effort to put a stop to, or at least put a brake on Diana's escalating foreign engagements and increasing popularity among governments across the globe, the royal courtiers decreed that the Princess was no longer permitted to use an aircraft of the Queen's Flight to make such journeys. These Queen's flight aircraft are for the specific use of the Queen and, importantly, whomsoever the Queen, with the advice of courtiers, decides should be permitted to use them. Until now, Diana had always been given permission to use the royal planes because they added prestige to the visit.

Informed of this latest restriction, Diana reacted with a wonderful pithy remark: 'They'll be cutting off their noses next!'

To Diana, it was just another hurdle to overcome. It seemed the palace had failed to take into account her stubbornness and determination. She saw the withdrawal of the royal aircraft as yet another deliberate ploy to cut her out of the Royal Family and make her life as difficult as possible. However, the facts were beyond contention. Throughout the 1990s, Princess Diana was almost alone among members of The Firm in garnering goodwill for the monarchy. The Queen's crude attempts to stop Diana's remarkable success in winning the hearts and minds of foreign governments, charities and ordinary people was neither logical nor reasoned. It appeared that in acting against her daughter-in-law, the queen was also risking the good name and reputation of the House of Windsor and the British people in the eyes of foreign governments and their citizens. It also demonstrated the desperate levels to which the British monarchy was prepared to sink in a bid to put an end to Diana's dramatic success overseas. Courtiers would argue that the Queen was simply making sure that Diana was not usurping the power and authority of the British monarch.

In any case, Diana took the initiative and ordered her staff to contact wealthy individuals she had met and ask them if they had an aircraft she might borrow. Diana offered to pay for these flights at a reduced rate, but on virtually every occasion the wealthy owner happily offered the plane, plus crew, at no charge, believing it was a privilege to have been asked.

As a result of such bargaining, the Queen, due to persuasion from the Prime Minister, agreed that Diana could visit Argentina. Diana's less formal relationship with the British Monarch might make the visit less 'tricky' than if the Queen or Prince Charles undertook a tour of that country, as Britain and Argentina had fought a bloody war over the Falklands Islands only thirteen years earlier. Princess Diana had engineered an invitation from Argentina for her to carry out charitable work in Buenos Aires. She was also keen to visit South America, where she had never been. Rather wickedly, she saw this tour as a golden opportunity to conquer the country where Prince Charles was particularly popular and where he had enjoyed visiting. The Argentines had a passion for his favourite sport, polo.

Once again, the visit was a great success and once again Diana was invited to meet the country's Head of State, President Menem, who hosted a lunch for a few of his most important ministers and senior officials. Diana was impressed. She had chalked up another resounding success, causing even deeper furrowed brows back at Buckingham Palace. The Argentines loved her and turned out in thousands to give her a wonderful South American welcome. Diana beamed and waved, loving the adoration. The British press corps once again hailed her triumphant tour, emphasizing that Diana had done more to restore good relations with the Argentine nation in a couple of days than Foreign Office officials could have achieved in years.

Since the official separation, Prince Charles and his advisers at Highgrove had been trying to marginalize the Princess in the same way as the Queen, Prince Philip and Buckingham Palace courtiers had done. Charles was certainly more than irritated to find Diana usurping his role in his beloved Argentina and more annoyed still to read in the papers that she had been received with such acclaim and affection. To Charles, it seemed that his estranged wife had virtually succeeded in sidelining him – the Prince of Wales and heir apparent – rather than the other way round.

'Every time I pick up a bloody newspaper,' he was reported to have said in one outburst, 'I see Diana disporting herself in some far flung part of the globe and receiving rave reviews in the papers while it seems no one is interested in seeing me at all. I'm meant to be the bloody Prince of Wales, for God's sake!'

Diana knew nothing of these outbursts and continued her globe-trotting often wondering, what effect her travels and subsequent rave reviews was having on Charles and the rest of the royals.

In early 1996, Princess Diana was invited to Hong Kong by the multi-millionaire socialite David Tang, who had widespread business interests in both Hong Kong and mainland China. Tang was perhaps one of Hong Kong's most famous entrepreneurs who seemed to revel in the limelight of glamour and fame. He was also legendary in supporting numerous charitable institutions, including the Leprosy Mission.

Once again, Diana was in her element, acting her part as princess and fundraiser extraordinaire in stunning fashion, appearing happy and elated throughout the three-day tour. On all occasions she was smiling, radiant and charming – and the people loved her. At a dinner attended by Hong Kong's rich and famous, Diana managed to raise $500,000, which was channelled through her Charities Trust, mainly to the Leprosy Mission. During the day, Diana worked, visiting hospitals and dealing with the appalling social problems leprosy caused. Once again, she showed her empathy with the sufferers as well as her professionalism in providing photo opportunities, which only helped the cause when they were published around the world. Indeed, this Hong Kong visit should have been a template for her own future as a semi-detached royal, touring the world and persuading wealthy people to part with their money for charitable causes to benefit the poor, the sick, the hungry and the dispossessed.

But it was not to be.

She was happy to perform this role of charity fundraiser occasionally, but she wanted to be involved with more vital, important work where her involvement could have a more dramatic, lasting effect on major issues.

The issue that Diana had been searching for to galvanize her life and give it *real* purpose arrived on her desk in the autumn of 1996, when her friend Mike Whitlam, Director-General of the International Red Cross, asked her whether she wanted to become involved in the highly political issue of anti-personnel land mines. From that October day until her death some eleven months later, banning anti-personnel landmines became her great crusade. Diana was prepared to go anywhere, see anybody, and use her influence in any way necessary to push through a worldwide ban.

She accepted the argument of those seeking a ban that AP mines were nothing less than an evil attack on the innocent of the developing world. What appalled and angered her was that she had been led to understand that nothing had been done to stop the production of AP mines, or their use, although politicians and generals were fully aware of the awesome facts – that a staggering 26,000 people, many of them children, were killed or maimed each year by such mines.

Diana's interest in the mine issue had actually begun a year earlier, on the 125th anniversary of the British Red Cross, of which she was patron. She was supposed to be taking a high-profile role in events being planned for the celebration, but Buckingham Palace frowned on the idea of Diana being the sole royal representative on such a high-profile anniversary. Palace officials argued that as Diana had decided to retire from official public duties, she should not be permitted to star in the Red Cross celebrations. Diana was livid, but there was little she could do. She talked over the issue with Mike Whitlam who understood that her involvement in the celebrations would give enormous impetus to the event and bring about far greater public awareness for the charity than if any other royal took the leading role. So a compromise was reached.

It was decided that Diana would become involved in only one aspect of the current Red Cross campaign – the thorny issue of landmines. 'That struck an immediate cord in her,' Mike Whitlam said. 'But because of the situation, it was decided that she would play no major part in our celebrations on the home front but would concentrate instead on the mines issue. She was delighted.'

He went on, 'We sent her videos, photographs and reading material. Some of the videos were truly horrifying, showing footage of children and adults who had lost an arm, a leg, a foot or half a face in AP mine accidents. The photographs pulled no punches. The videos also showed the excellent work being carried out by Red Cross volunteers, doctors and specialists who were carrying out wonderful work helping amputees.'

It was after seeing such harrowing material that Diana told Mike, 'I am prepared to do anything, anything at all, if I can help put a stop to the production and use of landmines. I will make speeches, attend meetings, travel wherever you like to highlight this grotesque trade which kills and maims so many innocent children.'

Diana did not reveal to Mike that she had shown some of the gory photographs to her sons William, then aged fourteen, and Harry, then aged twelve, and discussed the issue with them in some detail. Harry asked her with childlike innocence, 'Mines kill children, don't they, Mummy?'

The concern of her sons motivated Diana even more to help in any way she could to rid the world of landmines. Here, at last, was an issue of great humanitarian interest that she totally believed in. She hoped it would bring her the credit she craved. Diana talked passionately whenever the issue was raised and she read and learned by heart all the arguments put forward as to why landmines should be banned.

She asked for more material and studied the papers and the details of different types of landmines until she had attained a good working knowledge. She also studied the worldwide problems involved in tracing, finding and destroying the mines. In many Third World countries, for example, searching for the misplaced mines sometimes began years after they had been laid. She understood the primary problem – no maps had been kept by the armies laying the mines and, as a result, no one knew precisely where they were buried – which led to many people, including children, were being killed and maimed each year.

By a stroke of good fortune, the premiere of the film *In Love and War,* produced by Lord Richard Attenborough, was to be screened in London at the end of 1996. Attenborough approached Mike Whitlam, asking whether the Red Cross might be interested in highlighting the film. Whitlam immediately saw this as a golden opportunity to promote their campaign to ban landmines and discussed the idea with Diana, knowing that involving her in the film premiere would create extensive media attention. He wrote to her asking if she would be interested, and she jumped at the idea. It was exactly the opportunity she had been waiting for. The premiere was a great success and afterwards Diana told Whitlam that she would be prepared to travel anywhere in the world if he thought it might help the cause.

Her next trip was to Angola in the early part of 1997 to meet young victims of landmine incidents. Diana was eager to make this trip. It meant a lot to her in terms of her own personal ambition to be accepted as a world player tackling serious issues. Whitlam explained, 'She wanted her visit to Angola to be a working tour. She wanted no high profile meetings with government ministers, no official dinners. She didn't want to pack any posh dresses. She wanted to travel light, taking only jeans and a few shirts.'

As expected, press and television cameras followed.

Emotive pictures of innocent, seriously injured children all but killed in landmine accidents made front page news in the papers and heartrending footage on television screens around the world. Those pictures of Diana, Princess of Wales, comforting child victims propelled the landmine issue to the centre of political agendas throughout the western world.

In Angola, Diana saw for herself the extent to which landmines hindered aid and development and caused tragedy for thousands of refugees seeking to return to their villages. She met children and adults horrendously mutilated by anti-personnel mines and realized the desperate need for aid to enable the wounded to live normal lives.

Demand for a worldwide ban on the manufacture and use of anti-personnel landmines had been slowly gathering supporters over the years, but the pictures of Diana holding mutilated young victims catapulted the issue into the living rooms of ordinary people. For the first time, the silent majority took note and demands for action on this issue forced governments to address it as a matter of urgency and promise action. Suddenly, banning landmines was an issue at the forefront of people's minds and the voters were not prepared to take 'no' for an answer.

The Canadian government had been trying to persuade governments everywhere to address this issue for some years, so naturally they agreed with the ban. The Nordic countries also responded positively, as well as those developing nations whose people were suffering terrible injuries and loss of life from the exploding mines.

Throughout the developed world, however, the arms lobbies and the military were fighting a rearguard action against such a ban. From a military viewpoint, the politicians accepted the arguments of their generals: the use of mines was a necessity, required to protect their armies. The generals convinced their politicians that if anti-personnel mines were laid correctly, with every mine diligently recorded on a map, there was no danger to civilians because they could be removed by the army when the danger or the war was over.

The International Red Cross, however, pointed out that for some countries it was too late – many armies in Third World countries did not keep accurate records and maps. It was the manufacture and sale of mines to irresponsible governments and warring factions that caused the problems and the thousands of deaths and injuries each year. The Red Cross argued that laying anti-personnel mines had become an ethical issue, which the world's responsible governments now had a duty to face.

By 1996, many western governments had accepted that the laying of landmines had become a moral issue but many countries were not prepared to stop the production and sale of anti-personnel mines unless an internationally recognized worldwide ban was enforced.

The International Red Cross reported that deaths and injuries caused by landmines had escalated since the 1970s. Other non-government agencies have also noted the increase. From 1979 to 1997, the International Red Cross manufactured 100,000 prostheses for 80,000 amputees in 22 countries. Much of that was for amputees in Cambodia, Afghanistan and Angola. Since the end of the Angolan civil war, when landmines were laid randomly over a 20-year period, the IRC fitted 1,550 new amputees with prostheses. It gave Afghanistan 600 wheelchairs and 6,000 pairs of crutches. This covered only a fraction of the number of victims who needed help.

The IRC insisted that nearly all these horrific injuries were occurring in countries with very low incomes, so that those maimed could never receive the help or treatment for their injuries without outside assistance. As a result, the vast majority of maimed people in developing countries were condemned to a life of abject poverty and wretchedness, unable to work or care for themselves.

Across the developing world, voluntary organizations have been at work for years clearing mines. The Red Cross, the Cambodia Trust, Motivation, Power, The Halo Trust and The Mines Advisory Group have all been involved in the clearing of mines and caring for the maimed and wounded in a number of countries including Afghanistan, Angola, Bosnia, Cambodia, Chechnya, Laos, Mozambique, Sri Lanka and the Sudan.

These voluntary organisations needed someone to highlight the plight and the appalling results of laying landmines indiscriminately. They were desperate for someone who could combine a high profile with compassion, bringing the attention of the world to the problem. No politician or organization had the image or the mass appeal necessary to grab the attention of the international media and demand action.

Even after Diana's Angolan visit, some nations continued to hold out against the Canadian Government's efforts to persuade all nations to sign a draft treaty outlawing the use of anti-personnel mines. But the tide was turning against them. Across the world a total of one thousand non-governmental agencies in 60 countries joined the campaign to outlaw these indiscriminate weapons.

Six months after visiting Angola, Diana readily agreed to visit Bosnia where the IRC reported that increasing numbers of people, including many children, had become victims of landmines laid during the horrific ethnic wars in the former Yugoslavia during the 1990s. Once again the photographs and the TV footage revealed the full horror of the effect of laying mines indiscriminately. On this visit Diana also heard some horrifying stories of wounded children, related through interpreters.

Viewers were touched when they saw Diana sharing a birthday cake with a little boy named Hamic who lived outside Tuzla, one of the cities most affected by the war. Hamic had lost both feet when he stepped on a landmine. He had no idea who Diana was. She was just a young woman dressed in blue jeans and a white shirt, who came in, sat next to him, held his hand and cuddled him like his mother did. Hamic was fascinated by the television cameras, the photographers and their equipment.

Diana was deeply affected by this mission, fighting back tears as she spoke to widows and orphans, to parents who had lost their children as a direct result of anti-personnel mines. Through this mission Diana had found herself; found a cause that would give meaning to her new life outside the Royal Family, outside fundraising and outside Britain. When she flew back to Britain from Bosnia at the beginning of August 1997, she committed herself to helping the International Red Cross in any way she could to help bring about a worldwide ban on mines.

In fact, it was Diana's death some three weeks later that helped bring forward the treaty dedicated to banning the use of landmines. Two weeks after she died, representatives from 100 nations met in Oslo, the Norwegian capital, to sign the treaty. The final document was signed in Ottawa, the Canadian capital.

In October, some six weeks after her death, the

campaign to ban landmines received the final accolade when it was awarded the Nobel Peace Prize. The Norwegian Nobel committee said the $1,000,000 award would go in equal parts to the International Campaign to Ban Landmines and to Jody Williams, the campaign co-ordinator. They had, the Nobel committee said, 'started a process which, in the space of a few years, changed a ban on anti-personnel mines from a vision to a feasible reality'.

Diana had known before her death that the campaign was a success and that a treaty was about to be signed banning the future use of landmines. To her this was the most important and rewarding achievement of her entire life. But some powerful people were far from happy. Until Diana, Princess of Wales, had entered the arena they believed it was possible to sideline the anti-mine campaign. But Diana had inspired ordinary people who, in turn, created a furor in many western capitals in support of the ban. She had demonstrated her remarkable power in the twinkling of an eye by appealing directly to voters over the heads of politicians and gaining their wholehearted support for a fundamental change of policy towards mine-laying.

In her naivete, Diana had upset a number of factions which were taken aback by the speed at which her intervention had accelerated a mines ban. Jubilant, Diana knew none of these problems. Now she determined to follow up this extraordinary success with a new challenge, a new project, another high-profile issue that would once again grab the world's attention. Unknown to nearly all those around her, Diana had found that new project, one that would send shock waves through the capitals of the western world. And once again she was keeping this secret to herself.

Chapter Eleven
The Day of Reckoning

The world knows how Diana spent the last day of her life. Waking on Mohammed al Fayed's luxury yacht the *Jonikal* with her lover Dodi Fayed, she decided to take one last swim in the warm blue waters of the Mediterranean before flying to Paris on the way back to London. They sped the *Jonikal* around to a nearby cove. But as the couple splashed about, enjoying their privacy, a motor launch packed with paparazzi headed towards them. The Fayed bodyguards in another launch confronted the photographers and asked them to respect Diana's privacy and leave. They refused, using their customary excuse – that they were simply making their living and should be allowed to do so unhindered.

Les Wingfield, one of Dodi's trusted private bodyguards said, 'We tried to appeal to their better nature but they didn't want to listen. They were determined to stick around and take pictures of Diana and Mr. Dodi together. There was nothing we could do.'

Annoyed that their swim had been interrupted, Diana and Dodi headed back to the *Jonikal* moored at the jetty of the exclusive Sardinian resort of Cala di Volpe on the Costa Smeralda. They showered and ate a light breakfast on the deck bathed in morning sun. They had some time to spare and Diana lay around the deck sunbathing until lunch, keeping out of sight of the photographers who were kept out at sea away from the port.

Diana had arranged to be back at Kensington Palace on the morning of Sunday, August 31, because William and Harry, who had been staying with their father at Balmoral, were due to fly to London that afternoon. On the spur of the moment, Dodi suggested to Diana that they fly to Paris so they could both do some shopping. Diana liked that idea and planned to buy some presents for her beloved boys. Little did she realize that the reason Dodi wanted to stop over in Paris was that he planned to buy her an expensive ring – an engagement ring – and propose to her that night. For weeks his father, Mohammed al Fayed, had been urging his son to propose to Diana, despite the fact that Dodi had little or no reason to suppose Diana had ever contemplated marrying him. But he would carry out his father's wishes.

Diana enjoyed herself with Dodi. She found him fun, upbeat and enjoyable company, happy to do whatever she wanted, when she wanted.

She had first met Dodi, the 42 year-old playboy, erstwhile film producer and eldest son of Mohamed al Fayed, the owner of top London store Harrods, ten years earlier when his polo team, sponsored by his father, had played the Prince of Wales' team in the final of the Harrods Cup at Windsor Great Park. It was Diana who presented the winner's trophy. When she met Dodi again, she had no real idea of his life or his background, except the fact that his Egyptian father owned Harrods and his mother was Samira Khashoggi, sister of the billionaire international arms dealer Adnan Khashoggi.

Dodi was a playboy who wanted to become a film producer, the more to enjoy the company of beautiful young actresses and all aided by the financial muscle of his father. He led a typical Hollywood rich-kid lifestyle, trying to break into films, setting up his own film production company, Allied Stars, when he was only 23 years old. He flashed his money around, drove expensive cars and dated young starlets. He also became addicted to cocaine and was a steady drinker.

On numerous occasions Mohamed al Fayed had offered his villa in the South of France – the Castel Sainte Terese – for Diana's use, primarily because it was secluded, hidden from any paparazzi and patrolled by Fayed's own bodyguards. Fayed thought it a perfect holiday home for Diana, William and Harry. His invitations to Diana had first come through Raine, Earl Spencer's second wife, a director of Harrods International. Until the summer of 1997, Diana had always declined. But her beach holiday with Wills and Harry the previous year had been an unmitigated disaster, primarily due to the infuriating attentions of the paparazzi, who not only discovered the exact location of their holiday villa, but spent days and nights camped nearby, their intrusive lenses forever trained on the terrace leading from the villa to the swimming pool. During that holiday, Wills and Harry deliberately remained out of sight inside the villa because they did not want to give the photographers a chance of taking any pictures. In the end, Diana cut the holiday short and returned to London, furious at the press intrusion.

In the early months of 1997, Dodi, spurred on by his father, invited Diana to dinner. He took her to his penthouse apartment in London's Mayfair only a few hundred yards from Buckingham Palace. Dinner was cooked by his father's chefs, the meal served by a young waitress and the wine by a butler. Diana was impressed, and she was enchanted by this Moslem man whom she found gentle, fun and, shortly afterwards, an accomplished, passionate lover. As ever, she tried to keep this new relationship a secret from the ravenous British press and she succeeded. Diana came to appreciate that Dodi had the money which she now recognized was absolutely necessary to ensure that she could enjoy a secluded existence, assisted by bodyguards, chauffeurs, blacked-out motor cars.

From the very beginning, however, Diana felt uneasy with Dodi, feeling he lavished her with too many expensive gifts. It seemed that he was trying to 'buy' her love and that left an unpleasant taste in her mouth. Diana had never wanted anyone to own her. She decided that the cause was his experience with the young starlets of Hollywood, whom she believed were only too happy to receive presents from wealthy men.

Diana came to feel obliged to buy Dodi presents in return to show her appreciation for his generosity. She would have preferred that they simply enjoyed each other's company, being together because they wanted to be together. Yet she would usually give him the benefit of the doubt for a somewhat quirky reason – his given name, Emad, translated from the Arabic, means 'someone you can depend on'.

It was in the early summer of 1997 that Mohamed al Fayed once again offered his St. Tropez villa to Diana, suggesting that his son Dodi would be on hand in case of trouble from paparazzi. Dodi would stay in the fisherman's cottage on the beach some 200 yards from the villa. This time, Diana jumped at the invitation for this was a way she could enjoy a free and easy holiday with Wills and Harry in privacy, while in the dead of night she could visit her lover for a few hours before stealing back to her bed in the villa as dawn was breaking.

Dodi had fun with Wills and Harry, though he had never met them before. He was happy to play rough-and-tumble games with them in the pool. Occasionally, Diana would invite him to take lunch with her and her sons on the terrace and sometimes he would dine with them. On a few occasions, after the boys had gone to sleep, Diana and Dodi took moonlit walks along the deserted beach. Most evenings they sat and chatted on the terrace over a bottle of wine and Diana would visit Dodi's cottage from time to time, after her sons had gone to bed.

Diana and the boys also had the use of the *Jonikal*, Fayed's magnificent yacht, and the boys thoroughly enjoyed running all over it, inspecting the cabins and the crew quarters as well as taking turns at the wheel. The boys were allowed to roam the yacht at will, so unlike the times they had spent aboard the royal yacht *Britannia*, when they had to obey strict rules.

They all had a wonderful carefree holiday, swimming in the warm Mediterranean, taking rides in the *Jonikal* and sunbathing back at the villa. Most important of all; there were no photographers about. When she returned home Diana told close freiends, 'That was the best holiday I have ever had in my entire life.'

Three weeks later, and to everyone's surprise, Diana and Dodi flew from Stansted Airport near London on a Harrods Gulfstream jet for a six-day cruise aboard the *Jonikal*. They visited Monte Carlo and the island of Corsica. Their days were spent visiting quiet coves, swimming in private, lazing about the yacht and dining on board under the stars. In fact, this second holiday had been planned several months earlier. Once again, they enjoyed a quiet

peaceful time and only once did the paparazzi capture
their quarry on film.

The couple were caught on camera by an Italian
photographer, Maro Brenna, who snapped them with a
long lens, producing the grainy, out-of-focus photograph
which has since been named 'The Kiss'. It seemed from
that picture that Diana was becoming seriously involved
with Dodi. In reality, she wasn't; she was simply enjoying
a romantic summer with a generous, wealthy playboy
whose company she enjoyed and whom she had discovered
was quite a stud.

But that single photograph set the tabloid press
speculating furiously about Diana's intentions towards
Dodi. Was she in love with him? Would they marry? Where
would they live? Would Diana ever leave her children?
Would there be any religious problems? After Diana's
earlier infatuation and unrequited love for the heart
surgeon Hasnat Khan, her friends had reached the
conclusion that, for whatever reason, she had decided that
she rather enjoyed the company of Moslem men.

For many years, Diana had a close friendship with a
woman who became almost a second mother to her, Lady
Annabel Goldsmith, wife of the late billionaire Sir Jimmy
Goldsmith. For more than twelve years Diana had enjoyed
Lady Annabel's hospitality at her beautiful Queen Anne
home at Ham, near Richmond, some fifteen miles from
Kensington Palace. Diana loved taking Wills and Harry
there for a Saturday or Sunday lunch when other children
and their parents would also be invited. Annabel's home
was open house and the meals were often taken in the
large kitchen with much chatter and noise as the children
scoffed their food, watched over by their adoring mothers.
After these meals, sometimes attended by 16 or more

people, Diana would insist on doing the washing up, insisting that she even do the pots and pans. Other mothers protested but Diana would insist. 'It'll do me good,' she would say with a laugh as she rolled up her sleeves, pulled on the rubber gloves and set to work.

Lady Annabel's daughter Jemima, who was the apple of her father's eye, had fallen in love with Imran Khan, the former Captain of the Pakistani cricket team. A tall, handsome, intelligent Oxford-educated young man, Imran had a well-earned reputation as a lady's man. Most of his adult life he had lived in Britain, except when playing cricket for his country. Jemima and Imran fell in love and married, though Sir Jimmy wasn't too happy that his beloved daughter had decided to marry a Moslem and live so far away in Pakistan. But Annabel knew that Imran made her daughter happy and they enjoyed a wonderful loving relationship. In Pakistan, Imran founded a hospital for cancer patients and decided to enter the problematic world of Pakistani politics.

Even after Jemima left Britain to live in Pakistan, Diana and Annabel frequently chatted on the phone and sometimes visited each other. Over the years they became close friends, and Diana put great faith in Lady Annabel's judgment because she was so natural, so honest, had oceans of common sense and gave sound advice.

Annabel warned Diana that she didn't believe Dodi was the right man for her. That concerned Diana for she already had some doubts herself, particularly the fact that she felt certain Dodi had become addicted to cocaine, a fact which Diana certainly didn't like. She also didn't like the fact that Dodi was a 'Daddy's boy', obedient to everything his father suggested. She presumed that was because 'Daddy' held the purse strings. She also had qualms about the stream of presents Dodi kept giving her because she believed most of them had probably come from Mohamed. Sometimes she felt uneasy, suspecting that Mohamed al Fayed was using his fortune to try and 'buy' her for his son. She also realized that if she ever married Dodi, the greatest beneficiary would be Mohamed himself, who might then believe he was on almost equal footing with the Royal Family. In reality, Diana had no intention of settling down with Dodi, as Lady Annabel would later confirm, despite al Fayed's contention that Diana and Dodi were on the point of becoming engaged.

At first, Diana had certainly enjoyed Dodi's company, his jokes, his sense of fun and his ability to make her laugh. But she came to suspect that the jokes he was making and his constant patter were the same as he had used on many other women. In time, Diana came to see him as a professional lover who took pride in seducing beautiful women with his charm, his jokey personality and his father's money. Toward the end of their summer fling, Diana discovered that the more time she spent with Dodi, when they weren't having sex, the less interested she became in the relationship.

Throughout their relationship Dodi had apparently not informed Diana that he had been married before, even though the marriage had lasted only eight months. Nor had he told her that just before their summer holiday in St. Tropez with Wills and Harry he had become engaged to a beautiful American model, Kelly Fisher, 31, who had also spent a holiday with him on the *Jonikal* a month before. Indeed, as Dodi was romancing Diana on the *Jonikal*, Kelly Fisher's lawyers issued a statement saying that Miss Fisher had met Dodi Fayed in Paris in 1996 and they had travelled together, staying in London, Paris,

California and New York. He agreed to pay her $500,000 in pre-marital support, for she had abandoned her modelling career to be with him. Allegedly, Dodi had promised to marry her the following year and buy her a house in Malibu Beach, California. He had also given her a cheque for $200,000 which bounced. Diana learned this from reading the British newspapers, just before her fateful journey to Sardinia.

Meanwhile, Diana's good friend Rosa Monckton, the president of Tiffany & Co. and wife of Dominic Lawson, the then editor of the *Sunday Telegraph,* invited Diana to accompany her on a short Mediterranean cruise only days after she returned from holiday with Dodi. Rosa Monckton confirmed after Diana's death that they had discussed her relationship with Dodi and Diana had led her friend to understand that she had no plans whatsoever to marry her playboy lover, though she happily admitted to enjoying a fun and passionate summer with him.

Dodi's father, however, thought differently. He was convinced that Diana was seriously involved with his son. He pushed Dodi into buying a ring for her and suggested that while handing it to her, Dodi should also make a proposal of marriage. Even if Diana said 'no' to marriage, there was a possibility that she would have found the stunning and expensive ring irresistible and accepted it as a generous gift from her lover. Such outward signs of affection and commitment as accepting a ring from a lover can persuade people that a relationship has serious intent.

It was not to be.

Diana's last hours began as the Harrods jet landed at Le Bourget at 3:20 p.m. after a 90-minute flight from Sardinia. Dodi was also on board, as well as a number of bodyguards, including Trevor Rees-Jones and Les Wingfield. Waiting on the tarmac was Gamma photographer Romauld Rat, a large, softly-spoken and respected photographer, who was there with five other photographers. They snapped away as Diana and Dodi disembarked and clambered into the black Mercedes 600SEL leased by the Ritz for ferrying VIPs around Paris. Henri Paul, deputy chief of security at the Ritz, a man well known and trusted by Dodi Fayed, was also waiting to welcome the couple.

As is customary in Paris and Rome when high-profile celebrities make an appearance, the paparazzi gave chase on motorbikes and in cars. Les Wingfield described the journey: 'A black Peugeot came from behind, overtook our vehicle and then slammed on the brakes, forcing us to slow right down. The guys on the motorbikes then came up on either side of the Mercedes and began snapping away at the Princess. The Peugeot then controlled the speed at which we could drive into Paris.'

On the way to the Ritz the couple stopped off at the Villa Windsor, the house where the Duke and Duchess of Windsor had lived for many years before their deaths. Mohamed al Fayed had bought the lease on the substantial, detached French mansion in the exclusive Bois de Boulogne for £4,000,000 and spent a further £20,000,000 modernizing, refurbishing and redecorating the beautiful house.

At the Ritz, they managed to evade photographers at the front of the hotel by driving to the service entrance at the rear. They went to the prestigious Imperial Suite and Diana ordered tea and later had her hair done. Two hours after their arrival, Dodi slipped out, accompanied by two security guards, and crossed the Place Vendome to Repossi, the jewellers. Later that evening, a diamond ring was delivered to Dodi at the Ritz.

At 7 pm, Diana and Dodi left the Ritz, once again using the service entrance in the Rue Cambon, but this time the photographers were ready. Diana and Dodi were driven to Dodi's private apartment just off the Champs Elysee and, as the couple arrived, some 15 or more photographers moved toward them and a scuffle developed on the doorstep of the block of apartments. Punches were thrown, cameras knocked away. The paparazzi were objecting to being physically manhandled and prevented from taking their precious pictures and, in turn, the bodyguards didn't like being physically assaulted by the paparazzi. The atmosphere was heated. Before the evening was over the relationship between the bodyguards and the paparazzi would get much worse.

When they returned to the Ritz, Diana and Dodi were met by a phalanx of photographers – perhaps 30 or so – as well as a swelling crowd of people, tourists and sightseers who had heard Diana was staying at the Ritz. As with half the world, they were curious and wanted to see her.

Les Wingfield later described the scene: 'We unlocked the car doors and got the couple out. We were immediately surrounded by about a dozen photographers who jostled us, coming within a couple of feet of Diana, shooting away in her face. Some were aggressive, others were OK.'

But as this melee developed, behind the scenes a secret intelligence operation, professionally planned and meticulously carried out, was swinging into action. It would end some hours later in the deaths of Diana, Dodi Fayed and their driver Henri Paul. The operation had been planned some months before after discussions at the

highest level had been held involving MI5 and the French
D.S.T. – La Direction de la Surveillance du Territoire –
the French equivalent of MI5. The United States Central
Intelligence Agency had also been informed of the plot.
An agreement had been reached. It had been accepted
that Diana had become a serious liability to those whose
duty and responsibility it was to protect their nations
against any threat from any quarter. Usually, of course,
such threats come from terrorism, espionage or subversion
– not from one of the world's most adored and glamorous
superstars who was at the height of her fame.

The decision was made that since Diana was a British
citizen, MI5 should take responsibility for organizing,
planning and carrying out her killing. Diana's alleged threat
to the status quo of international relations came from the
fact that she had become political dynamite, a naïve, well-
intentioned and very persuasive young woman, innocently
wielding great personal power among the electorates of
the western world. Diana's involvement in the International
Red Cross campaign for ridding the world of anti-personnel
mines had been astonishingly successful. Pictures of Diana
in minefields in Angola and Bosnia, and further pictures
of her chatting to children maimed by AP mines, had
touched the hearts of the western world and at the time
of her death it was all but certain that a worldwide ban of
those mines would come into force, despite fierce
objection and opposition from defence chiefs throughout
the west.

Flushed with this extraordinary success, Diana decided
to use her power to aid the plight of the world's refugees.
It was almost certain that with the assistance of the
International Red Cross and other agencies dealing with
refugees the world over, Diana could move from one

refugee problem to another, bringing her own magical brand of political pressure to bear on nations of the developed world to sort out these intractable problems, which never seemed to reach a sensible conclusion.

It was accepted and recognized that Diana's involvement in any particular refugee problem would bring enormous pressure to bear on politicians from their electorates and the media to alleviate whatever problem she highlighted. And there was real concern, if not dismay, among the three security intelligence agencies that if Diana was pictured with a group of wretched, poverty-stricken Palestinian children in a hovel of a refugee camp in Gaza or the West Bank, there was no telling what might be demanded by voters around the world. As always, security intelligence agencies were concerned with maintaining the status quo; Diana was concerned with the plight of refugees and her new ambition to become the world's number one ambassador for humanitarian issues.

Diana let friends know that if the Royal Family refused to permit her to be a roving royal ambassador, she would seriously consider moving to another country, perhaps France or the United States, and setting up a permanent home there. Diana had told friends, 'I am deadly serious. This is no idle threat for I am determined to do the job for which I believe I am uniquely equipped. And if the royals won't let me carry out that work, then I will go and live where I can.'

MI5 were well aware that Diana had become a serious liability and an increasing embarrassment to the British Royal Family. Without a doubt, she had succeeded in becoming the nation's favourite royal, even supplanting the Queen from her customary position as the most popular and respected royal. The British people had shown how much they loved Diana and they whole-heartedly supported anything and everything she said and did. The public enthusiastically endorsed the contentious issues Diana raised in her *Panorama* interview, where she overstepped the bounds of her position as a royal princess. In suggesting that some of the royal courtiers treated her as the 'enemy'; in suggesting the Prince of Wales was unfit to be King; and, lastly and most importantly, in criticizing the Queen for not changing and modernizing the monarchy and its relationship with the British people, Diana had gone too far. Some people, including her own Private Secretary Patrick Jephson, had described her famous speech as 'suicidal'.

Diana didn't give a damn what critics had to say about the *Panorama* interview because the newspapers showed that the British public were right behind her, agreeing with all she had said. But there were others who had taken offence at her remarks and accusations. And there were still more who believed she had taken a step too far. What, they would ask, might she do for her next trick? It is little wonder, therefore, that the death of Princess Diana bore all the hallmarks and fingerprints of a classic security service operation.

MI5 were, of course, aware of Diana's ongoing affair with Dodi Fayed, the information being supplied by the police and Special Branch. For some years MI5 had been kept informed as to Diana's whereabouts, her habits and, more important, the men in her life. At some point during the summer of 1997 a decision had been made – if Diana continued in her ambitions to raise her international profile, and in particular, to concentrate on the politically-charged Palestinian refugee issue, it might become necessary to take the ultimate action.

Until the late 1960s, Britain's intelligence and securities agencies, which had been set up before World War 1, had a virtual *carte blanche* in decision-making regarding people they believed should be removed from society. They did not have to seek advice or permission from the political establishment or the Head of State when it came to making those decisions.

During the late 1960s, however, Prime Minister Harold Wilson decided this practice had to cease and that in future reasons had to be argued and permission sought from the Home Secretary or the Prime Minister before such action could be taken. That has remained the policy of all successive British governments. Crucially, however, the intelligence and securities agencies retained their decision-making privileges if, in their opinion and for whatever reason, they believed the security of the state was at risk.

The 1994 Intelligence Services Act placed the functions of the Secret Intelligence Service (SIS) and the Government Headquarters (GCHQ) on a statutory footing for the first time. It also established a group of senior parliamentarians, reporting to the Prime Minister, who looked into the expenditure, administration and policy of the intelligence and security agencies. Greater openness was also introduced and a new Official Committee was set up to examine the plans of the Security Service and review its work. Of course, this did not mean that MI5 and MI6 had to reveal top-secret information to the committee, nor have they done so.

With Britain's media renowned for their dogged pursuit of issues that gripped the nation and sold newspapers, MI5 were not keen to undertake such a delicate, controversial and high-profile operation in Britain. They were well aware that if there was the faintest whiff or suggestion of MI5 involvement in Diana's death, the media would pull out all the stops in an effort to establish the truth. It was therefore preferable for such an operation to be undertaken overseas.

The fact that Dodi's father owned the Ritz in Paris as well as the Duke and Duchess of Windsor's former home in the Bois de Boulogne led MI5 to the conclusion that there was every probability that Diana and Dodi would visit Paris from time to time to continue their affair in private – out of sight **of** the tenacious British Press. After consultations with their counterparts in the D.S.T, the decision was taken to make preparations for the operation in Paris. They needed a plan that could be put into action within days, if not hours. Over the years, security agencies have frequently used the fatal car crash as their most favoured method of arranging the 'accidental' death of those they want to target. Throughout Europe, a hundred people or more die every day in road accidents. The fact that people die in car crashes has come to be accepted in all western civilizations and, as a result, raises fewer questions than any other method of removing unwanted citizens.

M15 contacted the D.S.T in Paris, saying that they needed a car for an operation they were planning. By pure chance, in the spring of 1997, the D.S.T. obtained a Mercedes, used on a regular basis by patrons of the Ritz. This car, leased to the Ritz by a car company named Etoile Limousine, was used to ferry guests to and from airports and, when required, for shopping and sightseeing. The D.S.T. was now using the vehicle to eavesdrop on the occasional distinguished visitor and also keep an eye on distinguished V.I.Ps thought to be possible targets for terrorists.

They arranged for the Ritz's black Mercedes S280 – license number 688 LTV 75 – to be stolen by professional car thieves. In return for their assistance, the thieves were given permission to take whatever they wanted from the vehicle and then dump it. On April 20, the car was stolen from outside the fashionable Taillevent Restaurant in Paris. Sixteen days later it was discovered stripped and abandoned outside the city. The wheels and the tyres were missing as well as the inner workings of the doors. Also stolen was the all-important electronic 'brain', which controlled the car's vital functions, including the power steering, the electric windows, the speedometer, the anti-lock braking system and the six-cylinder 195 brake horsepower engine. The total cost of repairs: £13,000.

By June, the Mercedes was fully repaired and back in service. In the meantime, D.S.T. technicians had secretly installed sophisticated tracking devices and transmitters. The tracking device transmitted detailed information of the car's exact whereabouts directly to a VDU map back at headquarters. A voice-activated transmitting device had also been installed, which meant that all conversations inside the vehicle could be overheard and recorded back at base. A fail-safe tracking device – a backup mechanism – was also installed in case either of the other two failed.

It was decided that this Mercedes would be used for the fatal operation of August 1997. Meetings and discussions took place with senior D.S.T officers and a plan of action agreed. Officers visited the site of the proposed crash, approach routes were discussed, necessary speeds measured and dry runs made in another Mercedes S280 car. Experienced police drivers considered the entrance to the chosen site – the Alma Tunnel – was such a narrow, awkward approach that driving at speeds in excess of 50 miles an hour created problems for the driver. That was the reason why the Paris highway authorities had applied a speed limit of 37 mph on the approach to the tunnel beneath the Pont de l'Alma.

Back at the Ritz on that fateful night, Diana and Dodi made their way to the hotel's Espadon Restaurant where Diana ordered her last meal, roast turbot garnished with dried seaweed and seasonal crispy vegetables. From the neighboring dimly lit bar, she could hear the pianist playing romantic melodies which included, 'You Must Remember This'. After finishing their main course, Diana and Dodi left and went upstairs to their suite. It was 10:15 p.m.

At about the same time, Henri Paul arrived at the hotel, alerted by a phone call asking him to return because Diana and Dodi were planning to leave the Ritz after dinner and drive to Dodi's apartment off the Champs-Elysee.

The MI5 team and their D.S.T. counterparts had been alerted after Diana and Dodi arrived in Paris that same afternoon. They were ordered to pre-arrange their tasks for that night because it was believed the operation would take place in the next 24 hours. They were also warned that if Diana and Dodi changed their plans and did not spend the night at Dodi's apartment, the operation would be called off.

Officers from both MI5 and the D.S.T. took up positions outside the Ritz, two or three posing as photographers, others mingling with the excited crowd eager to catch a glimpse of Diana. Their task was to create a fuss, to excite the crowd, to keep the photographers busy and to create an atmosphere of confusion.

D.S.T. technicians were working on the Mercedes S280 earlier in the evening. The world has always been surprised, indeed taken aback by the fact that neither Dodi nor Diana

231

was wearing a seat belt when they were found in the back of the crashed Mercedes. Diana's friends, her former police bodyguards, and anyone who had ever travelled with her in a car knew that she was meticulous about 'belting up' before each and every car journey. Diana would always insist on William and Harry 'belting up' before the car they were travelling in had even started to move. And, when the lads were older, she would frequently check to see if they had secured their seatbelts correctly.

It is beyond comprehension that as the Ritz security officer Henri Paul accelerated to speeds in excess of 100 miles per hour as he raced through the near-deserted streets of Paris, neither Diana nor Dodi would have quietly sat back and *not* made any attempt whatsoever to secure their seatbelts. Everyone who ever knew Diana well has never been able to provide a satisfactory answer to that conundrum.

And therefore it is highly likely, in fact highly probable, that Diana did fasten her seatbelt on that fateful journey. The safety belts on Mercedes cars are made to the highest standards. The anchorage of those belts is tested to a remarkable degree. And yet on that night both Diana's and Dodi's seatbelts failed. The only conclusion that can be drawn is that someone tampered with the seatbelts that night.

As with all bodyguards, it is their duty to ensure that their VIP passengers are 'belted up' before they commence any journey. Of course, it is possible in the heat of the moment that Trevor Rees-Jones forgot to tell them to secure their belts or, as has been suggested, Dodi may have told him that it didn't matter. But that is unlikely, very unlikely, for Trevor Rees-Jones is a professional who knew his duty. And it was his duty that night, as on all other occasions when he was escorting Diana, to ensure she belted up on each and every journey. He would simply not have permitted the car in which they were traveling to even begin the journey unless Princess Diana had secured her seatbelt. The very fact that Rees-Jones secured his own safety-belt during the journey as the Mercedes sped through the streets of Paris adds even greater mystery to the fact that Diana never, apparently, secured her seatbelt.

It is also an insult to Trevor Rees-Jones' professional reputation to suggest that if, as had been presumed, neither Dodi nor Diana had 'belted up' that night, he would not have warned them to fasten their seatbelts, especially in the light of how fast Henri Paul was driving.

Following Diana's tragic death, experts specializing in the causes of deaths and serious injuries suffered by car passengers in road accidents expressed the belief that if she had been wearing her seatbelt on that night, there was every probability that she would have survived the crash, especially as she was sitting in the rear of the car and was furthest away from the front near-side of the vehicle which sustained the initial impact. Surgeons who deal with the broken bodies of car accident victims every day are of the belief that despite the speed the Mercedes was travelling that night, it would have been very unlikely that Diana would have suffered the injury which was mainly responsible for her death – a torn pulmonary vein – if she had been wearing a seatbelt.

In fact, the D.S.T. technicians who were working on the Mercedes that day, on orders from MI5, had been 'fixing' the seatbelts of the rear passengers. This process of 'fixing' seatbelts is remarkably simple, well-known and frequently used, not only by those working for security agencies, but also by many personal bodyguards who spend much of their life sitting beside a driver in the front of a car while the person they are guarding sits in the back. The reason for needing a quick safety-belt release is that bodyguards may be called upon to take action within a split-second and having to undo a seatbelt, which takes two hands, wastes precious seconds.

The pin which secures the seatbelt in position across the person's lap is filed down. In the event of a bodyguard wanting to take immediate action and leap out of the vehicle, he only needs to thrust his body towards the door and the seatbelt breaks loose without the need for him to even touch the belt. And this filing process, usually carried out with a power grinder, can be adjusted to any degree. If the person wants a rapid release, more of the pin is filed down; and conversely, if the person wants some protection, the pin is only gently filed which means a greater effort has to be made before the safety pin flies loose, but still with no need to use the hands.

This was the operation that the technicians were carrying out on the seatbelts on the back seats of the Mercedes that night.

Since the fatal crash, much of the blame has been attached to Henri Paul, the 41-year-old security officer who had worked for the al Fayeds for six years. Balding and stocky, the 5ft 5in. native of Brittany looked ten years older than his years. A former pilot in the French Air Force, Paul spent most of his evenings after work drinking moderately and socializing in the bars and small clubs around the centre of Paris where, as a gifted musician, he would happily play the piano in exchange for free drinks. Paul, who spoke fluent English and German, was also a paid informant for both the D.S.T. and the DGSE

(Direction General de la Securite Exterieure), the French equivalent of MI6. His handlers asked him to keep an eye on certain guests at the Ritz and inform them if certain people they were interested in booked a room or suite at the hotel. Henri Paul would frequently meet his French handlers in one of his Paris haunts and have a few drinks with them.

In 1988, he dated Laurence Pujol, a petite, young blonde secretary at the Ritz who had a two-year-old daughter Samantha. A year later, they were married and the three set up home. Paul was happy for he adored little Samantha. But in 1992, and for reasons unknown, Laurence wanted an end to the marriage and she and Samantha moved out. A heartbroken Henri Paul turned once more to his 'social drinking' in the bars around Paris.

Following his death, there have been conflicting stories about Henri Paul and the part his drinking may have played in the crash that killed Diana. Some considered him a social drinker; others said that he was a heavy drinker and still others suggested he was an alcoholic. However, his former wife Laurence insisted that she had never seen him drunk, claiming that he drank only one or two glasses of wine a night. And she had no reason to try and protect Henri Paul's good name. Friends who claimed to know Paul well reported that, like many middle-aged lonely Parisian men, he was a habitual drinker, but never showed any signs of inebriation.

But in 1996, a year before the fatal car crash, it seemed Henri Paul had become worried about his drinking problem and went to see his doctor, Dr. Dominique Melo. It emerged after the crash that Dr. Melo had prescribed Paul Aotal, a popular drug in France for alcohol abuse. He was later prescribed Tiapridal to combat aggression, as well as the anti-depressant Prozac. Despite warnings to stop drinking, however, French police investigators concluded that Henri Paul continued to drink, though in moderation.

Investigative journalists quoted friends and acquaintances who had said they saw Henri Paul take a drink or two on that fateful August evening but no one suggested he was in any way drunk. And police were unable to confirm these reports. Some staff at the Ritz allegedly claimed that Henri Paul drank alcohol that night as he waited for Diana and Dodi to appear, but this also has never been confirmed. Nor did the French police investigating the accident trace any witnesses who had in fact seen Henri Paul consuming alcohol. Dodi's personal bodyguard Les Wingfield gave evidence stating that he had not seen Paul take a single drink that evening. However, on the night of August 30, some witnesses at the Ritz reported seeing Paul in a 'happy and somewhat excited' mood, yet no one reported that he looked drunk or acted as though he had been drinking. Indeed, no evidence whatsoever has been brought to light even suggesting Henri Paul had been drinking or was drunk on the evening of August 30.

Throughout the time Paul was at the Ritz there has never been a single piece of evidence proving that he drank that evening or was in any way drunk. He spoke to Dodi and Diana by phone but they did not report anything untoward in his speech. On arrival at the Ritz, Paul parked the Mercedes with no suspicion of drunkenness; Trevor Rees Jones spoke to him in the hotel but had no suspicion he was under the influence.

However, unknown to hotel staff and others, shortly after arriving at the Ritz, Henri Paul was briefed at a meeting with one of his intelligence handlers. He was told that the *gendarmerie,* the Paris police force, had a plan that night to prevent photographers from following Diana and Dodi after they left the Ritz. He was told the police had been ordered to give the couple some privacy and save them from further press harassment. Henri Paul was instructed to drive the Mercedes S280 while the other Mercedes, a much larger 600 model, would be used as a decoy car. At that vital meeting, Henri Paul was also given precise instructions as to which route he was to take to Dodi's apartment, where the couple planned to spend the night. Importantly, the route Henri Paul was told to drive was not the most direct route to the apartment, nor the fastest.

Paul was also informed that there would be no police patrol vehicles checking his speed and that he should drive as fast as possible in order to escape the photographers on their scooters and motorbikes. Henri Paul was told to phone Dodi in his suite, tell him of the plan and impress on him that the plan of escape from the Ritz, and that the route to be taken had been devised by the Paris police to prevent further harassment. From Dodi's actions and instructions that night it seems he agreed to the plan.

Despite the late hour, there were 30 to 40 people still mingling about outside the Ritz, waiting for Diana to emerge, beside the 15 or so photographers who had waited patiently most of the evening. Parked by the door was the Mercedes 600, the driver and the bodyguards. Hotel staff were constantly popping in and out of the main entrance as if checking all was in place. Some of those standing around in the cool of the summer evening and posing as pushy cameramen and eager spectators were in fact British and French intelligence agents.

At 12:15 am, hotel staff announced to the waiting

photographers that Diana and Dodi would be out in five minutes. Photographers and members of the crowd pushed forward toward the entrance, creating a sense of excitement and expectation. Bodyguards and Ritz staff stepped outside ready to prevent the photographers getting too close to Diana as she took the short, five-yard walk to the waiting car. There had already been two scuffles between bodyguards and *paparazzi* that day, and the situation had become heated with much pushing, shoving, shouting and heated exchanges. The atmosphere outside the hotel was electric.

But Diana and Dodi didn't appear. Once again, they had used the exit at the back of the hotel where Henri Paul was sitting in the Mercedes S280. Only one photographer was there. In no time, staff helped Diana and Dodi into the car, Trevor Rees-Jones jumped into the front passenger seat and Henri Paul gently accelerated away.

Gamma photographer Romauld Rat recorded later, 'As I arrived at the lights which had been at red I saw the Mercedes with Diana and Dodi inside pull away. As the Mercedes increased speed along the road beside the River Seine we all dropped back, unable to keep up. At that stage I believe the Mercedes must have been doing in excess of 80 mph and it was accelerating further away from us.'

Drivers entering the Alma Tunnel veer slightly towards the right before the road dips down to the left and straightens out. The road has a slight camber and there are no crash barriers, just massive concrete columns some three feet in diameter on the driver's left side and a wall on the right.

As the Mercedes carrying Diana and Dodi accelerated

into the tunnel, one or two of the chasing photographers later gave evidence that they saw a bright flash of a light coming from inside the tunnel. They said the light was too powerful, too bright to be the headlights of a car or the flash of a photographer's camera. It was that sudden, intense flash of light, momentarily blinding Henri Paul, that made him lose control of the speeding Mercedes. The vehicle smashed into the third concrete column with a horrendous crash that sounded almost like an explosion. It bounced off the column, careered further along the tunnel and then crashed almost head-on into the thirteenth column some 20 yards further on before spinning 180 degrees, finally coming to rest against the wall on the right side of the tunnel. The vehicle was a tangled, bludgeoned mass of metal and the roof caved in almost to the level of the bonnet. The left side of the front end, which had taken the brunt of the impact, had been pushed back some three feet, but the back seats and the rear of the car were relatively intact.

Dodi Fayed and Henri Paul, who were both on the left side of the vehicle, died instantly– principally from massive trauma to their chests and heads. Diana, tossed about all over the inside of the car as it spun violently 180 degrees, was lying severely injured on the floor of the car, facing backwards between the front and rear seats. She was semi-conscious and, at first appearance, it didn't seem as though she was seriously injured. This was the message the late night duty officer at the British Embassy in Paris was told some 30 minutes after the crash. He immediately passed this information to Buckingham Palace staff on weekend duty, who telephoned Balmoral so that Prince Charles, who was staying there with Wills and Harry, could be informed.

The flash of brilliant light had come from the back of a white Fiat Uno which was seen travelling at a normal speed in front of the speeding Mercedes, in the same lane and travelling in the same direction. As the Mercedes raced into the tunnel, someone in the rear seat of the Fiat Uno, allegedly alerted via a wireless link, informing the occupants that Diana's Mercedes was approaching, flashed the blinding light directly into the eyes of Henri Paul. Those high-intensity strobe lights, used by NATO forces, are designed to blind and disorientate people for a few seconds. Driving at speed, Henri Paul didn't stand a chance.

The mystery of the white Fiat Uno has never been satisfactorily explained. The one certain fact is that the car clipped by the Mercedes was definitely a Fiat Uno, confirmed by paint technicians from Fiat of Italy. It seems extraordinary, if not unbelievable, that the Uno was never discovered and, more importantly, that if the Uno driver was an innocent participant in the crash, why didn't he or she come forward and tell the police what had in fact happened? It is beyond belief that the driver was unaware that the police were searching for him or her. The news of the crash and Diana's death was on every radio and television broadcast for days in France and every other European country.

As a result, the suspicion remains that the Fiat driver involved in the crash was not simply an innocent person caught up in the tragedy but, more plausibly, a knowing participant in the whole affair. This deduction points to the only possible conclusion; that the car crash was no accident of fate but a carefully planned and well-executed operation to kill Diana.

The entire trip from the Ritz to the crash scene had

taken under three minutes – and it would have taken about seven minutes if Henri Paul had kept to the legal maximum speed. That short time span gives a fairly accurate assessment of how fast Henri Paul must have been driving for most of the journey.

Within minutes there was chaos and confusion at the crash scene as 20 or so photographers and their drivers came to a halt near the tangled mass of metal that had been the Mercedes. The non-stop wail of the Mercedes horn, magnified in the confines of the tunnel, added to the chaos and people tried to make themselves heard by yelling above the ear-splitting noise. The photographers immediately went to work, flashing away both outside and inside the wrecked and battered vehicle. Romauld Rat, who held a first-aid certificate, checked inside the vehicle to see if anyone was alive and realized immediately that both Henri Paul and Dodi were dead. But, on closer examination – checking their pulses – he discovered that both Diana and Rees-Jones were alive but barely conscious.

It was by chance that some three minutes after the crash, Dr. Frederic Mailliez, 36, and an American friend Mark Butt, 42, were returning from a birthday party and chanced upon the crash scene. Dr. Mailliez, an experienced emergency physician, was employed by a private on-call medical service. Having quickly checked the four people in the car, Dr. Mailliez confirmed that only Diana and Rees-Jones were alive. He called for two ambulances and resuscitation equipment and ran back to the Mercedes with the only piece of medical equipment he found in his car, a self-inflating oxygen mask. He clambered into the back of the vehicle and held up Diana's head so she could breathe into the mask.

Five minutes after the crash, two police officers on patrol, flagged down by motorists, arrived on the scene. They called for ambulances and more police support and then tried to usher away the photographers, who were still clicking away, and the group of interested bystanders who had arrived on the scene.

Dr. Mailliez would say later that at that time he believed Diana's injuries were not life-threatening for there was very little blood coming from her nose or mouth. There were no other visible injuries. He later confirmed that Diana had even mumbled an incoherent word or two.

Six minutes later, the first ambulance arrived and Dr. Mailliez moved away from Diana so that the ambulance crew could take over. Minutes later he drove away from the scene, reasonably confident that both Diana and Rees-Jones would survive. As he drove away, Dr. Mailliez had no idea the young blonde woman was the Princess of Wales.

The ambulance crew quickly ascertained that Henri Paul showed no sign of life, so they concentrated on trying to save Dodi. But after fifteen minutes trying to resuscitate him, Dodi was pronounced dead.

It is now acknowledged by most surgeons and doctors that if Diana had been rushed to the nearest hospital within minutes of the crash, it is likely that her life would have been saved. Recovery from such a severe injury is rare and is possible only through immediate hospital treatment. Ironically, if the crash had occurred in Britain it is possible that Diana's life might have been saved although, as a consequence of the injury, she may have suffered permanent brain damage.

In France, car crash victims are stabilized at the scene before being taken to the hospital. That is why French ambulances are equipped more like mini operating theatres on wheels and are staffed by a fully qualified physician and nurse. In Britain, of course, the practice is to get the victim to hospital as quickly as possible and that is why British ambulances are staffed with paramedics.

Diana was carried to the waiting ambulance parked in the tunnel a few yards from the Mercedes and immediately placed on a respirator, but both her pulse and blood pressure were weak. Both continued to deteriorate. The decision was made to stabilize her before leaving the crash site, but after 40 minutes it was decided there was no option but to take her to the nearby Pitie-Salpetriere Hospital when Diana suffered a sudden and major heart attack. She was revived only by external heart massage. The ambulance moved at a snail's pace so that the medics could continue their life-saving work for they didn't want to further risk worsening the condition of the weakening Diana.

She was still unconscious when she arrived at the hospital and once inside the operating room she suffered another heart attack. An emergency thorocotomy (surgical opening of the pulmonary vein) revealed a major laceration to the left pulmonary vein. Damage to such a major blood vessel will usually cause a patient to bleed to death very quickly. Twelve doctors surrounded the operating table. Some surgeons worked on repairing the laceration, others took it in turns to pump her heart manually, while others pumped blood and other liquids into her bloodstream.

But after two hours of both internal and external massaging of her heart, Princess Diana was pronounced dead at 4:00 a.m. Paris time on Sunday, August 31.

Chapter Twelve
Facts, Fantasy or Deception?

Judge Herve Stephan, the French judge detailed to investigate the crash that killed Diana, Dodi and Henri Paul, and his associate magistrate Marie-Christine Devidal concluded after a full investigation and interviewing many witnesses, that the three died 'as the result of an accident, rather than a deliberate act'. Importantly, they went on, 'This was because the driver of the vehicle was drunk and under the effect of medicine incompatible with alcohol; a state which did not enable him to maintain control of his vehicle while driving at high speed on a difficult part of the road, and also having to avoid a vehicle travelling in the same direction at a slower speed'.

French police provided evidence that the Mercedes S280 was travelling at a speed somewhere between 74 mph and 97 mph when it entered the Pont d'Alma tunnel, and at between 59 mph and 69 mph when it hit the first pillar.

It is probable that the most telling piece of evidence given to Judge Stephan were reports of the blood samples taken from Henri Paul's body by qualified hospital staff who handed the results to Commander Jean-Claude Mullez, the senior investigating police officer working on behalf of Judge Stephan. These samples showed that Henri Paul's blood alcohol level was very high.

When this evidence was made public by Judge Stephan

the world's newspapers proclaimed that a drunken, hapless Henri Paul was the person responsible for the death of Diana and Dodi and that speed was a contributing factor. That evidence has been accepted as fact by the vast majority of people who have followed each and every turn of this extraordinary saga.

And yet there was not a single piece of evidence put forward to Judge Stephan to suggest that prior to the accident Henri Paul had been drinking or was drunk. Indeed, French detectives tried in vain to find a single witness who was in the Ritz that night who could confirm or even suggest that Henri Paul had seen drinking or was the worse for wear. Everyone they interviewed who remembered seeing Henri Paul that night said they had no reason to believe that he was not sober. It should be noted that if anyone – Diana, Dodi, Rees-Jones, or any members of the Ritz staff – had thought for one moment that Henri Paul was under the influence of alcohol, he would most certainly not have been permitted to drive that night. But no one made any such suggestion that Henri Paul had been drinking or was unfit to drive. Indeed, CCTV pictures, shown later in television news bulletins across the world, revealed a sober Henri Paul walking about the Ritz foyer, fully in control of himself, standing around waiting for Diana and Dodi to make an appearance and, on occasions, chatting to people. At one point Henri Paul was seen speaking to Les Wingfield, one of Dodi's trusted bodyguards who has said that he had no reason to think Henri Paul was drunk or that he had been drinking. And Wingfield knew that Henri Paul was the man chosen to drive Diana and Dodi home that night. If Wingfield had the slightest suspicion that Paul was under the influence of alcohol, he would never have permitted him to drive his boss Dodi or Princess Diana anywhere that night. He would have found another driver.

Indeed, if anyone present at the Ritz that evening, whether a guest or a member of the hotel staff, had the slightest suspicion that Henri Paul had been drinking it is most unlikely he would have been permitted to drive Diana and Dodi. But no one has ever come forward to support the allegation that he had been drinking. The only piece of evidence was forensic, an analysis of his blood taken after the accident.

Millions of television viewers who have watched the CCTV footage of the Ritz foyer that night witnessed Henri Paul stooping down to tie his shoe laces. At no time was there a hint the man was inebriated. And for a man in his 50s to stoop and tie his shoelaces when inebriated to the extent that medical evidence has suggested he was drunk that night it would have been virtually impossible for him to do so. But he tied both laces immediately and with no stumbling, fumbling or falling about.

Despite the medical evidence obtained from the blood samples undertaken by qualified medical staff from Henri Paul's body some hours after the crash, the truth of the matter is that Henri Paul had *not* been drinking that night and at no time was he under the influence of alcohol.

The French investigators under the jurisdiction of Judge Herve Stephan, who gathered the medical evidence, produced the results of blood samples taken from Henri Paul's body, the second blood sample being taken some hours after the first.

The first analysis of blood taken from Henri Paul's body by Dr. Pepin showed that alcohol (ethanol) was present in amount 174mg/100ml and the later sample taken by Professor Ricordel showed 187mg/100ml of blood. Such levels of alcohol in the blood, which were three times over the French drink-drive limit and twice over the British limit, would produce marked effects on the person whether they were driving or not. The finding that Henri Paul had a high level of alcohol in his blood was first made by the Paris prosecutor's office on September 1, the day after the fatal crash.

Lawyers for Mohamed Al Fayed, Dodi's father, sought an independent analysis of the blood samples but Judge Stephan refused. However, the judge ordered new tests in a bid to counter any future challenges. Blood, hair and bone marrow were drawn and examined on September 4 with the entire procedure recorded on video.

Small traces of tiaprise, used to treat pain or aggression, sometimes in chronic alcoholics, were found. So was a therapeutic dose of fluoxetine, the key active ingredient in the anti-depressant Prozac. The Public Prosecutor's Office commented, 'Care in the use of these medicines is habitually recommended to drivers'.

The Public Prosecutor's Office also stated that analysis of protein transfer in M.Paul's blood produced results which were 'compatible… with a chronic alcoholism over the course of at least a week'. And yet, bizarrely, the autopsy also revealed that Henri Paul's liver was normal for a person of his age with no forensic evidence pointing to alcoholism. According to Henri Paul's former wife, his family and his friends he was not a heavy drinker and never had been and, to all intents and purposes, led a quiet life. His father, Jean Paul also refutes that his son was a heavy drinker or ever had been. He confirmed that his son took his job at the Ritz very seriously, adding, 'The family remain absolutely convinced that our son had not been drinking that night'.

Adding weight to his family's claims that he was not a heavy drinker, it has been confirmed that Henri Paul had successfully passed a stringent, rigorous medical examination only a few days prior to his death for the annual renewal of his pilot's licence. If, indeed, Henri Paul was such a heavy drinker he would most certainly never have passed such a medical examination for the licence renewal.

One of his blood samples allegedly showed 20.7 per cent of blood had combined with carbon monoxide, a distinctly high-level. According to Commander Jean-Claude Mullez carbon monoxide was inhaled when the driver's air-bag inflated on impact. But this was impossible because the Mercedes Benz car company publicly asserted that their airbags do not contain carbon monoxide releasing chemicals. In addition, it is customary for French firefighters to wear carbon monoxide detectors, yet none of the firefighters attending the crash scene reported detection of the deadly gas.

Since that piece of evidence was crushed after a single telephone call to Mercedes Benz the suggestion that Henri Paul's blood had combined with carbon monoxide has been quietly forgotten, leaving people asking from where did this piece of totally inaccurate information come from and how was it possible for the Commander to produce as factual evidence such an erroneous blunder.

Commander Mullez later said the information he had been given concerning the allegation of carbon monoxide in Paul's blood was a genuine error, a mistake. To many of those believing Diana's death was a deliberate act carried out by professionals or security forces, such an error as that made by Commander Mullez simply lends weight to their contention that her death was not accidental.

Analyzing the proportion of alcohol in blood from such samples is simple but reliance on the analytical results is fraught with difficulties. The problem arises because of difficulties in establishing by chemical analysis of blood the proportion of alcohol in the blood of a person *prior* to his death, particularly when the person has suffered a violent death, so violent that body organs were ruptured or mangled, permitting the stomach contents and intestine yeasts to mix with the blood. Indeed, such was the case with the injuries sustained by Henri Paul as reported by doctors who carried out the post mortem on his mangled body; his organs were severely ruptured.

In violent deaths the bloodstream can become contaminated with stomach contents, including yeasts, and this results in the production of alcohol through the fermentation of blood sugar into alcohol (ethanol), even before the blood sample is taken. It is a very rapid process, a matter of minutes rather than hours. As a result, alcohol can be formed in the blood prior to blood samples being taken.

There is a further possibility of this fermentation process taking place. Unless specific preparation of sample bottles has been carried out with a suitable preservative added to the sample bottles, and the bottle sterilized, fermentation also occurs within the sample bottle, thus generating alcohol. The usual preservative is sodium fluoride.

It is common practice in France that in such circumstances as a road crash fatality, when sample bottles are not immediately available, then vials are used instead. These vials usually contain heparin as an anti-coagulant. But this substances has no anti-fungal activity so will not prevent or inhibit fermentation. As a direct consequence some or all of the alcohol detected by analysis of post mortem blood can have been formed *after* death.

These facts have been known for many years. They came to light when blood samples of trainee fighter pilots were analysed after they had been killed in violent deaths when their aircraft crashed. Tests of their blood revealed alcohol of about 180mg per 100 ml of blood; yet it was known for certain that these pilots had not taken any alcohol whatsoever prior to flying.

In the case of Henri Paul, however, there is even further proof that the alcohol in his blood was caused by fermentation after his death. The second test, taken some hours later, should have recorded less alcohol because of evaporation. Instead, it found more, strongly suggesting that alcohol was created between the two readings. There was a difference of eight percent, a marked difference in such findings.

One of the world's leading authorities on this fermentation process following a violent death, is Dr. Jim Sprott OBE a New Zealand scientist who has conducted investigations into a number of young aircraft pilots killed in violent deaths in the 1970s. Dr. Sprott has also given expert professional evidence at inquests involving drivers killed in high speed car crashes when the analysis of post mortem blood revealed alcohol, in about the same quantity as Henri Paul – of approx 160-180 mg of alcohol per 100ml of blood.

Dr. Sprott wrote a detailed report to the Royal Coroner Michael Burgess and asserted that in his opinion, 'the alcohol in Henri Paul's blood sample was created by fermentation after Mr. Paul died as the contents of his gut mixed with the sugars in his blood'.

In other words Henri Paul was *not* driving under the influence of alcohol. Indeed, this new fact accurately reflects the CCTV images of Henri Paul taken while waiting in the foyer of the Ritz immediately prior to driving Diana and Dodi on their fateful journey. In those CCTV pictures which the world has witnessed showed no evidence or signs that Henri Paul was under the influence of alcohol. This means, of course, that the cause of death handed down by the French Coroner – that the accident was caused by Henri Paul driving at excessive speed while under the influence of alcohol – was incorrect and can no longer be sustained.

Indeed British detectives discovered the restaurant bar where Henri Paul enjoyed his last meal on that fateful night. The owner of 'Le Grand Colbert' restaurant in Paris, not far from Paul's home told detectives that Henri Paul was in his usual quiet, relaxed frame of mind. He ate a two course meal and enjoyed a single small glass of wine. The owner reported that Paul was a frequent diner at his bar and he had never seen him have more than one or two glasses of wine. He was always pleasant, quiet and unobtrusive, sometimes accompanied by a woman or an occasional male friend but often than not eating alone. He had never seen him drunk or even slightly tipsy.

Lord Steven's team of detectives are examining the possibility that the only reason why forensic doctors examining Paul's blood after the crash reported finding high levels of alchohol in the specimens was because the blood sample might have been replaced by another. It would of course have been so easy for a member of the DST or MI5 to organise such a replacement.

Though of no real consequence, it is also odd for a man who was allegedly an alcoholic that when the French police searched Henri Paul's apartment they found only two old bottles of Ricard and 240 cans of diet coke!

Henri Paul may have been driving at excessive speed though there has never been any official police report suggesting at what speed the Mercedes was travelling at any time from the moment the Mercedes left the Ritz hotel to the crash site in the Alma tunnel. Comment has also been made in many quarters that it seems somewhat odd that no police car or motorbike escorted the Mercedes that night when Diana and Dodi had undergone intensive paparazzi attention throughout the few hours they spent in Paris.

Some witnesses alleged Henri Paul drove away from the Ritz at high speed, others reported that he drove away at a normal speed. CCTV evidence showed the Mercedes pulling away at a reasonable speed. However, there was no CCTV footage along the route Henri Paul chose that night and, though there were a number of automatic police cameras on the route they took, allegedly none was working.

In January 2004, following the opening of the inquest into Diana's death by the Royal Coroner, still further doubts were raised by senior British police over the authenticity of Henri Paul's blood samples, adding yet more controversy to the doubts which seem to have bedeviled many areas of the evidence surrounding Diana's death. The British police were not confident that the forensic evidence obtained by the French authorities because they had failed to carry out DNA tests to prove that the specimen of blood tested for alcohol actually belonged to Henri Paul. As a result, of course, it is now impossible for the authorities to establish whether or not the blood tested did in fact belong to Henri Paul or to someone else.

It has been suggested by some who believe Diana and Dodi were murdered that the blood sample purported to have been taken from Henri Paul's body was swapped for blood from a drunken motor-cyclist who also died that night in a crash in another area of Paris. But there has been no evidence to substantiate that theory.

Chapter Thirteen
Diana's Secret Mission

Diana's newfound status as an international icon gave her a real buzz, a wonderful feeling of achievement and success. She felt good about herself, and the plaudits she read in newspapers and magazines gave her a feeling of real elation. Sometimes, Diana would read something in the press about herself or watch herself on television, and then leap to her feet and walk around the room clenching her fists, her face wreathed in smiles, a look of excitement and determination in her eyes. 'Done it, done it' she would mutter quietly to herself between clenched teeth. Her visits to minefields in Angola and Bosnia were the two most momentous events of Diana's life because she felt she had finally achieved something to be proud of. The feeling of elation gave her was like nothing she had ever experienced. Within months Diana convinced herself that she could now successfully tackle almost any humanitarian issue she wanted.

Until that moment, Diana had been craving the adoration of the media and, even more so, those hundreds and sometimes thousands of ordinary men, women and children who came to support and cheer her whenever she stepped out into the public arena. Slowly but surely, however, Diana began to believe the hype that she was receiving from around the globe; pictures, stories and articles about her and her life, her projects, her humanitarian spirit in innumerable newspapers and magazines and, of course, television news and magazine programs. Praise and acclaim were heaped upon her, and descriptions ranged from 'Angel of Mercy' to 'Saviour of the Innocents'.

This gave her a feeling of both power and real achievement. She had never before felt so confident or successful, not even at school and never since. Diana came to believe that there was nothing that she could not achieve and, in proving herself to the world, she had succeeded in two of her main aims that she had dreamed of for some years – to destroy Charles' reputation and to dominate the royal scene. Indeed, it must be said that Diana had achieved these aims within a matter of a couple of years. She had also ruined Charles' reputation with the great mass of the British people and she was fast reducing both the roles of the Queen and Prince Philip to bit players as they went about their dutiful royal tasks as they had done for the last forty years. But now the crowds who attended royal events when the Queen and Prince Philip were present were becoming ever smaller.

Diana knew that she had become not only the most popular royal in modern times, and she now believed the newspaper hype that she had become the most sought after person in the western world. As Mike Whitlam explained, 'In reality, there were only three world figures in the 1990s who would be welcomed in the great majority of countries for their ability to capture the imagination for humanitarian causes: Mother Teresa, Nelson Mandela and Princess Diana. That was all.'

Throughout the 1990s, when royal tours and visits to foreign and commonwealth countries were discussed amongst diplomats, the only person the host nations wanted to see was Diana. A number of governments readily turned down the suggestion of solo visits by Prince Charles and they even found excuses for not hosting official royal tours or visits by the Queen and Prince Philip. Of course some official royal visits, scheduled years before, did take place, but new invitations were becoming fewer. However, if there was the faintest possibility that Diana would visit a country, for a day or a week, the red carpet was immediately thrown down, celebrations organized and there would be an almost tangible feeling of excitement and expectation in the air for weeks before her arrival. Diana loved such attention.

Following her legal separation in 1992, Diana was fully aware that she was succeeding in her ambitions to a far greater extent than she ever thought possible. Until that time, she had been in awe of the Queen, behaving in a shy, even timid manner in the royal presence. She did however respect the Queen's remarkable workload and dedication to duty, but now, somehow, Diana had succeeded in pushing even the Queen, the Head of State, to a subsidiary role. She began to really enjoy, even revel, in her new found status. Now Diana was carrying the flag, the one person in Britain whom the rest of the world admired, and many loved. In her heart, Diana rejoiced at her remarkable achievement, revelled in her newfound fame and wallowed in the adoration to which she readily and happily exposed herself. It was the most extraordinary achievement, particularly for a shy, reserved, poorly-educated girl who had left school without passing a single exam, who had never held down a proper full-time job in her life and who, through adversity and her own determination, had proved herself to be a remarkable young woman.

And it wasn't simply her glamorous, movie star qualities, her beauty, her radiant smile or her acting ability. Diana succeeded so triumphantly because she cared for people and she showed she cared. She was happy to be seen with victims of AIDS, touching and holding the victims of this terrible disease which was frightening because it killed so many innocent people; she loved holding and helping destitute, starving children in third-world countries or caring for Leprosy victims. And the reason she became so dedicated to helping those children was because she knew it would open people's hearts and their purse strings, bringing some comfort and maybe hope to those poor afflicted victims who had little food and no education, no future and little chance of a better life.

But even Diana wasn't that pure, straightforward or honest. On occasions when she left the hospital or hospices where she had been chatting, touching or holding AIDS patients, she would wave goodbye with a look of sadness and compassion in her face, get into the car and, tell her chauffeur, 'Get me back to the palace quickly so I can have a hot bath and feel clean again.' It might seem churlish, even offensive to reveal such negative characteristics, but that was the real Diana; she wasn't totally without a stain on her character.

However, Diana's new found position of power would only last a short while. Unknown to the princess the forces ranged against were becoming ever more fearful of her power to influence people's opinion and to persuade the *hoi poloi* – electors the world over – to listen to her arguments and blindly follow her lead. By the mid-1990s, to those in positions of power and influence in Britain, Europe and the United States, Diana had become a so-called 'unguided missile' for there was no telling where or when she might strike next, giving her support, opinion or influence to any cause.

Diana had no plan, no projects, no list of specific interests but she was now determined to continue the work she felt she was destined to undertake from the day she split from Charles. Since her 1995 divorce, Diana was even more confident that she had the popularity and natural authority to become an ambassador of good causes, roving the world, searching for causes to espouse, humanitarian issues to publicize and innumerable problems to solve.

But her life wasn't all roses. Throughout those last seven years of her life, Diana had reached the conclusion that she would never find true happiness with a man, though she might fall in love from time to time. She had thoroughly enjoyed most of her various love affairs and, by the early 1990s had come to realise that she could charm virtually any man wanted sometimes merely with a shy but deliberate glance, look or gesture. She liked doing that for it gave her a sense of real power. For a woman who had been so shy and introvert at the time of her marriage to the seductress and hussy of the 1990sthe change had been dramatic. And she knew that for the next few years she would continue to flirt and find men she fancied to tease, to titillate, to bed and to amuse her. Diana came to enjoy openly flirting and playing the scheming woman and not for one moment did she believe that it was wrong in any way to enjoy a love life with as many men as she wished. Once, she was known to say, 'It's my life and I can do what the hell I like with it.'

In some circumstances it seems that Diana didn't care a damn whom she hurt in her headlong pursuit of the men she wanted. One such example was Diana's famous public tangle with the English Rugby Captain Will Carling and his wife Julia. It was played out, blow for blow, in a glare of publicity gleefully fuelled by the tabloid press; Diana did not like the fact that someone's wife had the audacity to call her a 'homewrecker.' In the ensuing tussle for Will Carling's affections, Diana would refer to Julia as 'that little tart'. In that battle Diana showed she could be ruthless in her pursuit of a man but, in reality, she only wanted to show Julia Carling that she had not only met her match but had been forced to accept defeat.

For Diana, the Carling affair was perfunctory and brief though Diana did gain applause and recognition from William and Harry for bringing the English Rugby captain home on a number of occasions. For Carling and Julia, however, the affair was disastrous, destroying their marriage in a blaze of unwanted publicity. Understandably, Julia was angry and critical of Diana's behaviour in the affair but Diana seemed to take pride in winning the battle for Carling's affections. Then, almost overnight, as if to further humiliate poor Julia, Diana ditched him.

In her heart, however, Diana could count on the fingers of one hand the number of men she had truly loved. Of course, Hewitt was one, but Diana found him wanting, for she sensed he hadn't the courage or the willpower to go through with a marriage to her despite the fact they had a child to share. Diana understood Hewitt's nervousness, for he had come from a quite humble background, a stranger to the life of luxury, power and prestige enjoyed by most of his brother officers in the Brigade of Guards. Diana understood that Hewitt realized that he was treading on dangerous ground becoming involved with the Princess of Wales, the wife to the heir to the throne, and he did fear his army career was at risk. It made no difference to Diana. She simply lost all respect for him when he told her he didn't want to marry her. And Hewitt, somewhat besotted by Diana's interest in him, was upset when Diana turned his back on him for he had risked his entire army career for Diana, and had been carpeted and repeatedly warned by senior officers for refusing to end the affair.

Hewitt's fear for his future and his career proved accurate. In 1993 he chose to quit the army but, in fact, he was given little alternative. Following the initial warning in the 1980s, Hewitt had been strongly advised on numerous occasions to end the affair but, urged on by Diana he had continued their affair. But his loyalty to Diana was not returned, for once Diana came to the conclusion that Hewiit had no stomach for a fight, preferring to quit the army rather than stand and fight and face the consequences, she quickly lost interest. Hewitt was devastated.

Within a matter of weeks Diana began indulging herself in a number of other love affairs. And the more she met, socialized, dined, partied and bedded other men she more she came to see the flaws in Hewitt's one dimensional character. She came to understand that Hewitt was not as bright or intelligent as she had first thought; that although he might be courageous on the battlefield he hadn't the strength of character to take the decision she had wanted and needed in their early years together.

Despite their unhappy parting, Diana never lost complete interest in Hewitt. From time to time they enjoyed the occasional tryst together but there was never again any serious intent on Diana's behalf. Indeed, Diana rather used him, usually phoning him for a night of lust when she had no other men on hand to entertain her.

There were probably only two other serious loves in

Diana's life - Oliver Hoare and the heart surgeon Hasnat Khan. And both would disappoint her. Hoare did not want to become more closely involved with a woman whom, on occasions, he believed showed serious psychological problems. And Hoare was also fortunate in having a loving and beautiful wife waiting patiently at home for her man to finish his royal fling.

The handsome Hasnat Khan was far more interested in being married to his job and his career as a surgeon than the limelight, the glamour and the problems that marriage to Diana might have brought to a man who had dedicated his life to his work.

When Diana's heart was torn by her love for both Hoare and Khan and the subsequent feeling of rejection she hated, she would invariably turn to one or two close, personal friends in whom she kept faith. They were her ever-faithful friend and confidant Carolyn Bartholomew, her former flatmate and Lady in Waiting, and her dear friend Rosa Monckton. From time to time there were of course others, such as Sarah Ferguson and Kate Menzies as well as half a dozen other women, including some of her therapists, whom Diana would dally with for a while and then move on to others who had caught her imagination.

In the last six years of her life, Diana became particularly close to Rosa Monckton, the wife of Dominic Lawson, then editor of *The Sunday Telegraph* newspaper, after Rosa had given birth at six months to a still-born baby girl she named Natalia. In a moment of deep sorrow between the two women, Diana suddenly asked Rosa if she would like to bury baby Natalia in her private garden at Kensington Palace, a place which Diana always referred to as 'my little oasis'.

For a woman whose life was filled with drama and heartache, the internment of a baby in an unmarked grave in her own garden at Kensington Palace must rank as one of the most extraordinary occurrences in Diana's life. It was a thoughtful, deeply affectionate though, perhaps, somewhat bizarre offer of friendship. But Rosa loved the idea and, as a result, baby Natalia's body lies buried today against the garden's west wall.

At the graveside, Rosa read out a verse by Rabindranath Tagore, India's great poet and Nobel prizewinner, a poem that Diana came to remember by heart and to love.

> 'They who are near me do not
> know that you are nearer to me
> than they are.
> They who speak to me do not know
> that my heart is full with your
> unspoken words.
> They who crowd in my path do not
> know that I am walking alone
> with you.
> They who love do not know that their love brings you to
> my heart.'

As those lines were read out at the short funeral service, Diana once again revealed her huge capacity for unhappiness – one of the reasons she responded so openly to the suffering of humanity – and the tears flowed unchecked. That sign of such a profound friendship between the two women, who were roughly the same age, cemented their relationship and, as a result, whenever Diana was at a particularly low ebb she would usually turn to Rosa for comfort, solace and understanding. Rosa turned out to be one of Diana's true friends, recalling after her death, 'She used to bound down the stairs of Kensington Palace with a huge smile and arms outstretched. But she also had a dark side – that of a wounded, trapped animal who frequently asked for advice but rarely took it.'

Throughout her adult life, however, Diana's friends had not always proved so rewarding, though the greater part of the blame for that rested with Diana and her paranoia which she was never able to shake off or dispel. It was Diana's abnormal tendency to suspect and mistrust others that led to her lifelong tendency to make and break friendships with many people, nearly all of whom were women, and all usually for no good reason. The number of women to whom Diana showed great affection, trust, kindness and friendship exceeded a score or more in the last fifteen years of her life but these so-called friends would be dropped by Diana without rhyme nor reason. And the breakdown in the friendship would usually be sudden and immediate, leaving the friends bemused, disconcerted and somewhat unnerved by the lightning change in Diana's attitude to them.

Diana's infamous mood swings became legendary among her friends and those with whom she worked at Kensington Palace. Nearly everyone who came into regular contact with Diana either witnessed one or many of these mood swings or was at the receiving end of this quite bizarre treatment in which Diana's mood of the moment would gyrate from gaiety, laughter and happiness to a look that could kill or a comment which seemed designed to wound or ridicule the recipient. She could be cruel indeed, a trait which she would have hated if practiced on her by a friend or acquaintance. And these mood swings were still a part of Diana's personality through the last years of her life. No one to whom I have spoken could give sound reasons for these violent swings in her moods, most commenting with a shrug, 'That was Diana.'

The life of Diana can never be properly appreciated and understood without examining and evaluating her constant need for reassurance and the lengths to which she would go in her bid to control the so-called 'demons' in her head which caused her so much stress and anguish.

From her teenage years, Diana never enjoyed a peace of mind at any time of her life, and she would forever raise the matter with whomsoever would listen until many of her friends became rather bored with the repetitive conversation about the stress in her life, the problems she faced and her desperate search for cures for whatever ailment she was suffering at the time.

To that end, Diana approached a battalion of practitioners, including members of the medical profession, who were all invited to give their expert opinion, their suggested remedies or to exercise their particular skills on a variety of Diana's alleged ailments and her never-ending search for peace of mind in what she saw as her stress-filled life. But for the most part, those members of the medical profession who treated Diana came to the same conclusion – that Diana was simply indulging herself. She would read of the latest fad, some interesting therapy, a new remedy, attributes of an avant-garde treatment and would instantly set about finding out all the details before trying out the fad herself.

Aromatherapy was a constant interest and fascination to her and one that she indulged in at least once or twice a week over a period of some ten years or so. These sessions, undertaken in four different treatment centres in London, helped Diana feel more relaxed and happy with the world. Diana would experiment with a variety of oils allegedly providing whatever relief she requested at the time, though stress and mental fatigue were the main reasons she gave for seeking any of these treatments.

Acupuncture was another of Diana's favourite treatments and she became convinced that it was responsible for overcoming her bulimia, her anorexia nervosa and her nervousness in company. And she graciously credited one of her practitioners, Oonagh Toffolo with saving her life and her sanity.

Diana also indulged in colonic irrigation on a regular basis with Chrissie Fitzgerald at her London therapy centre despite the fact that she had medical advice telling her there was no need for her to undergo such treatment. She believed the irrigation therapy cleared out the 'angst' and the 'aggro' that constantly built up inside her, thus helping her become more relaxed and at peace with the world. She also enjoyed reflexology, which Diana believed drained the tension from her body.

And there were other treatments, which, at one time or another, calmed or interested Diana in her life-long quest for peace of mind. She put her faith in osteopathy, which aimed to correct supposed deformations of the skeleton, leading to disease. Her London osteopath, Michael Skipworth would receive urgent phone calls from a panic-stricken Diana asking for an immediate appointment because she was suffering from a severe headache. Diana came to believe that she suffered from migraines but was reassured that her headaches were not migraines. She would drive to Skipworth's surgery and found that after 30 minutes of his soothing hands her headache had disappeared. And so for a while Diana put her faith in him.

There were other treatments and indulgencies. At one time Diana came to rely on psychotherapy, introduced to her by her trusted friend and therapist Susie Orbach, with whom Diana enjoyed a rewarding relationship during the last four years of her life. Susie Orbach had co-founded London's Women's Therapy Centre when she returned after training as a therapist in the United States. Diana met Susie after reading one of her book's *Fat Is a Feminist* published in 1978. In that book Orbach identified the obsession with weight, shape, and food that haunts so many Western women and lays the blame squarely on men for controlling women within unequal partnerships. Diana related to this theory and even more so when she met and talked over her problems with the sensible, down-to-earth Susie.

To educated women Orbach's theory may have been commonplace but to the innocent, poorly-educated Diana who hardly ever read a book Susie was someone who understood Diana's problem personally and could offer sound advice through her own experience. Susie Orbach herself had once suffered from binge eating and its subsequent problems but had learned how to control and conquer those urges. Orbach, too, had an unhappy marriage at a young age. Diana believed she had finally met the one person who could *really* understand her, perhaps even shape her life and, as a result, Susie became her indispensable guru. Indeed, Diana became one of her keenest disciples and she came to rely on Susie Orbach's advice, discussing every problem, every aspect of her life and revealing many, but not all, of her most intimate secrets.

During psychotherapy, the patient transfers emotions

connected with people from their lives on to the analyst in a bid to deal with the past, and eventually forget those emotions that have caused the patient stress. Hypnotherapy can be used for many different aspects of a patient's health and Diana would seek the treatment in a bid to contain her stress level which she convinced herself she could never overcome. The third treatment – anger therapy – Diana sought after she came to realize that she lost her temper far too often and for silly reasons. She knew that she flew off the handle for no good reason and, in her frustration, would shout, yell, swear and rage around the apartment. It was a well-known fact in Kensington Palace that when the staff heard Diana raging about the place most of her staff would try to keep out of her way, fearing a high-velocity verbal attack surrounded by the most lewd, colourful language.

As a result, Diana lost faith in anger therapy because she found it wasn't working and her swearing and yelling fits of temper continued from time to time often for little or no reason. In the 1990s Diana discovered her own treatment to these mood swings. She would run to her bed, throw herself on the duvet, thump the pillows with her fists while burying her head in the pillows screaming at the top of her voice, the goose down drowning her cries of frustration. To her relief she found it worked better than any other therapy she had come across.

Like many members of the Royal Family before her, Diana would sometimes turn to astrologers, soothsayers, clairvoyants, mystics, palmists and card readers. She would frequently question friends about such people asking for recommendations and whether they thought the person would be suitable for her to visit. In the last few years of her life Diana visited many such people, both men and women, but believed that because they knew to whom they were giving their advice they would temper their true thoughts. She didn't like that. As a result, after such visits Diana would feel frustrated, never believing anything promising she was told but preferring to believe only the negative.

Diana would also use her visits to such fortune tellers to seek facts about Prince Charles and his future. She would ask them whether her husband's life was in danger; whether he would die in an accident; whether he would marry again; and whether he would ever be king. In his book, *Shadows of A Princess,* her secretary Patrick Jephson wrote, 'Yet she continued to heed her astrologers' predications, the more dire the better, particularly where the Prince (Charles) was concerned. Sure enough, she was rewarded with regular forecasts of helicopter crashes, skiing accidents and other calamities that obstinately refused to befall him ...'

It was after her legal separation that Diana first came to fear that there were people 'out there' who wanted her dead. And she would put considerable pressure on her fortune tellers demanding they tell her the truth of what lay ahead for her. As far as is known, none of them forecast an early death. As a result, she came to place little or no credence in their predictions, and yet, despite doubting their competence, Diana continued to seek their prophecies on a weekly basis right up to the time of her death.

But there were more down-to-earth friends and advisers who tried for years to wean Diana away from seeking advice from so many different sources, some of whom were dubious though others were well-meaning. As a result of seeking so much advice from so many different people,

Diana was constantly confused, leaping from one piece of advice to another. To some who knew Diana well her search for an answer to her supposed ills and problems was in reality a need for sympathy, empathy and attention from strangers who became so-called 'friends'. It was also her need for people to slavishly lavish attention on her – perhaps the only real benefit Diana gained from seeking the advice of so many diverse experts.

Following Diana's divorce, Patrick Jephson realized that the Princess needed a strategy of her own now that she was no longer a fully-fledged member of the Royal Family. He recognized that Diana had no experience in planning a public career for herself in the nation's life and, in late 1993 she was seriously contemplating, and sometimes discussing with friends and advisers, her wish to retire altogether from the public arena, living a totally private life away from the cameras, the media and public attention.

In essence, Diana had had enough. She was fed up with the *paparazzi* following her every step, her every move, seemingly only happy when she broke down in tears. The demands from various charities were increasing as they all realized that Diana's involvement in their particular charity brought in more funds and more interest from the general public. The pressure got to her. Diana would tell friends that she felt as though she was running on a treadmill that was accelerating at a faster pace each week. She was physically exhausted and wanted some peace for herself, and it was in this state of mind that she made her famous 1993 speech when she announced her partial withdrawal from public life.

That speech came as a surprise to almost everyone including her own friends and advisers. *'I hope you can find it in your hearts to understand and to give me the time and space that has been lacking in recent years ... When I started my public life twelve years ago I understood that the media might be interested in what I did. I realized then that their attention would inevitably focus on ...our private lives ...But I was not aware of how overwhelming that attention would become; not the extent to which it would affect both my public duties and my personal life in a manner that's been hard to bear...*

Diana's decision to cut the number of charities she openly supported struck those charities like a thunderbolt. They were aghast that the wonderful Princess of Wales, who had won the heart of the nation, could contemplate for one minute cutting herself off from the charities that relied so heavily on her for their very survival. These charity workers recognized that Diana brought real hope and a ray of light to so many disaffected, unhappy, sick, lonely and dying people everywhere and now she was throwing in the towel. They believed there had to be another reason for Diana's decision for it seemed totally at odds with Diana's love and compassion for people less fortunate. To some of the charity organisers responsible for raising the desperately needed funds, Diana's decision to quit meant that much of their work would have to be curtailed; some charities feared financial disaster.

And yet, it soon became apparent to those who worked with Diana that she wasn't really intent on finding time and space for herself at all. Within a matter of weeks Diana had thrown herself into other interests which she found more attractive than the annual round of what to her had become an endless succession of boring, fund-raising charity functions. The world scene had beckoned and Diana was keen to make her mark. Now that she had cleared her decks of mundane work in Britain she was ready to take on the world.

As a result of her decision to cut her work load, Diana's diary for 1994 was a virtual blank. All the planned visits, meetings, conferences and charity work she had agreed to carry out only weeks and months before had to be cancelled. Apologies were written, people were disappointed, events were re-organized or simply cancelled. For her part, Diana relaxed and enjoyed herself keeping fit, swimming and visiting her ever-growing list of therapists for her many and varied treatments and indulgencies. She also enjoyed herself with one or two lovers but more as an escape than anything else, and she soon tired of these men. In reality, she was still in love with her darling heart surgeon, Hasnat Khan.

In her heart Diana *really* wanted Hasnat more than any other man she had ever wanted in her entire life. And she didn't really know why she so loved him. She didn't even know what attracted her to him above every other man she had ever known or loved. She wondered if the attraction was simply that he spurned her many advances, refused her never-ending invitations to lunch, dinner, a drink or a night together in her bed at Kensington Palace.

Diana tried everything to persuade Hasnat that her love was real and that he was the only man she ever really wanted. But Hasnat spurned each and every endeavour Diana could come up with and always for the same reason; he was determined to spend his life working as a heart surgeon where he felt he could do some good in the world. On one occasion, Hasnat told Diana that nothing could compete with that, not even a woman as beautiful as her.

Throughout the '90s, Diana was frequently having informal chats with the energetic Mike Whitlam of the

British Red Cross, who had arranged and organized her visit to Zimbabwe to help highlight the plight of Africa's refugee children. He had also helped to organize her visit to Bosnia where she would be filmed and photographed calling for the worldwide ban on anti-personnel mines. Her Bosnia visit would prove another major success when she was filmed chatting to young victims of AP-mines about their courageous attempts to live normal lives with an arm or a leg missing, caused by exploding land mines. Once again, her presence in Bosnia, chatting to children maimed by mines, had a dramatic effect across the western world. Men and women everywhere took to the streets, demanding their governments back a worldwide ban on such mines.

Governments of every political persuasion found themselves under increasing pressure from their own electors to introduce such a ban despite pleas from their senior military staff to do no such thing. But the electors continued to press and governments felt they had little option but to support the ban.

Diana came to the conclusion that the campaign was now won and she revelled in the news stories and tv coverage all of which applauded her lead that had brought such a swift victory. It made her feel fantastic. She was confident, riding the crest of a wave and receiving the worldwide attention she loved. And, importantly for Diana, she had done this herself with no help whatsoever from Prince Charles, the Queen or any other member of the House of Windsor. That was the victory that was so sweet for Diana.

But now she wanted more. Mike Whitlam explained, 'Diana would come to see me and we would chat about the problems of the world. She always showed a great interest and concern for refugees, particularly the children, many of whom had no parents and relatives and whose life seemed forlorn and hopeless in the face of simply surviving in such a daunting environment without love, affection or anyone to care for them. Diana felt a natural affection for all refugees regardless of race, religion or colour because she felt for them, cut off from family and friends with no home, no country and no place to call their own. She felt in some way that she had a special affinity to refugees and we discussed many visits she might consider making to help the refugee problem wherever it occurred. We had organised a visit to Cambodia but diplomatic problems arose and we were advised by the British Foreign office that it would be inadvisable for the Princess of Wales to visit Cambodia of such a mission'.

It was during these talks in 1997 that Diana came to the conclusion that one of the world's most intransigent refugee problems was in the Middle East where millions of Palestinians, many of them children, had been living for some 25 years in makeshift refugee camps in the Gaza strip and the West Bank of the River Jordan.

She decided that she wanted to highlight what she understood was a heartbreaking situation, with children having to face a lifetime living in wretched camps as refugees with no future and no hope of a better future. In the same way as she visited Angola and Bosnia in a bid to bring an end to the use of anti-personnel, Diana now wanted to be seen and accepted as the world-wide ambassador for child refugees. She felt that she had finally discovered a mission in life, something really important which would entail visits to many countries in the world keeping herself in the limelight of world opinion while carrying out a task which the world could only admire.

The idea excited her and lifted her spirits.

She knew that her visit to Zimbabwe had created an interest in African child refugees and now she wanted to create a groundswell of sympathy for Palestine child refugees. She saw herself visiting a refugee camp on the West Bank and posing for pictures with the children, perhaps surrounded by hundreds of children, in an effort to raise awareness of their heartrending plight to the world at large. She felt certain ordinary men and women across the world would support her new humanitarian campaign as they had supported her land-mine ban.

Diana convinced herself that in helping child refugees she had found the cause which would promote her from being a stylish, glamorous, empty-headed princess to someone who earned the respect of people, regardless of their nationality, race or religion. Diana would never have compared herself openly with Mother Teresa, but she hoped that in this newfound work for refugees she might one day be seen as maybe a junior version of the sainted nun.

Mike Whitlam talked to Diana about the life and the work of Mother Teresa and about her universal appeal. 'Diana never for one moment compared herself to Mother Teresa but she admired her greatly. Diana was searching for a role, a big role for herself and she wanted that role to have a worldwide appeal. There was no doubt that she intended to become someone involved with charity work on the world stage. And she was prepared to do whatever work was necessary to reach that position. When Diana spoke like this there was a real determination about her ambition, which had to be admired. I do believe that had Diana lived she would have become a major player in worldwide charity work and, quite possibly, the refugee issue would have become her principal concern. She certainly felt great compassion for the children forced to live in terrible conditions in refugee camps everywhere.'

At the time of her death, at the age of only 37, Diana had begun to look at herself more critically in the mirror in the privacy of her bathroom. She was a mother of two children who was nearing forty and she knew that her looks would not last forever. At the time of her death she would laugh and joke about that fact and yet it gnawed at her mind. She understood it was time to change her image from that of the glamorous princess with 'cover-girl' looks to a more serious, concerned woman of the world who could tackle tough subjects.

AIDS had provided Diana with her first major worldwide cause to support and she knew that her efforts in that direction had brought her acclaim, not only from sufferers but from people in all walks of life who admired the fact that someone like Princess Diana had the courage to involve herself in a disease which many people shunned.

She leaped at the chance of highlighting the dangers of AP-mines and she was happy to stand behind the cause to ban them. And the more children she had seen maimed by land mines, the more she knew in her heart that here was another cause where she could make a real difference and win praise for doing so.

Now she hoped that she could prove herself once again as a roving ambassador for humanity – coming to the rescue of thousands of Palestinian children living a life of poverty trapped forever in squalid refugee camps. She believed in her innocence that she could bring them hope for a better future and even succeed in providing not only the necessities for their lives but also better education, better living conditions, better food and all in a more peaceful land.

She had little or no idea whether the Israeli or Palestinian authorities would permit her to enter such refugee camps on such a mission. Nor did she have any idea whether the British authorities or the Queen and her advisers would permit her to become involved in refugee causes. She didn't care.

Mike Whitlam explained, 'Diana never worried what Buckingham Palace would say after she had been stopped from visiting Cambodia. She told me not to take any notice of palace officials when they raised problems about her intended visit to Bosnia. They feared she may have been become embroiled in politics in pushing for a ban on mines, something which, understandably, Buckingham Palace always fought shy of. Diana would hear none of their objections, asking me to organise everything. In no uncertain terms she made it plain that she was determined to go to Bosnia and pose for pictures with children maimed by mines.'

Diana would probably have used the same no-nonsense tactics if problems had arisen of her intended visit to the West Bank. There would have been a necessity for her to obtain permission for such a visit from both the Palestinian Red Crescent and the equivalent Israeli charity. But before Diana had made plans for such a visit, she met her extraordinary death.

It is probable that the Israeli authorities would not have wanted Princess Diana to visit a Palestinian refugee camp, though it is highly likely that the Palestinians would have welcomed her with open arms. In her innocence and her ignorance Diana, of course, would not have spared a thought or cared a damn for the politics behind such a visit because she was only thinking of the humanitarian gesture she would be making to help the plight of so many child refugees. Diana didn't care a jot about the political and military concerns at the prospect of a worldwide ban on AP-mines, and she received rave notices from around the entire world for daring to take on the might of world leaders, the politicians, the world's major military machines as well as the all-powerful arms manufacturers. She was of course treading on dangerous ground.

Joyful at the media reception in many western countries to her new great idea to help the world's refugees, Diana simply did not have the guile or the experience to understand that in doing so she had inadvertently entered the cold, hard world of international politics. In her innocence, she was blissfully unaware that there might be people out there who would not welcome Princess Diana's selfless humanity and her unique and overwhelming persuasive powers to highlight politically sensitive matters.

Chapter Fourteen
Diana's Revenge

The almost audible sigh of relief from senior members of the Royal Family and their courtiers at the news of Diana's death changed to exasperation and tight-lipped anger a few days later when they were forced to sit and listen in silence to the oration by Diana's brother, Earl Charles Spencer at her funeral service in Westminster Abbey. Charles Spencer was merciless; delivering a harsh and acrimonious torrent of criticism.

His tribute – the most courageous and outspoken ever delivered at a royal funeral service – shook the Royal Family, but earned Lord Spencer huge praise from the tens of millions who listened to the oration. He caught the mood of the nation and the watching world brilliantly.

He began: *'I stand before you today, the representative of a family in grief, in a country in mourning before a world in shock. We are all united not only in our desire to pay our respects to Diana but rather in our need to do so. For such was her extraordinary appeal that the tens of millions of people taking part in this service all over the world via television and radio who never actually met her, feel that they, too, lost someone close to them.*

'Diana was the very essence of compassion, of duty, of style, of beauty. All over the world she was a symbol of selfless humanity. All over the world, a standard bearer for the rights of the truly downtrodden, a very British girl who transcended nationality.

Someone with a natural nobility who was classless and who proved in the last year that she needed no royal title to continue to generate her particular brand of magic.

'We have all despaired at our loss and only the strength of the message you gave us through your years of giving has afforded us the strength to move forward. There is a temptation to rush to canonize your memory; there is no need to do so. You stand tall enough as a human being of unique qualities not to be seen as a saint. Indeed, to sanctify your memory would be to miss out on the very core of your being, your wonderfully mischievous sense of humor with a laugh that bent you double.

'Your joy for life transmitted wherever you took your smile and the sparkle in those unforgettable eyes. Your boundless energy which you could barely contain.

'But your greatest gift was your intuition and it was a gift you used wisely. This is what underpinned all your wonderful attributes, and if we look to analyze what it was about you that had such a wide appeal, we find it in your distinctive feel for what was really important in all our lives.

'Without your God-given sensitivity we would be immersed in greater ignorance of AIDS and HIV sufferers, the plight of the homeless, the isolation of lepers, the random destruction of landmines. Diana explained to me once that it was her innermost feelings of suffering that made it possible for her to connect with her constituency of the rejected.'

'And here we come to another truth about her. For all the status, the glamour, the applause, Diana remained throughout a very insecure person at heart, almost childlike in her desire to do good for others so she could release herself from deep feelings of unworthiness of which her eating disorders were merely a symptom. The world sensed this part of her character and cherished her for her vulnerability whilst admiring her for her honesty.'

Earl Spencer went on to pledge that the Spencer family would do their utmost to protect William and Harry from being hounded by the press and he pledged that they would do everything possible to ensure her two sons were not totally immersed in duty and tradition. Those words were intended as a warning to the Royal Family not to stifle the characters and personalities of the two boys.

The speech, broadcast via loud speakers to the hundreds of thousands lining the streets of London, produced a huge emotional reaction. Many who lined the route to Westminster Abbey were in tears while millions more watched their television screens in the privacy of their homes with tears in their eyes. But applause greeted parts of Lord Spencer's speech, particularly when he vowed to protect William and Harry, suggesting that the Royal Family might not do so. At that moment it seemed the entire capital erupted in cheering and yelling.

So great and so spontaneous was the feeling that Earl Spencer had hit exactly the right nerve, that unbelievably, and without precedent, those friends as well as members of Diana's charities inside Westminster Abbey began to clap, and then to cheer Lord Spencer's words.

It was unprecedented in Britain for people to applaud at funerals but Diana's funeral was a unique occasion. The crescendo of applause in the streets could be heard inside the Abbey and the congregation began to join in. The applause began a crescendo which continued until almost everyone inside the Abbey felt the desire, indeed the necessity of joining the masses outside – prelates and peers, Presidents and Prime Ministers and even members of the Royal Family.

Some of those present believed Earl Spencer had gone too far. They argued that if he had a genuine concern for the Princess, he would never have issued such damning words. It was a brutal speech but nonetheless brilliant, speaking his mind to the world when one of the targets of his attack – the Royal Family – was sitting in front of him, unable to escape his withering criticism.

In fact, the Queen, Prince Philip and their senior courtiers took great exception to Earl Spencer's oration. In private they were furious, believing his attack was perfidious, bordering on treachery. They felt he had insulted them in suggesting the Royal Family would not take care of Wills and Harry and that if needs be the Spencer family would do so. It has not been by accident that from that day forth William and Harry have only infrequently seen Earl Spencer or any members of the Spencer family. Far from protecting the boys, who are now grown men, Earl Spencer has barely spent any time with them since. It has been made plain to him that William and Harry need no protection by members of the Spencer family for they are Windsors and would remain Windsors. Princes Charles has claimed responsibility for looking after them through their teenage and early twenties and he has forged a remarkably good relationships with them both.

Slowly but surely since that fateful funeral day the iron will of the Queen, backed by Prince Philip, has been exercised. No longer do William and Harry live the rather free lifestyle they enjoyed with Diana, but instead they have been persuaded to enjoy the traditional royal pursuits of the Windsors – playing polo and hunting, shooting, stalking deer and fishing, everything that Prince Charles has enjoyed throughout his life. And, save for polo, all these sports were those that held no interest for Diana, in fact, she tried to dissuade her sons from taking up any of them.

From the moment of Diana's death it seemed to many that the Royal Family were exhibiting behaviour patterns akin to a feeling of guilt. At the moment of Diana's death, Prince Charles, William and Harry were at Balmoral in Scotland with the Queen, Prince Philip and the Queen Mother enjoying the Windsor's customary late summer holiday. The Queen, Philip and their advisers decided the family should stay put and continue with their holiday rather than strike camp and head back to London to lead the nation in mourning the Peoples' Princess. Their only statement was that they were in mourning and 'deeply shocked and distressed' by the news.

The nation thought otherwise. Hundreds of thousands of men, women and children, most of whom had never seen Diana in the flesh, flocked to London in that first week, bringing flowers and messages of love and sorrow, leaving them outside the gates of Buckingham Palace, Clarence House, Kensington Palace and St. James's Palace. Most walked up and down the Mall as though lost and unsure how else they could show their sorrow for the young woman many had come to love. After a few days, the mourners, many with tear-stained faces, became angry and critical, their mood turned ugly and defiant, their unease directed squarely at the Queen. Newspapers took up the sentiment of the people. 'YOUR PEOPLE ARE SUFFERING, SPEAK TO US, MA'AM!' screamed the *Daily Mirror;* 'SHOW US YOU CARE,' the *Daily Express* urged and the *Sun* demanded to know, 'WHERE IS OUR QUEEN?'

The Queen even refused to fly the Royal Standard over Buckingham Palace at half-mast, despite the fact that thousands of flags on buildings across London were doing so. The public took that as an insult to Princess Diana, and their mood became even more restive. Some commentators warned of the possibility of mass civil disobedience leading to riots unless the Royal Family bowed to the demands of the nation.

Little did the nation know of the furious arguments taking place at Balmoral Castle. On the one side was Prince Charles, William and Harry; on the other the Queen, Prince Philip and Royal advisers. The Queen Mother tried to act as referee, sometimes supporting one side and then the other as the arguments continued. From time to time advisers were invited to give their views on the twin official formalities of precedence and protocol, both of which Diana had always resented, rejected and frequently ignored.

Charles, William and Harry wanted to fly to London and mingle with the vast crowds that were thronging the Mall and Kensington Gardens, but Prince Philip was vehemently opposed to the idea and, as usual on such occasions, the Queen sided with her husband. In such circumstances, of course, Prince Charles refused to disobey the wishes of his mother and, as a result, the family remained at Balmoral watching the extraordinary emotional scenes taking place in London. In particular, William and Harry desperately wanted to show their appreciation to the tens of thousands who had travelled to London to say 'farewell' to their beloved mother but Charles persuaded them that they must obey their grandmother's wishes.

In one of the most ferocious arguments during those few days, Prince Philip decreed that since Diana had taken the decision to leave the Royal Family some years before, an aircraft of the Queen's Flight should not be sent to Paris to bring back her body. He demanded that Diana's body should be returned like any other British citizen killed overseas, in a body bag on board a scheduled airline flight. Charles was apoplectic at the suggestion, outraged that his father could even consider such a proposal. Voices were raised, swear words exchanged, but Charles refused to back down. Charles threatened to tell William and Harry unless Prince Philip withdrew his proposal. Finally, Charles won the argument and he personally flew to Paris in an aircraft of the Queen's Flight and brought back Diana's body, the coffin covered in a flag of the Prince of Wales.

The Queen also followed Philip's advice over the funeral arrangements and decreed that Diana should only be awarded a simple, straightforward funeral with no pomp and ceremony. Charles and the Queen Mother disagreed totally. More arguments took place, but in the end Charles and his sons once more won the day, and Diana was given a funeral fit for a Royal Princess. Philip was furious at the decision, but then insisted on walking behind the gun carriage carrying Diana's body to Westminster Abbey with Charles, William and Harry. Of course, Philip had no alternative for if he had not done so it would have been seen by everyone that he was snubbing Diana's funeral.

As Charles, Wills and Harry daily pressed the Queen for permission to fly south to London, the Queen, rather pathetically, issued a statement saying that the family had decided to stay at Balmoral 'to comfort William and Harry in the loss of their mother'. Few of those who had flocked to London to mourn Diana, taking their children with them, believed that statement or the sentiment. The great mass of the British public had not been taken in. They were certain that the Royal Family was feeling guilty.

It took six days of argument, debate and

procrastination for Charles, Wills and Harry to persuade the Queen to permit them to fly to London. And even then Prince Philip believed the Queen should not have relented primarily because of the pressure building up in the national newspapers demanding action from the Queen and the Royal Family.

Finally, the Queen addressed the nation on television and relented to tabloid newspaper demands that the Union flag should be flown at half-mast above Buckingham Palace. At last, the Royal Family the Queen travelled to London and Elton John, a long-time friend of Diana's, was given permission to sing at her funeral. Diana's funeral was breathtaking, magnificent, traumatic and harrowing – not only for the million people who travelled to London – but for countless millions who watched the proceedings on television around the world, and silently wept.

Even in death, Diana succeeded in embarrassing the Royal Family. Neither the family nor their advisers had any idea how they should respond to Diana's death or the nation's shock, disbelief and sorrow that the young woman they had come to respect and, indeed, love had been killed in a stupid car crash in Paris.

Within days of the last tear being shed and Diana having been laid to rest at the Spencer family's ancestral home, the real work began for the royal minions. It was their duty to ensure that the memory of Princess Diana did *not* live on. And today, some six years after her death, their task is not yet complete. They are still striving to obliterate her name and her fame from the nation's psyche though time is, of course, taking its toll on peoples' memories.

Following her death, the British people desperately wanted to honour Princess Diana, many of whom believed she had been almost a martyr to the cause of kindness, generosity, love and affection in a world of hatred and prejudice. To that end they demanded that a magnificent memorial be erected on a prominent site in London so that future generations would not forget the Princess who had captured the hearts of their parents and grandparents. Prime Minister Tony Blair pledged that his Government would honour the Princess' memory. Memorial funds were set up and donations poured in from people from all walks of life. Everyone was invited to send in their suggestions for the ideal memorial for Diana. The Government's Diana Memorial Committee was formed under the chairmanship of the Chancellor Gordon Brown, its members selected from the great, the good and the privileged of British society. It was their duty to evaluate the various ideas and select the best to ensure that Diana's memory would be forever remembered.

This committee was given a list of odd criteria to test whether the chosen design would be acceptable. The criteria handed down were artistic merit, value for money and practicability; none of them aimed to help keep alive the memory of Diana. Since then, virtually nothing has happened.

Newspapers have badgered the principal Memorial Committee to reach a decision and let the nation know what was happening so that the Committee's memorial ideas could be subjected to debate and scrutiny. Reasons were given for the lack of progress, some pathetic, others downright insulting. To outsiders, this lack of progress is an insult to Diana's memory. But this lack of progress is deliberate, designed to frustrate the will of the mass of the British people until so that their social 'superiors' can decide what they believe is appropriate in such circumstances, made by those qualified to make the right decision. The argument of course was utter balderdash, a gigantic confidence trick perpetrated on the British people.

Many of the ideas submitted, some given prominence in newspaper columns, were mostly intelligent and apposite. They included a magnificent bronze statue of Diana to stand in Trafalgar Square; renaming Heathrow Airport *Princess Diana Airport* in the same way as New York's airport was re-named *John F. Kennedy* after his assassination, or re-naming a major London thoroughfare, a theatre, a sports stadium. All were quietly quashed. And today, the royal minions are still at work ensuring that memories will fade, the world will move on and the name of Princess Diana will eventually be forgotten, comprehensively trashed by the powers that be in the dustbin of history.

Five years after Diana's death the Committee reached their decision, and it was decreed their decision was final. The people's views and opinions of the committee's choice were not invited and, to give the decision credence, it was announced that the Queen had given it her approval. All neatly cut and dried, the will of the Royal Family and their advisers had triumphed. The British people wanted a full-size statue in a prominent place in London but their wishes were totally ignored.

Instead of a statue, an odd, rather incongruous, somewhat absurd type of fountain was selected, and this has been tucked away in a corner of London's Hyde Park, on the site of a disused pumphouse. The ring-shaped stone fountain, the size of four tennis courts, has apparently been designed to reflect the contrasting joy and turmoil of the Princess's life. However, few who visit the contraption, which keeps breaking down, see any relevance to Princess Diana's life. On one side of the fountain, water bubbles down a gentle slope, while on the other it cascades down, before the two streams converge into a tranquil pool. For visitors there is a small, simple plaque bearing Princess Diana's name and the dates of her birth and death. Nothing else.

Future generations will have no statue of Diana to admire and see for themselves what the beautiful, enchanting princess looked like; no idea of the impact that the princess made during the seventeen brief years in which she captured the hearts of the nation. Nor will people understand the impact Diana's fleeting life made on ordinary men, women and children who so admired her and gained strength from her courage and fortitude; and no understanding of the remarkable charity work she carried out bringing joy and happiness to people in many corners of the world which society had forgotten, sidelined, or neglected.

To many Britons, the choice of a so-called fountain was unacceptable. Those same people now believe the decision to select a fountain as the nation's principal memorial to Diana was based more on vengeance and retribution towards her than a realistic attempt to keep alive her memory. Still others believe the fountain was selected as an important part of the Royal Family's ongoing efforts to rid Britain of the memory of Diana as rapidly as possible.

However, there is one corner of an English field that will forever hold the essence of Diana. At Earl Spencer's ancestral home, Althorp, Diana's brother buried his beloved sister in an unmarked grave on a tiny wooded island in the middle of an Oval Lake. Oak trees surround the grave, shading the monument to her. It is wonderfully peaceful and quiet and, for three months every summer, the gates of Althorp House are thrown open, allowing visitors to view the tiny wooded island from a distance and also to visit an exhibition of Diana memorabilia including photographs, videos, gowns and frocks and, most nostalgically, her beautiful wedding dress.

However, some nine years after her death, Diana's memory continues to burn brightly in the lives of those unfortunates who need help and charitable support. Her favourite charities have been receiving substantial sums of money from the £50,000,000 raised by donations from the general public. Four principal categories of recipients were chosen to benefit –'displaced people', 'people at the margins of society', 'survivors of conflict' and the 'dying and bereaved'. In the words of its independent assessor: 'It has stuck to its principle of supporting less recognised causes against a number of odds and considerable pressure.'

Diana would have approved.

Bibliography

(All titles published in London unless otherwise stated.)

P.D. Jephson, *Shadows of a Princess.* 2000.

Inspector Ken Wharfe, *Diana. Closely Guarded Secret,* 2002.

Lynn Picknett, Clive Prince and Stephen Prior, *War of the Windsors.* 2002.

Philip Zeigler, *Mountbatten.* 1985.

Andrew Morton, *Diana. Her True Story,* 1992.

James Hewitt, *Love and War.* 1999.

Anna Pasternak, *Princess In Love.* 1994.

Nigel Blundell, *Windsor v. Windsor.* 1995.

Vernon Bogdanor, *The Monarchy and the Constitution.* 1995.

Basil Boothroyd, *Philip: An Informal Biography.* 1971.

Jonathan Dimbleby, *The Prince of Wales: A Biography.* 1994.

Tim Heald, *The Duke: A Portrait of Prince Philip.* 1991.

Robert Lacey, *Majesty: Elizabeth II and the House of Windsor*. 1977.

Elizabeth Longford, *Elizabeth R: A Biography*. 1983.

Trevor Rees-Jones with Moira Johnston, *The Bodyguard's Story: Diana, the Crash and the Sole Survivor*. 2000.

Ida Macalpine & Richard Hunter, *George III and the Mad-Business*. 1969.